Dead Soul Syndrome

Dead Soul Syndrome

A Biblical Alternative to the Nature of the Afterlife

JAY ALTIERI

RESOURCE *Publications* · Eugene, Oregon

DEAD SOUL SYNDROME
A Biblical Alternative to the Nature of the Afterlife

Copyright © 2010 Jay Altieri. All rights reserved. Except for brief quotations in critical publications or reviews, no part of this book may be reproduced in any manner without prior written permission from the publisher. Write: Permissions, Wipf and Stock Publishers, 199 W. 8th Ave., Suite 3, Eugene, OR 97401.

Resource Publications
An Imprint of Wipf and Stock Publishers
199 W. 8th Ave., Suite 3
Eugene, OR 97401
www.wipfandstock.com

ISBN 13: 978-1-60899-358-1

Manufactured in the U.S.A.

All scripture quotations, unless otherwise indicated, are taken from the Holy Bible, New International Version®, NIV®. Copyright ©1973, 1978, 1984 by Biblica, Inc.™ Used by permission of Zondervan. All rights reserved worldwide.

© 2010 Estate of Pablo Picasso / Artists Rights Society (ARS), New York.
Photo Credit: Art Resource, NY Museo Nacional Centro de Arte Reina Sofia, Madrid, Spain

*To Buzz, my brother in Christ,
who by example showed me to look past my own biases
and inspired me to study this topic further.*

Contents

List of Illustrations ix
Preface xi
Introduction xiii

Part One Hell

1. Defining the Situation 3
2. Dead Soul Syndrome 21
3. I'm Awake 40
4. "Well, Then, How Do You Explain . . . ?" 53
5. Problematic Passages 69
6. Death of All the Wicked 81

Appendix to Part One 109

Part Two Heaven

7. The Vocabulary of Heaven 113
8. Going to Heaven 122
9. Heaven Not Our Home 135
10. The New Spiritual World 147
11. The New Physical World 157
12. Redemptive and Judgmental Fire 170
13. Removal of the Curse 179
14. Ezekiel's Temple 187
15. New Jerusalem 203
16. Epilogue 221

Selected Bibliography 227

List of Illustrations

Figure 1—Biblical Holidays 131

Figure 2—Pangaea 165

Figure 3—*Guernica* 203

Figure 4—Arrangement of Tribes and Gates 213

Preface

WHEN A CHILLY WINTER day sets in, my wife frequently decides to make a big pot of stew. The first thing she does is cut up a lot of vegetables. She adds them to a large cauldron of water and turns on the heat. This is not soup yet. Next she adds bouillon broth, salt, and spices, but it is still nowhere near soup. At this point, it is merely wet, salty vegetables. It has to cook, but not just cook, because that could probably be done with very high heat at a rapid pace; rather, it needs to simmer. The way to make good soup is to let it simmer for several hours at low heat. Slowly the individual components give up their separate identities and become soup.

This book is a lot like soup. Some chapters came from Sunday school lessons that I did at my home church in a small town in rural Texas. The core skeleton of the hell topic was written not as a book but as a digest for myself. When I study a Bible topic, I find it helpful to write down corresponding verses and commentary thoughts, or else I forget where they were located or what they meant. "Digest" is a very appropriate word, because these notes helped me to digest the material that I was learning and retain it. It simmered for several years and gradually grew and grew, until one day not too long ago, I realized that maybe, just maybe, this could be a book.

In the pages of this book, I quote many Bible verses. Many authors only give references to Scripture. I suppose that is to economize on space. However, that practice makes it difficult for the reader to flip back and forth from the book to a Bible, which must be laid out on a table or couch nearby. I should have been from Missouri (I'm not), because I have a "show me" attitude when it comes to Bible verses. I need to see and read the verse for myself. Giving all of the verses in full, with context when appropriate, is a feature of this book. The verses are taken about 50 percent from the New International Version (NIV) and about 50 percent from the King James Version (KJV). It is not exact, and there is no particular system or rhyme for which translation was used on a particular passage. I like them both. For everyday reading and study, the NIV is my Bible of choice. I love the King James, too, and have no serious complaints about it. If that is your translation of choice, and you have acclimated to its unique voice, then may the God of heaven bless you. By reading God's holy word, in any language or any translation, you will increase. My advice for a brother or sister who has a preference for one particular translation over another would be to continue as you are in the grace of our loving God, but do not criticize or strike down others (see 1 Cor 7:18).

I owe many thanks to others in the production and creation of this manuscript. I credit my recently deceased mother, and my wife and other family and friends for their reviewing and proofreading of my atrocious spelling and grammar. I owe a debt of scholarship to many authors and theologians who have preceded me on the topic of the afterlife. I stand on their shoulders. Most of all, I have a humble, earnest gratitude to my savior Jesus, who by the Holy Spirit has strengthened my faith and built up my Christian walk.

The anonymous author of the book of Hebrews tells us that the resurrection of the dead and the study of eternal judgment are foundational, elementary doctrines (Heb 6:1–3). That after two thousand years so much debate and disagreement still surrounds this topic is ironic. I pray that the Great Physician (Mark 2:17; Luke 4:23) will anoint us with a healing balm of Gilead (Jer 8:22), so that someday soon there may be a consensus and unity within the church about this important set of doctrines. I do not necessarily insist that my interpretation is correct; I only insist that we hearken to Scripture, and not to tradition.

Introduction

Pastor Buzz hung up the phone and slumped into his chair. He had known David for several years. The man lived across the street from the church; however, he might as well have lived in Cambodia. David never came inside the church. Buzz had a bad feeling about this one. He had no reason or evidence to think that David had been a Christian. And now, David's wife, or rather his widow, had just requested that Buzz preach at the funeral on Saturday. David had died the previous night.

Any minister who has performed a few funerals knows the uneasiness Buzz felt. It is disturbing to officiate at the death rite ceremony of an unsaved person. Of course, we don't really know who is saved and unsaved, but we do have hints and impressions based on the fruit of one's life. Buzz thought to himself, *What should I say?* "Rest in peace" is not true, because the Bible says that nothing but shame and suffering will befall those who reject Christ. An uplifting word to the family is awkward, since as Bible-believing Christians, we believe that their loved one is now without hope and will be mercilessly tortured by an exacting God. The best strategy for most pastors, including Buzz—at this sad time when confronted with a funeral for an unsaved individual—seems to be a salvation message. It is an excellent opportunity to make God's offer of forgiveness heard once again to the living.

My questions are multitudinous. Everyone has thought about this topic, but few have taken the time to really study what the Bible teaches. What happens to people when they die? At what point does God exact his judgment and justice? What is the nature of a person's being? Do people possess a soul? What is the nature or substance of that soul? Do people immediately depart for the spirit world of the hereafter? Does the Bible support the eternal torment of the lost in hell as championed by the Roman Catholic tradition, or extinction and annihilation of the wicked in the lake of fire? Also, do Christians go to heaven; if so, when? What is the nature of eternal life for the redeemed? This raises a lot of questions for which the biblical text seems uninterested in even asking, let alone answering. This book is my personal Bible study to search out answers to these difficult questions.

First, so that you know who I am and where I am coming from: I am a conservative Evangelical Protestant, born again, rather fundamentalist, historically premillennial, moderately dispensationalist, Bible-believing Christian. I am decently educated and love to read, but have no formal seminary or theological training. My study is by reading and prayer. I was brought up Baptist; currently I attend a Full Gospel church.

I was brought up, as were most people of my background, with the traditional "real heaven and hell" teaching. I was taught that the human soul is eternal. Upon death, the saved go to heaven to forevermore be with Jesus, and the unsaved go to hell, a place of torment. After the great white throne of judgment, the lost/unsaved/wicked souls are cast into the lake of fire for an eternity of pain, suffering, and torment.

A number of years ago, I was challenged by a Christian brother who postulated the extinction theory for the wicked. I have scoured the Bible, both Old Testament and New Testament, for verses in favor of both damnation theories. I have used my Strong's and other lexicons to study the Hebrew and Greek, to the best of my amateur ability. I have researched ancient Jewish and Greek beliefs. We all hate it when we are wrong, but after pondering this, reading many books, and studying my Bible, I am now leaning toward conditional immortality. Humans are not inherently eternal, immortal beings. The only way for us to achieve immortality is through God's conditions—repentance and faith in Jesus Christ. Those who fail this goal will be forever destroyed.

I started out this study by simply listing all the verses I found that appeared to support the extinction theory. On a separate page, I wrote out all of the verses that supported eternal torment. The tome grew. It turns out that numerous books have already been written on the subject. I owe an acknowledgment to Edward Fudge, Robert Morey, LeRoy Froom, Arthur Pink, Harry Buis, Robert Peterson, and many others. My coverage of the extinction-versus-eternal-torment debate is pretty much a recap of what these men have already noted. I started noticing, however, a correlation between the extinction theory and soul sleep. Soul sleep is the idea that after death, people are unconscious, sort of like sleeping, until the resurrection. All of authors cited above touch on that topic, but none fully explore the interconnections and ramifications these doctrines have on each other. Although I am plowing an old field, I hope to upturn some new clods of fertile dirt on an age-old debate.

If you discover that you disagree with any or all of my hypotheses herein, please hold the complaint letters and the burn pile until after you have heard me through. If I did my job right as an author, I hope these doctrines will all knit together into a fabric. But to see the stitch work, you must read the entire book. At the end of the book I invite your comments and feedback. The older I get, the more I realize how little I know. I can learn from your thoughts, and I would deeply appreciate hearing from you. I have friends who only read books, watch TV news programs, or listen to radio talk shows that present the same point of view they already hold. I think they find some comfort in reinforcing their already-known belief. However, with this method of information gathering we are not exposed to anything new, nor do we learn anything fresh. Personally, I prefer to read books on topics that I know little about, or from perspectives with which I think I might disagree. I listen to political speeches from candidates I don't like. I don't want to be argumentative or to be contentious, I want to learn. By pushing the envelope of my horizons, I hope to expand my still small brain. So, regardless of your doctrinal position, please take notes of any perceived heresies presented herein, and at the end tell me all about it. If you present biblical data, I will agree with you and recant.

Before we get started, however, I would like to consider Eph 4:2–6:

> Be completely humble and gentle; be patient, bearing with one another in love. Make every effort to keep the unity of the Spirit through the bond of peace. There is one body and one Spirit—just as you were called to one hope when you were called— one Lord, one faith, one baptism; one God and Father of all, who is over all and through all and in all.

I consider this essay a relatively minor topic of doctrine. It is not relevant to salvation. If you are a believer, then the consequences of damnation do not apply to you anyway. If you are not saved, it is going to be ugly and unpleasant either way. Whether we snap to consciousness after a thousand years or really in just a split second after death is in the big picture a minor glitch to a heavenly future. Gloriously, we shall live and reign forever (Rev 22:5). No matter how much theorizing we perform, we cannot change or alter the nature of the afterlife. We must follow Paul's admonition above: to show love, meekness, and long suffering to each other. Some people, good Christians, have difficulty speaking about controversial topics without getting angry. They practically turn red with rage at the suggestion that their long-held beliefs may be incorrect. The disunity and hostility of Christians toward each other deeply saddens our Savior Christ Jesus.

Probably the most important reason for the first part of this study is that the concept of an everlasting hell has been a cause for the rejection of Christ. Bertrand Russell, twentieth-century humanitarian and philosopher, objected to hell (and rejected Christ) on the basis that anyone who believes in an everlasting hell is inhumane: "There is one very serious defect to my mind in Christ's moral character, and that is that He believed in hell. I do not myself feel that any person who is really profoundly humane can believe in everlasting punishment."[1] He has a valid point. I have encountered this objection in personal witnessing. Many people, including myself, have an emotional objection to the alleged torture and torments of eternity that are inflicted upon God's enemies. It appears disproportionate to their crimes.

Ellen G. White was the founder of the Seventh-day Adventist Church. Although I disagree on Sabbath keeping and *kasrut* dietary laws, I think she and her church are correct about this doctrine. They have this view on the doctrine of eternal torment: "How repugnant to every emotion of love and mercy, and even to our sense of justice, is the doctrine that the wicked dead are tormented with fire and brimstone in an eternally burning hell; that for the sins of a brief earthly life they are to suffer torture as long as God shall live."[2] Clark Pinnock[3] has similar comments that we shall investigate toward the end of chapter 6.

However emotionally intolerable the concept may be, I still believe that Scripture must be the supreme authority for our doctrines. Although it is impossible to remove all human biases from our thoughts, my goal is that with a thorough study of inspired Scripture, we can show the objection of Bertrand Russell to be pointless. I pray that through understanding of God's fair justice, more souls may be won to Christ. What a pity for someone to die without Christ because of a myth.

After a several-year period of studying the hell topic, I had exhausted my mental and literary abilities, as well as my wife's patience. Part 1 of this book is the result of that journey. Part 2 is perhaps an even grander undertaking. I slowly realized that the glorious eternal life that the Bible promises is truly a vibrant, biological, physical, bodily life in the resurrection, yet fully spiritual. The bodily resurrection is not denied by many Christians; however, it is woefully neglected to the point of nonrecognition.

Clearly, the pressing motivation for part 2 of this book is that the esoteric, spiritual theory of heaven, which has pervaded our thought for centuries, lacks in realism and understandability. Jesus tells us in Matt 6:1–20 that we build up treasure in heaven by our acts of righteousness. How many millions of Christians have been disillusioned and discouraged in this achievement due to a foggy, surreal view of the heavenly horizon? When I am packing suitcases for a vacation, I like to know where I am going and what the weather will be like. Do I pack shorts or a parka? Do I need bug repellent and sunscreen or a tuxedo and disco shoes? My vacation only lasts for a couple of weeks. Eternity is a bit longer. Shouldn't Christians inquire and strive to learn about the locale and conditions of our eternal home? The literal and solid substance of our glorified heavenly/earthly life should awaken our senses. It is just as real of a life as I currently enjoy.

As we review Scripture passages, a basic rule of interpretation should always be applied: compare Scripture with Scripture. Let the Bible interpret itself. We should not view the Bible as sixty-six different books; instead we should consider it as one book. It is unified and consistent. Scripture certainly contains great variety, and even different styles of penmanship, but the message is from the single mind of God. This canonical approach is the most solid basis of exegesis and is accepted by all schools of Bible study.

The most important question, which is key to the correct series of doctrines, is whether humans have an immortal soul. With the answer to this one question, the entire house of cards will fall.

ENDNOTES

1. Russell, *Why I Am Not a Christian*, 17.
2. White, *Great Controversy*, 469.
3 Clark Pinnock, an evangelical theologian, now retired, was professor at McMaster Divinity College, Hamilton, Ontario.

Part One
Hell

1

Defining the Situation

The Greek Connection

WE START OUR JOURNEY by traveling back to ancient Greece. Athenian philosophy has heavily influenced our Western belief system. Athens invented democracy, and Plato forged the concept of individual human rights. The spark of the gods, that immortal soul that humans possess, was Socrates' idea. He was the father of Western thought.

The concept of the immortality of the human soul comes from Greek philosophy. Greeks considered immortality to be an attribute of divinity. They felt that people possessed within themselves a small portion of this characteristic of the gods. Socrates (470–399 B.C.) had been on trial for the corruption of the youth of Athens. It was his joy to teach philosophy to the boys and young men of his hometown; however, his teachings became misaligned with the views of the Athenian state. He was accused of treason and corruption of youth. He was tried and condemned to death by drinking a silver goblet of hemlock. This was a culturally common method of executing condemned prisoners. Plato (428–348 B.C.), the most famous student of Socrates, records the scene in a dialogue called *Phaedo*. Phaedo, a young man's name, was another student of Socrates. The book is a dialogue between Socrates and Phaedo, mostly concerning the afterlife and nature of the soul. It also contains the famous death scene.

"The soul is perfectly and certainly imperishable, not only for this life, but forever" (*Phaedo* 105d). Socrates' and Plato's pagan Greek belief in the immortality of the soul became foundational to Western thought.

Modern European and American Christians take it for granted. However, the notion is not found in the Bible.

"The soul is immortal and indestructible, and in reality our souls will exist in Hades" (*Phaedo* 56). Hades was thought to be the abode of the dead; both good people and bad people went to Hades in the underworld. The deceased entered the underworld by crossing the river Styx, ferried across by the boat master Charon, who charged a small coin for passage. Pious relatives traditionally placed this coin under the tongue of the deceased before burial. The river Styx formed the boundary between the upper living world and the lower dead world. Hades was subdivided into regions. The virtuous went to the Elysian Fields; bad people went to Tartarus.[1]

Tartarus is a deep, gloomy place, a pit or abyss used as a dungeon of torment and suffering. While almost all the dead were said to go to other regions within Hades, the gods cast the very worst mortal sinners and immortal enemies (the Titans) into Tartarus for endless punishment. We speak more about Tartarus later.

By contrast, the Hebrew Bible was written, not by Greek philosophers, but by Israelites. An oriental Semitic race over one thousand miles from Greece, they were, until the Hellenistic period, unaffected by Greek myth and thought.

The Bible teaches that God alone is eternal. God alone is immortal. First Timothy 6:15b–16 states, "God, the blessed and only Ruler, the King of kings and Lord of lords, *who alone is immortal* and who lives in unapproachable light, whom no one has seen or can see. To him be honor and might forever. Amen" (emphasis added). First Timothy 1:17 also states, "Now to the King eternal, immortal, invisible, the only God, be honor and glory for ever and ever. Amen."

Genesis 3:19 says that man was created from dust and shall return to dust. The transience of life and the humble, dustly nature of man as a finite creation are stressed in Scripture:

Psalm 90:3a: "You turn men back to dust."

Psalm 103:14b (KJV): "He remembereth that we are dust."

Ecclesiastes 3:20b (KJV): "All are of the dust, and all turn to dust again."

Ezekiel 18:4b (KJV): "The soul that sinneth, it shall die."

Romans 2:7: "To those who by persistence in doing good seek glory, honor and immortality, he will give eternal life."

Second Timothy 1:10: "But it has now been revealed through the appearing of our Savior, Christ Jesus, who has destroyed death and has brought life and immortality to light through the gospel."

All of these verses say the same thing. The human being does not have any sort of innate immortality as a birthright. According to Rom 2:7 we must persistently seek it, which implies that we do not already have it. According to 2 Tim 1:10 immortality comes through the gospel, which also has the power to destroy death. Death is innately human, but immortality comes from God.

Solomon wrote in Prov 12:28, "In the way of righteousness there is life; along that path is immortality."

The implication is that other paths that are not righteous do not lead to immortality.

The human soul does not possess any form of eternal existence or immortality until God gives it to him. This is aptly called conditional immortality by scholars such as Fudge.[2] The human body and the human soul are created. They are finite and can be destroyed. Plato and Aristotle were just plain wrong. There is no spark of the gods that makes the human soul eternal and immortal.

The foregoing Platonic Greek theories of an immortal soul, be it noticed, are based upon the assumption that death does not mean death—that to die is to become more alive than before death. In Eden it was God who declared to our first parents, "Thou shalt surely die" (Gen 2:17 KJV). It was Satan who declared, "Ye shall not surely die" (Gen 3:4 KJV). Notice that the heathen, as well as the Christians, have accepted Satan's lie and correspondingly rejected God's truth. Do they not all agree with the serpent's statement, "Ye shall not surely die"? Do they not all claim that the dead are alive—much more alive than before they died? This, dear friends, has been our common point of mistake. We have followed the wrong teacher, the one of whom our Lord said, "'He abode not in the Truth,' and that he is the father of lies.—John 8:44" (KJV).[3]

What I am suggesting is nothing new. I believe that the idea of an immortal human soul is purely a pagan false doctrine that has snuck into Christianity through centuries of osmosis. Arnobius of Sicca lived in Tunisia in northern Africa in the late third century after Christ (c. A.D. 253–327). He wrote what is considered by many scholars to be the most remarkable patristic document now extant. In his treatise he affirms that the human soul "is not immortal by nature, but capable of putting on immortality as a grace." Arnobius clearly believed in final annihilation of the wicked.[4] Considering that he wrote in Latin, was thoroughly Roman, and was himself pagan before his conversion, this appears to be quite a major change in doctrine. Arnobius was postmortem declared a heretic and totally ostracized by the official church.

In the modern world, we no longer speak of the Elysian Fields. We no longer insert a coin under the tongue of a cadaver. But many of our thought patterns are fundamentally Greek. The mythology of Britain has also influenced us. The modern English concept of hell is more of Norse/Anglo-Saxon mythology than of Hebrew Scripture. From about A.D. 1200, the Norse religious poem *Prose Edda* describes "Hel" as an unpleasant abode for those unworthy of Valhalla, which is reserved for chosen warriors who die in battle.[5] This is the pagan origin of our English word "hell."

Additional Christian mythology comes from European literature. Dante's *Inferno* strongly influenced our understanding of hell. At times the descriptions seem like ancient torture chambers, with elaborate portrayals of suffering. Dante took the idea of levels of punishment in hell to dramatic extremes. In his circles of hell, each circle grew progressively worse. In one of the deepest circles, the heretics (notably Mohammed, founder of Islam) walked a loop and continually had their flesh ripped from their bodies.[6]

Dante's work appears to be one of the origins of the popular notion that demons torment and maliciously poke victims in the pit. That assumption is pure myth and has no biblical support. A popular book about hell is Bill Weise's *32 Minutes in Hell*, which has been mass-marketed and is available even at Wal-Mart. As we learn in the pages of this book, I don't believe Weise could have had a vision of hell immediately after death, as he purports. It maybe could have been an ultimate vision of Gehenna, but there are still some troubling contradictions with Scripture, not the least of which is that in Weise's vision he encounters demons who torment the lost and yet are seemingly unaffected by the hellfire themselves. Such a vision comes from Dante, not Scripture.

We won't even further consider it here.

Western European thought and the modern Evangelical Protestants for whom I write are primarily influenced by these mythologies—Greek, Norse, medieval. The people of ancient Israel, however, may have been influenced by Egyptian theology and Assyrian/Babylonian mythology.

Amazingly, through the power of inspiration, very little or none of this bleeds over into Old Testament texts. The superpowers of the ancient Near East all believed in the passage of the soul to the eternal afterlife. Egyptians wrote the *Book of the Dead* to guide the *ka*'s (soul's) passage through the underworld. Early Mesopotamians wrote the *Epic of Gilgamesh*, which similarly postulated the condition of the afterlife. Most human civilizations have believed in the eternal existence of the human soul as a deific being that transcends death. None of this mythology is characteristic of the God of Israel. When Scripture is read carefully and compared to itself, none of this myth can be found in the Bible.

When discussing the realm of the underworld, it is better not to use the word "hell." That English word is loaded, carrying its own presumed meaning and baggage. The word "hell" is heavily laden with literary and artistic associations that have accreted through the centuries. In order to attain a more original context, I suggest that we learn about the original Hebrew and Greek words. To understand more fully the state of the dead as mentioned in Scripture, let's examine the different Hebrew and Greek words that are frequently translated into English as "hell."

SHEOL

The original meaning of this Hebrew word may very well be lost to the centuries. It is almost pointless consulting a dictionary or concordance because the word now means what translators have for the last several hundred years thought it meant. For example, the *Brown-Driver-Briggs Hebrew and English Lexicon* (BDB) is a very traditional work. It was written and complied in the early years of the twentieth century. BDB is one of the primary, fundamental reference works that all good scholars (and also myself) refer to when researching a word. They list the definition for "sheol" as "the underworld ... whither man descends at death."[7] Similarly, and very picturesquely, John Davis's classic *Dictionary of the Bible* defines "sheol" as "a dark gloomy region, where the inhabitants pass a conscious but dull, inactive existence."[8]

On the other hand, the *Seventh-day Adventist Bible Commentary* claims that "sheol was used as a figurative expression denoting the place where men go at death. From a strictly literal point of view sheol may be equated with 'grave.'"[9] An additional witness agreeing with the Adventist view is William Smith in his *Dictionary of the Bible*, a classic of British scholarship from the nineteenth century. Hear him: "Hell . . . is the word generally and unfortunately used by our translators to render the Hebrew 'sheol.' The English word Hell is mixed up with numberless associations entirely foreign to the minds of the ancient Hebrews."[10]

The meaning of "sheol" has come to be what the dictionary author/editor wanted to print. All dictionaries and concordances are colored with bias. Whose dictionary do you use?

My view has come to closely follow the Adventist idea. However, do not jump to conclusions about my overall doctrine. (Read chap. 3 for some surprises.) Face it, we do not really know what the ancient Hebrews meant with the word "sheol." The best way to most fairly determine what the inspired word of God means is to listen to that very word. Allow your mind to be momentarily cleared of all preconceptions. Remove all indoctrinated thoughts, and let the Bible speak for itself. When studying several passages about Sheol, we must compare them to each other and nothing else.

The word "hell" occurs thirty-one times in the KJV OT; in every instance it is the Hebrew *sheol*. Unfortunately, the KJV is very inconsistent. *Sheol* is translated as "grave" thirty-one times and as "pit" three times. *Sheol* is the most common word in the entire Bible that is traditionally translated as "hell."

In medieval Old English, the related word *helan* meant to conceal; *helan* potatoes was to keep them in a shallow pit. The correct meaning of *sheol* is most likely the hidden condition of death. In the medieval context, the KJV translates correctly, but the word "hell" does not have that sense anymore in modern English. *Sheol* is a poetic term, and a better translation for the modern mind is simply "the grave." The KJV medieval translational error has been corrected in most modern English translations. Sheol is never to be understood as a place of consciousness, whether torment or bliss. Rather it is a place of silence, darkness, and no return. It is a place of no memory, no work, and no consciousness. This cannot be referring to a two-compartmented hades, as traditionalists understand. *Sheol* is the tomb, not literally—as in a cave or a hole in the ground where bones are buried—but poetically, as in gravedom.

In Gen 37:35 Joseph is alleged to have been ripped apart and eaten by animals, and in Jonah 2:1 the prophet of that same name drowns at sea. Neither of these had an actual grave or tomb that descendants could visit, yet Joseph and Jonah are said to have entered Sheol, the state of the grave. ("Sheol" is Strong's #7585.)

Let's consider some more citations:

Job 3:17: "There the wicked cease from turmoil, and there the weary are at rest." Notice that Scripture says that they are at rest, nothing about torment.

Job 10:20–22: "Are not my few days almost over? Turn away from me so I can have a moment's joy before I go to the place of no return, to the land of gloom and deep shadow, to the land of deepest night, of deep shadow and disorder, where even the light is like darkness." Job expects that he will go to Sheol.

Job 14:10–14: "But man dies and is laid low; he breathes his last and is no more. As water disappears from the sea or a riverbed becomes parched and dry, so man lies down and does not rise; till the heavens are no more, men will not awake or be roused from their sleep. If only you would hide me in the grave [*sheol*] and conceal me till your anger has passed! If only you would set me a time and then remember me! If a man dies, will he live again? All the days of my hard service I will wait for my renewal to come. You will call and I will answer you; you will long for the creature your hands have made." Job, however, also anticipates a bodily resurrection.

No one praises God from Sheol, so it is seen as an appropriate setting for the wicked and a sorrowful place for the righteous. However, all men have a common destiny in Sheol. In Gen 37:35, Jacob heard that his son, Joseph, had allegedly been ripped to pieces by wild animals and is already dead and currently in Sheol. Jacob lamented and said that he too would go in mourning down to Sheol to be with his son. Were Jacob and Joseph, patriarchs of Israel, in hell? No, they were to join their fathers in death. In 2 Sam 22:6 (and also in Ps 18:5) David says that "the cords of Sheol" coiled around him when Saul tried to kill him. Do you think that David, a man after God's own heart, was one step away from hell as he tried to outrun Saul in the wilderness? All men, godly and wicked, go to Sheol, because it is simply the grave and all men must die.

Psalm 116:3 (KJV): "The sorrows of death compassed me, and the pains of hell [*sheol*] gat hold upon me: I found trouble and sorrow." KJV readers sometimes misunderstand the pain, trouble, and sorrow seen in this verse. I have heard the suggestion that this verse is proof of conscious existence in Sheol, because here the dead experience pain, trouble, and sorrow. When read in context, this verse is very similar to 2 Sam 22:6 and Ps 18:5. David experienced these fears as he approached death. David was not actually dead; he was near death. He was gripped in fear that he may die. David was anguishing about the imminent loss of his life as Saul pursued him.

Psalm 6:5: "No one remembers you when he is dead. Who praises you from the grave [*sheol*]?"

Psalm 88:10–12: "Do you show your wonders to the dead? Do those who are dead rise up and praise you? Selah. Is your love declared in the grave [*qebar*], your faithfulness in destruction [*abbadon*, see comments below]? Are your wonders known in the place of darkness, or your righteous deeds in the land of oblivion?"

Psalm 115:17 (KJV): "The dead praise not the LORD, neither any that go down into silence."

Isaiah 38:18: "For the grave [*sheol*] cannot praise you, death cannot sing your praise; those who go down to the pit cannot hope for your faithfulness." Notice the parallelism, a common feature of Hebrew poetry. Sheol, death, and the pit are all repeated side by side, signifying their synonymous nature.

The Hebrew prophets understood the dead in Sheol to be weak and powerless, without thought or memory, without work or action. The citizens of Sheol sleep in unconsciousness.

Psalm 146:4 (KJV): "His breath goeth forth, he returneth to his earth; in that very day his thoughts perish."

Ecclesiastes 9:5–6: "For the living know that they will die, but the dead know nothing; they have no further reward, and even the memory of them is forgotten. Their love, their hate and their jealousy have long since vanished; never again will they have a part in anything that happens under the sun."

Ecclesiastes 9:10: "Whatever your hand finds to do, do it with all your might, for in the grave [*sheol*], where you are going, there is neither working nor planning nor knowledge nor wisdom."

Many Christians have presumed that Sheol before the time of Christ was a two-compartmented chamber consisting of Paradise/Bosom of Abraham and Hades. They claim to glean this idea from the parable of the Rich Man and Lazarus in Luke 16, which we study completely later. In reality, I think the origin of such Christians' thought is medieval Catholic or Greek pagan doctrine. Psalm 49:14 says of man, "Like sheep they are destined for Sheol." Do the sheep go to the Paradise compartment or to the torment of hades? Of course, animals go to neither, because Sheol does not mean "hell" as in our Greco-Roman mind frame. Sheol is the grave—not *a* grave, but poetically *the* grave.

Further evidence suggests that death was perceived as the end of existence during the Old Testament period (until the resurrection):

Job 7:9: "As a cloud vanishes and is gone, so he who goes down to the grave [*sheol*] does not return."

Job 7:21: "Why do you not pardon my offenses and forgive my sins? For I will soon lie down in the dust; you will search for me, but I will be no more."

Psalm 39:13: "Look away from me, that I may rejoice again before I depart and am no more."

The word "sheol" appears over sixty times in the Hebrew Scriptures. The KJV made the unfortunate mistake of being inconsistent in its translation. About half the time the translators rendered the word "hell," and about half the time they rendered the word "grave" or "pit." Either *sheol* means the place of departed dead spirits in the afterlife, or it means the grave. Picking its meaning on a verse-by-verse basis to accommodate one's doctrine is not the proper approach.

Old Testament–period (Iron Age) Israelites, at least the orthodox ones who followed the God of Abraham, did not have a developed concept of an afterlife because, as we see in upcoming pages, there was no afterlife; both the righteous and evil of all generations and all nations were in the grave awaiting their day. Numerous prophetic passages in the OT show the prophets promising a resurrection. However, the original authors may not have fully understood what they were writing; such is the power of inspiration. The consensus among scholars is that within orthodox communities, Israelites did not consider the dead "awake" in some other spiritual dimension. Death was the end of this life, not the start of the next life. This belief notwithstanding, there was undeniably an element in that culture of necromancy, demonic summoning of the dead, ancestor worship, offerings to the dead, baptizing for the dead, and other prohibited practices. For an excellent and detailed further study, see the books *Shades of Sheol* by Philip S. Johnston,[11] and *Judahite Burial Practices and Beliefs about the Dead* by Elizabeth Bloch-Smith.[12]

Those who choose to believe that *sheol* means a place of conscious departed spirits quote Isa 14:9 (kings in Sheol are excited at Nebuchadnezzar's arrival), Ezek 31:16 (a cedar tree goes to Sheol), and Ezek 32:21 (people in Sheol taunt Pharaoh for being mortal and having died). We review all of these verses shortly. These are highly poetic verses and do not point to a consciousness in the afterlife. If, however, they do represent literal awakeness after death, then they are in direct contradiction to verses declaring that those in Sheol do not know anything, think anything, or do anything. These contradictory verses include Ps 146:4; Eccl 9:5–6; and Eccl. 9:10, all quoted just above. There are *no other* verses concerning "sheol" that even remotely support a conscious theory. I am not withholding verses that do not agree with my pretext. They simply are not there. The idea that *sheol* represents an abode of conscious disembodied spirits comes from somewhere else, not from the sixty-five *sheol* verses found in the inspired word of God.

Abbadon is another poetic Hebrew word, a curious one (Strong's #011). It is used only six times in the OT. The word seems to mean destruction, a place of ruin. It is usually thought to be synonymous with Sheol, and I agree. Verses including *abbadon* are as follows:

Job 26:6 (KJV): "Hell [*sheol*] is naked before him, and destruction [*abbadon*] hath no covering."

Job 28:22 (KJV): "Destruction [*abbadon*] and death say, We have heard the fame thereof with our ears."

Job 31:12 (KJV): For it is a fire that consumeth to destruction [*abbadon*], and would root out all mine increase."

Psalm 88:11 (KJV): "Shall thy lovingkindness be declared in the grave? or thy faithfulness in destruction [*abbadon*]?"

Proverbs 15:11 (KJV): "Hell [*sheol*] and destruction [*abbadon*] are before the LORD: how much more then the hearts of the children of men?"

Proverbs 27:20 (KJV): "Hell [*sheol*] and destruction [*abbadon*] are never full; so the eyes of man are never satisfied."

"HELL" IN THE NEW TESTAMENT

"Hades" Rendered "Hell"

In the New Testament, the Greek word *hades* (Strongs #86) is used eleven times, including four times in Revelation. In Greek it best means "the unseen world." It corresponds almost exactly to the Hebrew word *sheol* and should be generally translated as "the grave." The word *hades* was chosen as a translation for *sheol* by the seventy-two rabbis who translated the Hebrew Scriptures into Greek, known as the Septuagint. The Septuagint was translated about three hundred years before Christ in the city of Alexandria, Egypt. By the time of the New Testament, *hades* was well equated with *sheol*. As proof, see the verses of the NT that are quotations or allusions from the Old Testament in which the inspired authors of Scripture render the Hebrew *sheol* into the Greek *hades*. Some examples follow:

Matthew 11:23/Luke 10:15: Jesus is speaking about Capernaum: "Will you be lifted up to the skies? No, you will go down to [*hades*]." This is a tribute to Isa 14:13–15: "You said in your heart, 'I will ascend to heaven; . . . But you are brought down to the depths of the pit [*sheol*]."

Acts 2:27 (KJV) and 2:31: "Thou wilt not leave my soul in [*hades*]" is a direct quotation from Ps 16:10 (KJV): "Thou wilt not leave my soul in [*sheol*]."

And in 1 Cor 15:54, 55 (KJV), "Death is swallowed up in victory. O death, where is thy sting? O grave [*hades*], where is thy victory?" is an allusion to Isa 25:8 (KJV), "He will swallow up death in victory," and to Hos 13:14 (KJV), "O death, I will be thy plagues; O [*sheol*], I will be thy destruction."

In Matthew 16:18 Jesus refers to the "gates of [*hades*]" while in Caesarea Philippi, which the KJV translates "gates of Hell." This is probably an allusion to Isa 38:10 ("gates of [*sheol*]),*" or possibly Job 17:16 ("bars of [*sheol*])." In the Isaiah passage, good King Hezekiah prays for healing from a serious illness and laments his early passing into death. Death is portrayed as a mighty city with impregnable gates from which no one escapes. It is a one-way road. Translators of the KJV correctly wrote this verse as "gates of the grave," because they, with their own preconceived biases, did not want to send righteous Hezekiah to hell. Jesus' statement is that his church will overcome that mighty gate, that one-way road, the unstoppable fate. The church will overcome death/Sheol/hades. This is evocative literature, using metaphor and imagery to stimulate the imagination. Precaution should be used not to literalize the meaning, as if Hezekiah and Jesus were literally describing the entrance portal to the City of the Dead in some otherworldly spiritual realm.

All four verses in Revelation utilizing *hades* do so in poetic parallelism, so common in Hebrew Scripture. Even though Revelation was written in Greek, the author was most probably a Palestinian Jew, whose mother tongue and cultural background were Aramaic or Hebrew.

Before we look at those Revelation verses, we need to spend a moment on understanding parallel poetry. The biblical style of writing poetry is not familiar to most readers, so the poetic intention is fully invisible. Parallelism is when the writer says one thing in two or more different ways. The first part of the verse is paralleled with the second part. The verse is not saying two different things, but one thing in two different ways. Often we overlook what the Bible is telling us because we are not recognizing what the poetry of a passage is attempting to convey. Even worse, sometimes we read extraneous things into a passage, because we do not realize the poetic construction. The Hebraic use of the conjunction "and" has been greatly misunderstood by the Western minds of modern Christians. The use of the word "and" linking death and hades in Revelation has certainly caused much confusion. We envision two separate entities both taking allied action. In English, rightly so: the word "and" between two items almost always conveys the meaning of two separate things, one after another. In Scripture, however, this word is used, as in standard Hebrew poetry, to link two statements as one. In other words, the first and the following are the very same thing.

The word "hades" is used four times in Revelation. Christ has the keys to death and hades (Rev 1:18), and they are said to follow the pale horse (Rev 6:8). Death and hades give up their dead at the judgment (Rev 20:13), and they are finally destroyed in the lake of fire (Rev 20:14). By pairing these two, death and hades, in a parallel sequence, John the Revelatee[13] is expressing their synonymy.

Revelation 1:18 is a particularly good example: "I am the Living One; I was dead, and behold I am alive for ever and ever! And I hold the keys of death and *hades*" (KJV: "hell"). Jesus says that he has the keys to hades. Keys let occupants out of their current habitation. Keys produce freedom. The risen Christ is pronouncing that through him there is freedom, escape, and release from death and the grave. If *hades* has a meaning other than the grave, if the KJV is correct, and *hades* means "hell," then that would mean that Jesus is intending to release the incorrigible wicked sinners from the pit. Remember, this verse is spoken by Christ in Revelation, c. A.D. 95, not by Jesus as he walked among us during his first advent. Proponents of the dual-chamber-of-hades theory claim that the bosom of Abraham (the good side) had been emptied and Jewish saints taken to heaven around the time of the resurrection, c. A.D. 30 The only souls left in hades by A.D. 95 (according to their own theory) are the lost sinners. Unless you subscribe to universalism (more on that later), it should be agreed that a scenario of releasing these prisoners would be impossible according to Scriptures such as 2 Thess 1:8–9 and Rev 20:14–15.

Hades, as used in the NT, does not mean "hell." It is a Greek translation of the Hebrew *sheol*. It is the intermediate state of the dead, after physical bodily death but before the promised bodily resurrection at the end time. Hades would be more appropriately translated into English as "grave." Since the word "hell" has strong Anglo-Saxon mythological connections to the pre-Christian pagans, it is not a good translation. The only instance of *hades* that requires further study is Luke 16, the parable of Rich Man and Lazarus, which we address shortly.

In the original languages, neither *sheol* nor *hades*, by their usage, context, or meaning, support the common concept of a two-compartmented intermediate abode of disembodied spirits as purported to be seen in the Lukan parable. But I'm getting ahead of myself; let us return to the New Testament words that are frequently translated to English as "hell."

"Gehenna" Rendered "Hell"

"Gehenna" (Strongs #1067) occurs twelve times: Matt 5:22, 29, 30; 10:28; 18:9; 23:15, 33; Mark 9:43-47; Luke 12:5; and Jas 3:6. Eleven of the twelve times, it was spoken by our Lord Jesus. It is the Grecian mode of spelling the Hebrew words translated "valley of Hinnom." This valley lay just outside the city walls of Jerusalem and served the purposes of a municipal sewer and garbage burning dump. The offal, garbage, and dead animals were emptied there, and fires were kept continually burning to consume utterly all things deposited therein. Sulfur, biblically known as brimstone, was added to assist combustion and ensure complete destruction. Gehenna was an unclean place. Ceremonially, it would be disastrous for a religious Jew to find himself wallowing in Gehenna.

Originally, the valley of Hinnom contained a Canaanite shrine called the altar of Topheth (2 Kgs 23:10). This is where sacrifices of living children were made to the demonically animated god Molech. Good king Josiah tore down the Topheth. Then to fully desecrate the area so it would not be used as a cultic center in the future, Josiah inaugurated the town dump in this local gulch.

The valley of Hinnom—Gehenna—is illustrating things future. I do not think that there is much debate among Christians about the meaning of Gehenna. It is clear that the defiled, abominable, wicked, and all of those unworthy of everlasting life were represented by the refuse and the filthy, lifeless carcasses cast into Gehenna outside the city—whose utter destruction was herein symbolized.

Gehenna is a metaphor for the second death and the lake of fire. The fire of Gehenna is used as a symbol of destruction, because fire consumes, turns to ash, and totally destroys that which is cast into it. If the traditional idea is correct—that the smoke-belching pit of hell does not consume the sinners, but instead preserves them in torment—then Jesus did not use a very good analogy. The local landfill consumes the waste; it destroys the waste; it turns the waste to dust and ash.

In closing, "*Gehenna* was a type or illustration of the Second Death—final and complete destruction, from which there can be no recovery; for after that, 'there remaineth no more sacrifice for sins,' but only 'fiery indignation, which shall *devour* the adversaries.'—Heb. 10:26, 27."[14]

LAKE OF FIRE

The Greek words *limne pur* mean "lake of fire." *Limne* is used many other times in simple reference to a lake, such as in Galilee. *Pur* is also used numerous times, seventy-four to be exact. Frequently the meaning is a simple fire, such as when Peter sat by a fire as Christ was being tried and denied his Lord (Luke 22:55), or when Paul shook off a snake into the fire (Acts 28:5). It is also used numerous times of a supernatural fire from heaven (Luke 17:29), hell fire (2 Thess 1:8), Holy Spirit as fire (Matt 3:11), Pentecostal tongues as fire (Acts 2:3), and so on.

These words together form the vision of a lake of fire, as seen by John in Revelation. It is mentioned five times, all near the culmination of the Apocalypse. Some believe that the vision of a lake burning with fire and brimstone (sulfur) is symbolic, as, undeniably, is much of the book. However, Rev 20:15 tells us that immediately following the great white throne judgment, all of the condemned will be cast into the lake of fire. I think it is real, and I think it is the same as Gehenna. I do not accept the figurative or spiritualization approach of the lake of fire that conceives it as nothing more than some mental anguish that is suffered. The lake of fire really is a place of literal roaring flames and burning sulfur. At a later point in this book, I will provide evidence for this assertion, but for now file that datum in the wee recesses of your brain. The lake of fire is what Jesus warned people about as he used the word "Gehenna" eleven times.

If *sheol* and *hades* depict the intermediate state of the dead, then Gehenna and the lake of fire depict the ultimate terminal state of those without Christ.

OUTER DARKNESS

Some verses appear to describe the geographical location of the lake of fire, Gehenna. Some have wondered, *How can a fire be dark?* Consider the following verses:

Matthew 8:11–12 (KJV): "And I say unto you, That many shall come from the east and west, and shall sit down with Abraham, and Isaac, and Jacob, in the kingdom of heaven. But the children of the kingdom shall be cast out into outer darkness: there shall be weeping and gnashing of teeth."

Jude 1:11–13 (KJV): "Woe unto them! for they have gone in the way of Cain, and ran greedily after the error of Balaam for reward, and perished in the gainsaying of Core. These are spots in your feasts of charity, when they feast with you, feeding themselves without fear: clouds they are without water, carried about of winds; trees whose fruit withereth, without fruit, twice dead, plucked up by the roots; Raging waves of the sea, foaming out their own shame; wandering stars, to whom is reserved the blackness of darkness for ever." See also 2 Pet 2:17, which is very similar to the Jude verse. As a matter of fact, these passages are so similar that I wonder who wrote first and who plagiarized. See also the parables of Jesus in Matt 22:13and 25:30.

These verses are metaphorical. They speak of expulsion and separation. This darkness to which the rebellious are cast should not be confused with the darkness of the pit Tartarus, where a literal darkness is possible.

TARTARUS RENDERED "HELL"

The Greek word *tartarus* occurs but once in the Scriptures, and it too is translated "hell." Second Peter 2:4 (KJV) reads, "God spared not the angels that sinned, but cast them down to hell [*tartarus*], and delivered them into chains of darkness, to be reserved unto judgment."

The word *tartarus* appears in Greek mythology as the name for a dark abyss or prison. In Greek the word is actually transliterated *tartaroo*, but in English is spelled "tartarus." Both spellings may be observed; it is the same word.

The Greek word *abussos* means "abyss" or "bottomless pit." Consider the similarity in the following verses:

Luke 8:30–31: "Jesus asked him, 'What is your name?' 'Legion,' he replied, because many demons had gone into him. And they begged him repeatedly not to order them to go into the Abyss."

Revelation 9:2–3a (KJV): "And he opened the bottomless pit; and there arose a smoke out of the pit, as the smoke of a great furnace; and the sun and the air were darkened by reason of the smoke of the pit. And there came out of the smoke locusts upon the earth."

Revelation 20:1–2: "And I saw an angel coming down out of heaven, having the key to the Abyss and holding in his hand a great chain. He seized the dragon, that ancient serpent, who is the devil, or Satan, and bound him for a thousand years."

I think the bottomless pit from which the demon locusts of the fifth trumpet appear, and the abyss in which Satan is bound during the millennium and the abyss to which legion begs not to be thrown, and the *tartarus* mentioned by Peter are all the same place. There is a real hell-like prison that contains demons. It is rather similar to the well-known pagan Greek myth. Everybody in the Roman world would quickly visualize Tartarus, from the myth of Homer's *Odyssey* (Greek, c. 1000 B.C.), Plato's many works (Greek, 400 B.C.), and Virgil's *Aeneid* (Roman, 50 B.C.). However, Peter used the word to describe a real place. Some demons have been locked up there for a very long time. Possibly they are the same demons who will be released to torment men during the fifth trumpet. It is possible that this is also the same as Gehenna/lake of fire, or maybe a chamber of that place.

A couple of additional difficult verses perhaps fit into the model of Tartarus:

First Peter 3:18–20 (KJV): "For Christ . . . being put to death in the flesh, but quickened by the Spirit: By which also he went and preached unto the spirits in prison; Which sometime were disobedient, when once the longsuffering of God waited in the days of Noah, while the ark was a preparing, wherein few, that is, eight souls were saved by water."

Jude 6 (KJV): "And the angels which kept not their first estate, but left their own habitation, he hath reserved in everlasting chains under darkness unto the judgment of the great day."

These are the same demons, I think. However, there is no mention, not even a hint, that humans are currently in Tartarus.

Some teachers believe that the 1 Peter verse above is claiming that Jesus preached the gospel of salvation to deceased human spirits in hell during the three days while he was dead. That interpretation makes several mistakes. First, there is no second chance for the dead. Second, Jesus could not have done this while he himself was dead (more on that thought later). Third, the spirits or *pneuma* are better interpreted as demons rather than humans. *Pneuma* is used in Heb 1:14 for ministering angels. An unclean *pneuma* speaks of a demon in Matt 8:16; 10:1; 12:43; Mark 1:26–27; Acts 5:16; 8:7; 16:16, and many other verses. The Bible never refers to human beings as "spirits." We have spirits, but we are not spirits. God, angels, and demons do not have spirits; they are spirits. So the better meaning of the word "spirits" in the phrase "spirits in prison" seems to argue for the spirits being something other than humans. Fourth, as we have already seen, humans are not conscious in hell, but are in the grave.

I admit that I lack an airtight explanation for the interpretation of this difficult passage (just like everyone else for the past two thousand years). I believe that a more biblically correct reading of that verse would be that at some point after the resurrection, Christ in the spirit went to Tartarus. In that place are demons that have been bound in chains ever since the days of Noah. They must have done something particularly heinous. (Some people speculate that they were involved in the "sons of God" having sexual relations with the "daughters of men" incident that resulted in the Nephilim found in Gen 6. Maybe, but that speculation is tangential to my point.) For whatever reason, these bad boy demons have been locked up and have had no contact with the outside world since before the flood. The word used for "preached" (*karusso*) means to proclaim in the manner of a herald. It carries a suggestion of formality and authority. Jesus publicly proclaimed and openly published the victory over death and sin that had become his because of his resurrection. This could not have happened while he was dead, before his resurrection (as many allege), because at that point he had not yet been fully victorious. According to the Apostle Paul in 1 Cor 15:14–19, without the resurrection, it is all vanity and a waste of time.

What befalls these demons in the Day of Judgment is beyond the scope of my afterlife study (although I think we both know the answer). My interest is in the afterlife condition of humans. We return in the next chapter to what happens upon death.

ENDNOTES

1. For further reading, see Homer, *Odyssey*, book 4.563.
2. Edward Fudge is considered by many the banner man for conditional immortality. See Fudge, *Fire That Consumes*.
3. Bible Truth Keys, *Where Are the Dead?* 10.
4. Lawler, *Ancient Christian Writers Series—The Case Against the Pagans*, book 2, 14–62.
5. Brodeur, *Prose Edda of Snorri Sturlson*, 16.
6. For further reading, see Dante Alighieri, *The Divine Comedy*, originally written ca. 1320. Mohammed's torment is in canto 28, vv. 30–31.
7. *Brown-Driver-Briggs Hebrew & English Lexicon to Old Testament*, 982.
8. Davis, *Dictionary of the Bible*, 286.
9. Nichol, *Seventh-Day Adventist Bible Commentary*, 3:999.
10. Smith, *Dictionary of the Bible*, 2:1037.
11. Johnston, *Shades of Sheol*.
12. Bloch-Smith, *Judahite Burial Practices and Beliefs about the Dead*.
13. 'Revelatee' might not be a real word in English. However, it is incorrect to call him John the Revelator, as is frequently heard. Jesus Christ is the one who made the Revelation, John received it.
14. Harvest Truth Database, "What Say the Scriptures Concerning Hell?" http://www.agsconsulting.com/htdbv5/r4553.htm (accessed March 8, 2010).

2

Dead Soul Syndrome

Particular Judgment

PARTICULAR JUDGMENT IS A common Christian doctrine which states that immediately after an individual's death, the Lord God justly decides that person's eternal destiny. In Christianity, the soul is generally said to go to heaven or hell—or, in Roman Catholicism, purgatory. The *Catholic Encyclopedia* notes, "Ecclesiastes 11:9; 12:1; and Hebrews 9:27, are sometimes quoted in proof of the particular judgment, but though these passages speak of a judgment after death, neither the context nor the force of the words proves that the sacred writer had in mind a judgment distinct from that at the end of the world. The scriptural arguments in defence of the particular judgment must be indirect. There is no text of which we can certainly say that it expressly affirms this dogma."[1]

Catholic theology, accepted by most Protestants through centuries of osmosis, supposes that "the particular judgment will be instantaneous, that in the moment of death the separated soul is internally illuminated as to its own guilt or innocence and then takes its course either to hell, or to purgatory, or to heaven."[2] Thomas Aquinas (A.D. 1227–1274), the greatest Catholic theologian, clearly defined this theory in the thirteenth century. His massive unfinished work *Summa Theologica* states as follows:

> I answer that, Even as in bodies there is gravity or levity whereby they are borne to their own place which is the end of their movement, so in souls there is merit or demerit whereby they reach their reward or punishment, which are the ends of their deeds.

> Wherefore just as a body is conveyed at once to its place, by its gravity or levity, unless there be an obstacle, so too the soul, the bonds of the flesh being broken, whereby it was detained in the state of the way, receives at once its reward or punishment, unless there be an obstacle. . . . And since a place is assigned to souls in keeping with their reward or punishment, as soon as the soul is set free from the body it is either plunged into hell or soars to heaven, unless it be held back by some debt, for which its flight must needs be delayed until the soul is first of all cleansed. This truth is attested by the manifest authority of the canonical Scriptures and the doctrine of the holy Fathers; wherefore the contrary must be judged heretical as stated in Dial. iv, 25, and in De Eccl. Dogm. xlvi.[3]

I guess Aquinas would think that I am a heretic. We modern Evangelical Protestants have been buying our philosophical groceries in the Catholic supermarket for so many centuries that we have taken some doctrines for granted without biblical support. The concept of particular judgment plays heavily to the sovereignty of the individual as advocated by Plato. Every person gets his own private judgment time with God, not a mass class judgment.

The only biblical passage used to support the doctrine of particular judgment is the parable of the Rich Man and Lazarus in Luke 16. The rich man, while in the excruciating agony of the flames, begs that his brothers be warned of the dangers of hades. Since his brothers are still alive on earth, the setting must be before the final judgment. Since he has received his just deserts, the rich man must have received a particular judgment. This is the only biblical text that solidly affirms a particular judgment. This text is also a classic example of moral rhetoric—not to be taken literally in any sense. We fully study this fascinating parable later. For now, suffice it to say, with my own moral rhetoric, that basing fundamental doctrines such as judgment and resurrection (Heb 6:1–3) upon a single passage—and one that is much disputed and admittedly difficult to interpret—is bankrupt hermeneutics. A doctrinal carpenter constructing a table to set great weight upon it should have four legs of the strongest oak. If his countertop of teaching has only a single leg of an aging soft pine (the picturesque and allegorical language of the parable), and if that solo support is heavily cracked, then we would be wise to sit at a different table before this one-legged contraption collapses.

Early church fathers did not all agree with particular judgment. Tatian of Assyria (d. A.D. 185) wrote *Oratio ad Graecos* (*Address to the Greeks*). His apology tries to prove the worthlessness of paganism, supports a strict monotheism, and clearly claims that all souls await the judgment. Tatian did not accept the natural immortality of the soul; to evidence this, he said, "The soul is not in itself immortal, O Greeks, but mortal. Yet it is possible for it not to die" (*Oratio ad Graecos* 13).[4]

Tertullian (c. A.D. 200) "argued against the pagan belief that the souls of the wise ascended into the heavens, or the belief among Christians that the souls of the faithful attain heaven before Judgment Day: 'How, indeed, shall the soul mount up to heaven, where Christ is already sitting at the Father's right hand, when as yet the archangel's trumpet has not been heard by the command of God . . . ?'"[5]

Vigilantius (c. A.D. 400), presbyter of Gaul (France), spent a number of years studying in Bethlehem. He returned to Gaul and, around A.D. 403, wrote a treatise against superstitious practices and Gnosticism. He argued against relic worship as well as the immediate advent of souls to their destiny. He believed that souls would arise at the resurrection of the body for judgment on the Day of the Lord.

Jerome (A.D. 347–420) was a contemporary and acquaintance of Vigilantius. Jerome is best remembered for translating the Hebrew and Greek Scriptures into Latin, called the Vulgate. The Vulgate became the recognized text of the Roman Church for the next one thousand years. Jerome disagreed with Vigilantius, and the former became one of the fathers of the Catholic doctrine of particular judgment. Jerome's treatise *Contra Vigilantium* expresses his belief. Jurgens notes that "Jerome sat down to write his *Contra Vigilantium* in a single night. It is not one of his gentler efforts. Jerome excelled in the dubious art of argumentation *ad personam*. He was perfectly capable of using the length of a man's nose to disprove the validity of his theological opinions."[6] (I hope that I do not come over that way with any opposing theories.) As translator of the Vulgate, Jerome was extremely influential in the Western church that would later organize into the Roman Catholic Church. His views have been accepted.

It wasn't until 1336, in the bull *Benedictus Deus* of Pope Benedict XII, that Thomas's and Jerome's view of particular judgment was pronounced as dogma. After their deaths, Tatian of Assyria and Vigilantius were declared heretics.

LAST JUDGMENT

I disagree with particular judgment, finding no biblical support for it. Only the doctrine of the Last Judgment is clearly supported in Scripture. It is also called the Day of the Lord, the End of Days, and the great white throne judgment. Few truths are more often or more clearly proclaimed in Scripture than that of the Last Judgment. Various OT prophets speak of the Day of the Lord (Joel 2:31; Ezek 13:5; Isa 2:12), in which the nations will be summoned to judgment. In the NT, too, the doctrine is oft repeated. The Saviour himself not only foretells the event but also graphically portrays its circumstances.

Matthew 25:31 says that it is when "the Son of Man shall come in glory . . . and separate the sheep from the goats."

The apostles give a most prominent place to this doctrine in their preaching:

Acts 17:31: "For he has set a day when he will judge the world with justice by the man he has appointed."

Be it known, Jesus has been appointed.

Romans 2:5: "But because of your stubbornness and your unrepentant heart, you are storing up wrath against yourself for the day of God's wrath, when his righteous judgment will be revealed."

Passages in Daniel and Revelation further support the doctrine of the Last Judgment.

Daniel 12:2: "Multitudes who sleep in the dust of the earth will awake: some to everlasting life, others to shame and everlasting contempt."

Revelation 20:11–13: "Then I saw a great white throne and him who was seated on it. Earth and sky fled from his presence, and there was no place for them. And I saw the dead, great and small, standing before the throne, and books were opened. Another book was opened, which is the book of life. The dead were judged according to what they had done as recorded in the books. The sea gave up the dead that were in it, and death and Hades [the grave] gave up the dead that were in them, and each person was judged according to what he had done."

If particular judgment is correct, even though there is no clear Bible verse directly supporting it, then what is the point of the Last Judgment? Why go through it all over again? Catholic theologians wrestling with this problem have not denied the Last Judgment's existence, but they have denied its legitimate verdict. Thomas Aquinas formulated the official church position, which has been subliminally accepted by the majority of modern Evangelical Christians—although I would wager that they have not seriously thought it out or researched the Scripture. The argument claims that the Last Judgment is not a literal trial, as those who have already died are either in hell or heaven (or purgatory) as a result of their particular judgment upon their individual death. The Last Judgment instead will occur after the resurrection of the dead and the reuniting of the body and soul. The sins and previous judgment verdict for each person will be made public to the entire assembled world before their status in eternal life or eternal damnation is resumed.[7]

Where is all that in the Bible? Instead reread Rom 2:5, printed just above. In the "day of God's wrath," his judgment will be revealed. I find no biblical support for particular judgment. I find no reason to suppose that the Last Judgment, so frequently mentioned, is not a real judgment. It will be a mass judgment of all people who have ever lived. However, only those accused of a crime—sin—will be arraigned. Revelation tells us this will occur at the great white throne judgment. Thankfully, Christians, all the redeemed, will have no part in these proceedings.

FACE ONE'S ACCUSER, AND INNOCENT UNTIL PROVEN GUILTY

The U.S. Constitution is an amazing document. Many of its precepts and articles have a basis in the Bible, coming from Mosaic law. The Sixth Amendment, known as the Rights of the Accused, includes the confrontation clause and presumption of innocence. This doctrine gives accused people the right to face their accuser as well as the right to hear and reply to the accusations of their crime, and implies (along with the Fourteenth Amendment on due process) that the defendant shall be held innocent until proven guilty by a court of law. God's law to Moses similarly required that criminal trials be fair, with representation and an opportunity for rebuttal:

Deuteronomy 19:17–19 (KJV): "Then both the men, between whom the controversy is, shall stand before the LORD, before the priests and the judges, which shall be in those days; And the judges shall make diligent inquisition: and, behold, if the witness be a false witness, and hath testified falsely against his brother; Then shall ye do unto him, as he had thought to have done unto his brother: so shalt thou put the evil away from among you."

God will come face to face with those whom he accuses of a crime.

Consider these other OT verses as well:

Deuteronomy 7:10: "But those who hate him he will repay to their face by destruction; he will not be slow to repay to their face those who hate him."

Psalm 50:21: "These things you have done and I kept silent; you thought I was altogether like you. But I will rebuke you and accuse you to your face."

Micah 6:1–3: "Listen to what the LORD says: 'Stand up, plead your case before the mountains; let the hills hear what you have to say.' Hear, O mountains, the LORD's accusation; listen, you everlasting foundations of the earth. For the LORD has a case against his people; he is lodging a charge against Israel. 'My people, what have I done to you? How have I burdened you? Answer me.'"

The main purpose is to ensure that all people have the opportunity to face their accuser and that none should be tried in absentia—that is, the accused must be present when any accusation is heard, lest there be false witnesses. (See also Exod 22:10–11 and John 7:51.) So shall it be at the great white throne judgment. Each person present will face God, who is the accuser. I believe that sinners will have the opportunity to defend themselves. In Isa 43:26, God says, "Review the past for me, let us argue the matter together; state the case for your innocence." God is reasonable and fair. God will actually listen to the wicked and give them a legal chance. The Last Judgment is not a kangaroo court. However, at the great white throne, sinners will be speechless. In the presence of the Holy One, who bears no false witness, they will be without excuse for their crimes.

So then, if it is agreed that people's souls will be judged en masse upon Judgment Day, at some time yet in the future; and that this will be a fair and legitimate trial with all opportunities afforded to the accused; and if it is agreed that particular judgment is a medieval Catholic fabrication under Platonic influence, then it must follow that lost souls are not currently in a contemporary hell. Why?

Because Numbers 35:12 prohibits sentencing of a criminal before fair judgment has run its course: "They [cities of refuge] will be places of refuge from the avenger, so that a person accused of murder may not die before he stands trial before the assembly."

Deuteronomy 17:2–6 is similar:

> If a man or woman living among you in one of the towns the LORD gives you is found doing evil in the eyes of the LORD your God in violation of his covenant, and contrary to my command has worshiped other gods, bowing down to them or to the sun or the moon or the stars of the sky, and this has been brought to your attention, then you must investigate it thoroughly. If it is true and it has been proved that this detestable thing has been done in Israel, take the man or woman who has done this evil deed to your city gate and stone that person to death. On the testimony of two or three witnesses a man shall be put to death, but no one shall be put to death on the testimony of only one witness.

This stands in accordance with our sense of fairness. Do not punish until guilt has been established, or to use a modern English and American phrase, innocent until proven guilty. It was commanded to the Israelites. I think God will follow his own rules. While I have heard the argument that God is above the law, and we can't know God's ways, this weak claim is that God is under no obligation to play by rules given to people. That would make God a liar, saying one thing and doing something else. I believe the rules given to Israel are characteristic of God's own character. No one will taste the punishment of Gehenna fire until after the great white throne judgment. The subterranean fire pits as depicted in a *New Yorker* magazine cartoon will have to wait for their members to check in.

BODY, SOUL, AND SPIRIT

I believe in the Trinity of God. However, God's unity is more important and should always be stressed. This is, however, a different doctrine that I do not wish to probe here.

It is widely taught within Christian churches that a human being is a tripartite trinitarian being, consisting of three separate parts, yet one holistic individual. Body, soul, and spirit are the three parts of a person's self. Genesis 1:26–27 says, "Then God said, 'Let us make man in our image, in our likeness' . . . So God created man in his own image, in the image of God he created him; male and female he created them."

God is a Trinity, so his jewel of creation mimics that quality. God, however, has no body. God is a spirit, according to John 4:24. That spiritual image was originally created into humankind. A verse in 1 Thessalonians supports humans' tripartite nature: "May your whole spirit, soul and body be kept blameless at the coming of our Lord Jesus Christ" (5:23b).

I have pointed out in other passages that sometimes biblical writers, especially of Hebrew Scripture, use parallel repetitions to drive home their thought. Some Christians believe that there is no difference between body, soul, and spirit. It is a poetic way of emphasizing a person's whole nature, but not to be understood as a tripartite being. However, the church at Thessalonica was made up of "some of the Jews . . . and a large number of God-fearing Greeks" according to Acts 17:4, so I think it is reasonable that Paul wrote in Greek style to this majority-Greek congregation. He saved the Hebrew poetry for the Jews. Paul advocates in 1 Cor 9:20 of finding common ground with those to whom he is reaching out. Hence, I find it likely that this verse does contain a bulleted list of three separate components. We all know what the body is, but what is the difference between soul and spirit?

According to the author of Hebrews, soul and spirit are distinct and can be separated from each other: "For the word of God is living and active. Sharper than any double-edged sword, it penetrates even to dividing soul and spirit, joints and marrow; it judges the thoughts and attitudes of the heart" (4:12).

Early-twentieth-century dispensationalist Baptist pastor Clarence Larkin described man as a trichotomous being made up of body, soul, and spirit. He then proceeded to compare the threefold nature of man to the three sections of the Israelite tabernacle. The "Courtyard" represents his body, the "Holy Place" his soul, and the "Most Holy Place" his spirit. Larkin pointed out that in 1 Cor 3:16, our bodies, too, are the temple of God.[8]

Let's start with the easy one. The body is that structure of corporal flesh and bones. It is all of our fingers, legs, torso, and head. It, of course, includes brain, heart, lungs, and all of the other inner parts. Genesis 2:7 tells us that man was formed out of the dust of the earth. Sure enough the elements and molecules that make up our bodies—such as oxygen, hydrogen, nitrogen, and carbon—are all common to the crust of this planet. *Geviya* and *etsem* are the two most common Hebrew words used, but there are half a dozen different words translated as "body" in English. In Greek, the most common word is *soma*. All of these words for body can be either a living body or a corpse.

Let's go back to Genesis 2. After God formed Adam, his body was still lifeless until God breathed the breath of life into Adam's nostrils. Adam became a "living soul," or in Hebrew, a *nephesh*. The soul, in this context, is the animating force of the body. The soul is the essence of consciousness. The difference between a living person and a dead person is the life force, or the soul. There is really no chemical difference between a cadaver and a living person; they are both 70 percent water, and the carbon and trace minerals are basically the same. They both contain lipids, proteins, hormones, and enzymes. The only difference is that the life force—maybe some sort of electrical impulse—has gone from the corpse. Scientists really are not quite sure exactly what this life force is. The soul gives sense and motion to the body. Unfortunately, "soul" is a confusing word. It is used here, in this verse in the KJV, to mean the vital life force. Yet in everyday English we tend to think of the soul as the spiritual side of people that communicates with God. The same English word has two entirely different meanings. *Nephesh* is the Hebrew word so often translated as "soul," but is also translated as "human being," "life," or "creature." The word *nephesh* is very common; it appears over seven hundred times in the Hebrew Scriptures. Every time it refers to the life of the being—never a spiritual dimension. The Hebrew is consistent.

Nephesh is even used of animals. For instance, Gen 1:21 states, "So God created the great creatures of the sea and every living and moving thing [*nephesh*] with which the water teems, according to their kinds, and every winged bird according to its kind." Most Christians would agree that brute beasts do not have a soul or spiritual nature to communicate with God.

According to Lev 17:11, "For the life [*nephesh*] of a creature is in the blood, and I have given it to you to make atonement for yourselves on the altar; it is the blood that makes atonement for one's life [*nephesh*]." The *nephesh* or the life is in the blood; for this reason we are not to eat the blood of any creature. Jehovah's Witnesses actually take this to the extreme. They believe that since the soul—the vital force—is in the blood, all medically necessary blood transfusions are prohibited, because it is giving away your vital force. More realistically, I think that this passage means exactly what it says: the life of the being is the blood. Since God alone is the giver and taker of life, the blood is not ours to ingest. No comment by Scripture about surgery. Upon studying the Bible it becomes apparent to me that *nephesh* or "soul," as the word is used here, is not dualistically existent apart from the body, but holistically intrinsic to life.

The KJV says that when Rachel died, her soul departed at death. This is a good example of where the confusion sets in. We get from the Patrick Swayze movie *Ghost* the vision of a spiritual essence coming up out of and pulling away from the dead body. Genesis 35:18 (KJV) states, "And it came to pass, as her soul [*nephesh*] was in departing, (for she died) that she called his name Benoni: but his father called him Benjamin." A better understanding would be that she died when her life ceased. The word "soul" is not a proper translation for the word *nephesh*. "Life," "being," or "vital force" would be better. The NIV, NASB, and other modern translations have made this semantic correction.

The third part of man's being is the spirit, the spiritual nature that we frequently call the "soul." Our words are mixed up. *Nephesh* is translated as "soul" about 475 times in the KJV (in the other 250 occurrences of the term, it is rendered as "life," "creature," "being," etc.). The word "soul" is more appropriately reserved for this spiritual dimension, not for the life force that is common to animals as well as man. Some people—such as Jehovah's Witnesses, Seventh-day Adventists, Bible Students, and others—deny that humans have a soul, a dualistic element, a transcendent self, or a spiritual nature at all. But I feel that a separable component (only separable by God) is needed to complete this picture.

Jesus tells us in Matt 10:28 that the body and soul are two separate natures: "Do not be afraid of those who kill the body but cannot kill the soul. Rather, be afraid of the One who can destroy both soul and body in hell [*gehenna*]." The soul Jesus is referring to is the immaterial transcendent self.

See also 3 John 1:2 (KJV): "Beloved, I wish above all things that thou mayest prosper and be in health, even as thy soul prospereth." The adverbial phrase "even as" (*kathos* in Greek) indicates a comparison and a distinction between the physical body and the spiritual soul.

Paul had some type of spiritual out-of-body experience, as he reports in 2 Cor 12:2–4 (KJV): "I knew a man in Christ above fourteen years ago, (whether in the body, I cannot tell; or whether out of the body, I cannot tell: God knoweth;) such an one caught up to the third heaven. And I knew such a man, (whether in the body, or out of the body, I cannot tell: God knoweth;) How that he was caught up into paradise, and heard unspeakable words, which it is not lawful for a man to utter."

John also had an out-of-body experience, related in Rev 4:1–2 (KJV): "After this I looked, and, behold, a door was opened in heaven: and the first voice which I heard was as it were of a trumpet talking with me; which said, Come up hither, and I will shew thee things which must be hereafter. And immediately I was in the spirit: and, behold, a throne was set in heaven, and one sat on the throne."

The three parts of a person's nature—body, soul, and spirit—should more correctly be called body, life force, and spirit/soul. The verse in Hebrews that mentions dividing the soul and the spirit means to separate the life force from the spiritual nature. God has a fillet knife that only he can wield, with which he can cut the life force and spiritual soul apart.

DEAD SOUL SYNDROME

We come now to the part of our study that gives this book its title. I believe that the spiritual nature of people—the third element of our being, the spirit/soul—is dead. I call this Dead Soul Syndrome. In Gen 2:17 (KJV), God tells Adam, "But of the tree of the knowledge of good and evil, thou shalt not eat of it: for in the day that thou eatest thereof thou shalt surely die." Notice that God told Adam that the *very same day that he sins*, he will most definitely die. I encourage you to check the Hebrew. It says, *yowm akel muth muth*. The KJV translation above is well justified. Adam's heart, however, kept ticking after he swallowed. His *nephesh*, or life force, continued for more than 900 years after that fateful day. But since God cannot lie (Num 23:19; Heb 6:18), we must believe that Adam did in fact have some element of his nature that immediately suffered death (absence of life) upon his ingesting the fruit.

Some theologians have postulated that Adam's death that same day should be understood in context with 2 Pet 3:8 (KJV): "But, beloved, be not ignorant of this one thing, that one day is with the Lord as a thousand years, and a thousand years as one day." These theologians would claim that when Adam died at 930 years old, it was still within one of God's days.

Peter is quoting from Ps 90:8, which is expounding the eternal and omnipotent nature of the Almighty. In context, Peter's point in the epistle was for believers to be patient with the timing of the Second Coming. Peter, or the psalmist, is not revealing a code language to decipher the hidden meaning of prophecies given thousands of years ago in Genesis.

rise in the resurrection at the Last Day. What a stark contrast from the Pharisaical and Gentile myth of life after death. Oddly, Jesus did not offer any comforting words about her brother already being in the presence of God. Instead, as a token that he would raise men and women at the Last Day, and that he possesses the keys to the grave, Jesus went to Lazarus's tomb and cried with a loud voice (John 11:39), "Lazarus, come forth." Now, Jesus didn't say, "Lazarus, come down." Let's suppose that what some people believe is true—that Lazarus died and went to heaven—and that Jesus said instead, "Lazarus, come down." And Lazarus, up in heaven (now if it were me, I would have done this), says, "Lord, I've been up here four days, and I'm not coming back. I am in Gloryland, Lord. I really don't want to come back to that sinful world!" If anybody could have had a near-death experience, it would have been Lazarus! If anybody could have had an experience to report to us what it's like (not for a few seconds but for four days) after death, it would have been Lazarus, but Lazarus said nothing about life after death. Why not? Because he was sleeping, awaiting his justification.[9]

Similarly, Jonah prayed right before he went to Sheol in Jonah 2:1-9. People have often wondered how Jonah could have survived for three days inside a fish. We get the cartoon vision from Disney's movie of Pinocchio and Gepetto inside the whale on an intact raft with a lantern burning. This is definitely not the real-life case with Jonah. I do have faith, and I believe that the account of Jonah is historical fact.

Whenever I go fishing and am cleaning the catch, I like to dissect the stomach. I find crayfish, small perch, and other animals inside a snug muscular membrane. The contents are bathed in gastric juices. Everything inside is dead. Inside the stomach of Jonah's fish would have been similar. There would be no air to breathe. I think Jonah actually died. He went to a watery grave in the sea and was resurrected as a prefiguring of Christ. Christ used Jonah's three days in Sheol as proof of Christ's own Messiahship, because Christ also spent three days in Sheol. Jonah is unique in that he is one of the few people who have gone to Sheol and returned. He wrote an inspired book about the experience. Jonah's description of Sheol matches what we have already learned. Water engulfed him. Seaweed wrapped around his head. He drowned in the belly of a fish at the bottom of the ocean to which he sank. However, when he returned, he gave no flatliner experience of what life is like in the hereafter.

This absence of Jesus', Lazarus's, and Jonah's comments about life of the soul immediately after death is certainly not proof of its nonexistence in that day, but it does seem interesting and strange.

DEAD PEOPLE TALKING

A couple of OT verses at first read appear to say that dead people are conscious and talking in hell (*sheol* as translated by KJV). Immortal soul advocates often use these verses to show that humans have a life (of some sort) immediately after death. One such verse is Isa 14:7–10:

> All the lands are at rest and at peace; they break into singing. Even the pine trees and the cedars of Lebanon exult over you and say, "Now that you have been laid low, no woodsman comes to cut us down." The grave [*sheol*] below is all astir to meet you at your coming; it rouses the spirits of the departed to greet you— all those who were leaders in the world; it makes them rise from their thrones—all those who were kings over the nations. They will all respond, they will say to you, "You also have become weak, as we are; you have become like us."

Isaiah has been prophesying that Babylon will destroy Judah. Now in chapter 14, he turns the tables. This comforting chapter tells that God will destroy Babylon. This passage is a taunt against the king of Babylon (Isa 14:3). The very last part of this passage above has another dead king talking (v. 10). If, however, this is read in context, the passage, I believe, is obviously poetic and figurative. In verse 8 the cedar trees are rejoicing that he is dead. Do trees literally rejoice? In verse 9, past generations of kings stand up from their thrones in *sheol* ("hell," per KJV). Do kings really get a throne in hell? This is beautiful poetry, but it is not literal. This is not Scriptural proof that dead people are talking and conscious. The point is that the world will rejoice at the fall of Babylon. A side note of interest is that this passage is entirely prophetic. In Isaiah's life Assyria was the great power. Babylon had not yet even risen to world-stage prominence.

Another example states that from within the grave the mighty leaders will be talking and conscious: "From within the grave [*sheol*] the mighty leaders will say of Egypt and her allies, 'They have come down and they lie with the uncircumcised, with those killed by the sword'" (Ezek 32:21).

This is a prophecy against Egypt. During the last days of Judah, before Nebuchadnezzar invaded, Egypt was a "staff of reed" (Ezek

29:6). In other words, Egypt was an ally that acted tough, promising to protect Judah against Babylon, but in fact was weak and no match for the Babylonians. Pharaoh actually turned on Judah and helped the Babylonians when Nebuchadnezzar forced his hand. When the last kings of Judah leaned on Egypt, she broke—hence "staff of reed." That is why Egypt is being judged and cursed. The first half of Ezek 32 likens Egypt to a sea monster, maybe a big crocodile. The text says that it was written on the first day of Adar (twelfth month). The sea monster is yanked out of the river (the Nile, of course) and rots on the shore. This is symbolic. Pharaoh is a man, not really a sea monster or a big croc. The point is that he thought he created the river; he was too big for his britches, so God knocked him down a few pegs.

The second half of Ezek 32, verses 17–32, was written two weeks later: "On the 15th of the [same] month." The mighty leaders of Earth are astonished to see Pharaoh joining them in Sheol. More dead people talking to each other, just like in Isa 14. The words here are poetic, not doctrinal. Death, and implicitly Sheol, is the great leveler of all. Great and small, slave and free, all people will die. The poetic point is that if you mess with God's people, you're going to pay.

A further poetic image is found in Ezek 31. In this passage the king of Assyria or possibly the pharaoh of Egypt is compared to a majestic tree, more beautiful than the trees of Eden, in which birds and animals take refuge and find food. In Ezek 31:15 the mighty tree is chopped down and sent to Sheol. Are there trees in hell? Certainly not; this is poetry. It is not to be taken literally.

COMPROMISING ON SOUL SLEEP

Compromise can be a good thing. My intention here is not to mean settling short of your standards. Instead, by compromise, I mean to honestly and openly review both sides of a dispute. I am cursed with the ability to see both views in an argument. When I read a book on eternal torment by an author such as Robert Morey,[10] I think to myself, *Wow, he has a good point*. Then when I read Edward Fudge,[11] who is an extinctionist with soul-sleep tendencies, I think to myself, *Wow, he has a good point*. I'm not wishy-washy, and I don't vacillate. I think both opinions—the conscious soul advocate and the soul sleeper—have some truth and some error.

THE PROBLEM WITH SOUL SLEEP

As I mentioned in the Introduction, there seems to be a correlation between the extinction theory and soul sleep. At least most modern sources that believe in one also appear to believe in the other. I think the connecting link, the bridge between extinction and soul sleep, is the common rejection of immortal soul philosophy.

If the soul is immortal, if it is true that the soul cannot die, then obviously eternal conscious torment must follow. Also, it becomes logically necessary to allow for an intermediate habitation place for deceased disembodied souls of both the righteous and the wicked. The cornerstone of the foundation of this belief system is that all people's souls are immortal. Both the regenerated righteous and the unrepentant wicked are spiritually/soulfully alive. That point would be assumed before reading any biblical text. It is the framework from which doctrines emerge, but as previously discussed, it is invalid. Even the noted Dr. Robert Morey, who has written what conservative traditionalists consider to be "the most comprehensive Biblical study of the subject,"[12] concedes in his book, "Until solid evidence is presented to the contrary, we shall begin with the assumption that some part of man survives death."[13] We should never base our faith and doctrine on assumptions, but instead the word of God.

Likewise, those who postulate human mortality surprisingly fall into the same logical trap, but heading in the opposite direction. If the human soul is nothing more than the life force of the body, then it is destined to die without God's gracious intervention. Soul sleepers universally deny the tripartite nature of human composition. The structural bedrock of this belief system is that people do not possess any type of soul/spirit as a dualistic part of their nature. This is the framework and assumption from which they proceed. So the soul sleeper concludes that the soul, or life force, of people—both righteous and wicked—ceases to exist or at least ceases any sort of viable consciousness after physical death. All people, wicked and righteous, await the resurrection. This is where I think the soul sleepers have gone awry. From Martin Luther to Samuele Bacchiocchi,[14] I think they fail to differentiate between the saved and the unsaved. All Scriptures, both Old and New Testaments, draw stark distinctions between these two species of people. The soul-sleeper belief implies that the Holy Spirit–filled soul of Christians is incapable of transcending death.

Most all soul sleepers allege that humans have no spirit/soul, as in a separable dualistic spiritual nature apart from the body. *Nephesh* is, as we have previously studied, simply the essence of life and no more. I don't think it is that simple. "Soul" in English has a variety of meanings, and I affirm that one of them is a dualistic spiritual nature that can exist consciously apart from the body. However, it lives only by the power and grace of God.

The immortal soul philosopher relies heavily on NT language. Such philosophers tend to cast aside dozens of OT passages (see the following chapters), relegating them to the bottom cupboard of obscure, unused verses. Soul sleepers aren't much better. They rely far too heavily on Ecclesiastes and Sheol language. The only NT verses that they care to quote reflect Jesus or Paul referring to the "sleeping" of the dead.

I perceive a dichotomy wherein immortal theorists have the other side of death half right (transcendent life and immediate felicity of the righteous), and sleepers have it half right too (unconsciousness of the disincarnate minds of the lost within any parallel dimension).

My studies bring me to the tentative conclusion that immortals and sleepers are both partly correct and partly mistaken. I say "tentative" because as I have stressed throughout this manuscript, I don't know everything. (According to my wife, I hardly know anything.) I am always reading and learning more. If someone can show me biblical evidence counter to my theory, then I hope to be among the first to humbly change my opinion.

As this book continues, we learn how to synthesize these views. I present nothing new, as I mentioned in the beginning. I am rehashing material with a very warm skillet and ample oil from past theologians, yet I hope to brown up a fresh batch of fritters with some unique seasoning not yet sampled. May the Spirit of the Almighty God help me to believe and accept fully at face value the scripture of both Testaments.

ENDNOTES

1. McHugh, "Particular Judgment."
2. Ibid.
3. Thomas Aquinas, *Summa Theologica*, Supplement 69:2.
4. Canright, *History of the Doctrine of the Soul*, 133.
5. Chapman, "Tertullian."
6. Jurgens, *Faith of the Early Fathers*, book 2, 206.
7. Thomas Aquinas, *Summa Theologica*, Supplement 88:1.

8. Larkin, *Dispensational Truth or God's Plan and Purpose in the Ages*, 169. This book is a classic with many excellent charts.

9. Modified from Ball, "What Happens to My Soul When I Die?"

10. Morey has written with great authority in his book, *Death and the Afterlife*.

11. Fudge, *Fire That Consumes*.

12. Morey, *Death and the Afterlife*. Front cover credit by Dr. Walter Martin.

13. Ibid., 69.

14. Dr. Samuele Bacchiocchi, now deceased, was a Seventh-Day Adventist scholar and author of many books. His compelling book on this topic is *Immortality or Resurrection?*

3

I'm Awake

THIS WHOLE CHAPTER IS probably more aptly connected to part 2 of this study, rather than part 1. We are going to talk about the soul of the saved residing in heaven after death. Part 2 is specifically about heaven. However, this news—that the soul of the redeemed has been made alive—is so joyful that I cannot wait. I want to yell it from the mountaintops.

I think "soul sleep" is a misnomer. For my purposes, I have proposed the term "Dead Soul Syndrome." It is a disease that has affected all people (except Jesus) ever since Adam. I believe that the soul/spirit of the unsaved is truly dead; however, it is not yet extinct. A resurrection will occur— either in this life upon salvation for glory, or in the next life for damnation. Gloriously, there is a cure for Dead Soul Syndrome, and we need not wait until the end of earthly time to enjoy good health in our soul. The cure is made ready in Christ Jesus for those who believe today.

During this age of grace, we are given a super-special blessing that OT saints did not enjoy. The Holy Spirit (the third member of a unified singular Godhead; remember, I'm a trinitarian) lives within our spirit/soul. Our body is God's temple. Just as the overpowering *kaboud shekiniah* (dwelling of glory) was in Solomon's temple, so, too, is God within our soul, quickening it to life.

In 1 Kgs 8:10–11 (the same story appears in 2 Chr 5:14), Solomon dedicates the temple, and the glory of God settles within the Holy of Holies. There is a cloud that is so thick that the priests must cease ministering for a while. Moses had this same experience on Mount Sinai (Exod 24:6). God's glory was powerfully manifested upon the mountain in Arabia with a thick cloud, thunder, lightning, and minor earth tremors. In both of these cases, the magnificent power of the Almighty God—the One who created the universe, the One who holds together the bonds of atomic particles in his hand—dwelt or abode with men on planet Earth. This was again seen in the pillar of cloud and fire that settled upon the tabernacle while Israel wandered in the wilderness. The Hebrew word for tabernacle comes from the word for dwelling (*shekan*). God dwelt with men.

In the New Testament, Paul tells us in 1 Cor 6:19 that our body is the temple of the Holy Ghost. The dwelling place of God is no longer within a building, a structure of bricks and mortar. Today, during the age of grace, the dwelling place of the Almighty is within the soul of Christians. Think about how awesomely powerful this is. The pillar of fire and the cloud of His glory are within us.

Ephesians 2:22 states, "And in him you too are being built together to become a dwelling in which God lives by his Spirit." (See also 1 Cor 3:16; 2 Cor 6:16.) Jesus tells us in Mark 16:18 and again in Matt 10:8 that we have the power available to raise the dead, cast out demons, and heal the sick. This is almost unanimously untapped.

Jesus explains to Nicodemus in John 3 about being born again. This is the quickening of the soul upon salvation. The new birth is the revitalization of the human soul. The soul goes from being dead, a victim of Dead Soul Syndrome since the fall of Adam, to being alive. The soul is resurrected spiritually by the power of the Holy Ghost. For the Christian, the soul or spirit lives once again; Dead Soul Syndrome has been cured. We are once again a living triune being of body, soul, and spirit. A few verses serve as examples:

Second Corinthians 5:17: "Therefore, if anyone is in Christ, he is a new creation; the old has gone, the new has come!"

John 6:63a: "The spirit gives life" ("quickeneth" in KJV).

John 14:16–20: "And I will ask the Father, and he will give you another Counselor to be with you forever—the Spirit of truth. The world cannot accept him, because it neither sees him nor knows him. But you know him, for he lives with you and will be in you. I will not leave you as orphans; I will come to you. Before long, the world will not see me anymore, but you will see me. Because I live, you also will live. On that day you will realize that I am in my Father, and you are in me, and I am in you."

Colossians 2:13 (KJV): "And you, being dead in your sins and the uncircumcision of your flesh, hath he quickened together with him, having forgiven you all trespasses." See also Rom 8:11.

Just like Adam's original soul/spirit before the fall, we have a living spirit. When a Christian dies, the life force (*nephesh*) dissipates into nothing, as the blood is poured out upon the ground. The mortal body goes into the grave and decomposes. At the rapture or second coming (depending on your eschatology), the body will be resurrected from the grave with an incorruptible glorified body as promised. Upon death, the living soul/spirit of the Christian immediately enters heaven to be with the Lord.

Interestingly, there are far more verses to study and work with concerning the final fate of the lost than there are about the interim destiny of the redeemed. Everyone agrees that the saved will have everlasting life, glorious and bountiful, throughout all of eternity. But verses that speak of the interim preresurrection period, and our exact location, are somewhat scarce.

I do, however, find a few good verses to support the immediate translation of a Christian's soul in the New Testament.

Philippians 1:23–24: "I am torn between the two: I desire to depart and be with Christ, which is better by far; but it is more necessary for you that I remain in the body."

Second Corinthians 5:6–9: "Therefore we are always confident and know that as long as we are at home in the body we are away from the Lord. We live by faith, not by sight. We are confident, I say, and would prefer to be away from the body and at home with the Lord. So we make it our goal to please him, whether we are at home in the body or away from it."

Hebrews 12:22–23: "But you have come to Mount Zion, to the heavenly Jerusalem, the city of the living God. You have come to thousands upon thousands of angels in joyful assembly, to the church of the firstborn, whose names are written in heaven. You have come to God, the judge of all men, to the spirits of righteous men made perfect." Notice that the spirits of righteous men are at the same location as God, the heavenly temple prototype, and the angels.

Revelation 6:9: "When he opened the fifth seal, I saw under the altar the souls of those who had been slain because of the word of God and the testimony they had maintained." (Note: This is postrapture, if you subscribe to such, but still pre–second coming. More on this vision in heaven later in part 2.)

Revelation 7:9: "After this I looked and there before me was a great multitude that no one could count, from every nation, tribe, people and language, standing before the throne and in front of the Lamb. They were wearing white robes and were holding palm branches in their hands." I believe that this scene must also be before the second coming, because the scene is in heaven and the saints are standing before the throne of God. After the second coming, as we shall learn in much greater detail in part 2 of this book, the saints will stand and dwell on earth, not heaven.

In 2 Cor 12:1–4, Paul is describing a vision that he had in the third heaven, the abode of God, and is unsure whether he left his body, indicating the life and vitality of his soul. His options were that maybe the experience had occurred bodily or maybe the event was in spirit only, which he calls "out of body." Paul does not know which way it happened. If the trip to heaven was "in body," then either he physically and bodily went to heaven just as Jesus had ascended in bodily form or maybe he received a vision in his body while still planted on earth. If the trip to heaven was not in body, then Paul left his body behind and went to heaven in spirit alone. Paul considers this a possibility. I'm inclined to think that Paul probably made this trip in his spirit, that living portion of his being. But since Paul himself is unsure, I certainly cannot know.

Colossians 3:4 (KJV): "When Christ, who is our life, shall appear, then shall *ye also appear with him in glory*" (emphasis added).

First Thessalonians 4:14–16: "We believe that Jesus died and rose again and so we believe that *God will bring with Jesus those who have fallen asleep in him*. . . For the Lord himself will come down from heaven, with a loud command, with the voice of the archangel and with the trumpet call of God, and the dead in Christ will rise first" (emphasis added).

Note that the dead are with Jesus. They are still 'asleep' or dead yet they return with Christ, so they have some sort of consciousness. The Greek word *syn* is used in both of these verses in Colossians and Thessalonians, translated as "with." The preposition means beside or accompanying.[1] We will not bother to list other verses that have been used to make this point. Such verses as Jude 14 and Rev 19:14 have been interpreted by some to show that humans will march with Christ in the second advent. Although I accept that conclusion, those particular verses may very well speak of angels, not people. In Matt 25:31, the Lord told his disciples that holy angels will accompany him when he returns in glory. However, the verse above, 1 Thess 4:14, does not indicate angels. It clearly says that those who have fallen asleep (died) will also accompany Christ in his majestic return to earth. It will be quite a parade. Thousands of disciples, martyrs, and saints will be riding on white horses leading a host of angels. Praise God, I am confident that I, too, will be present in this march, although I'll probably be on a small pony near the back of the crowd.

NO JUDGING OF THE SAVED

Saved Christians have no guilt. The righteousness of Christ is accredited to us, so we need not concern ourselves with the Last Judgment or the law of refuge. Christians are not charged with a crime (sin), receive no judgment, and have no sentencing. See Rom 8:1–2: "Therefore, there is now no condemnation for those who are in Christ Jesus, because through Christ Jesus the law of the Spirit of life set me free from the law of sin and death."

The judgment seat of Christ is not exactly a judgment. There is no criminal proceeding with a verdict and sentence. The Greek word used for our life-reviewing event in Rom 14:10 and 1 Cor 5:10 is *bema*; it is never used in reference to the Last Judgment. A different Greek word, *krima*, is used in reference to the Last Judgment and the great white throne judgment. Another Greek word often used for judgment of the unsaved is *dikaioma*, which refers to legal proceedings that have discerned justice by the force of law (verdict). Christians are not subject to this judgment. Paul says in 1 Cor 6:5–7 that Christians should not take fellow Christians to court. Surely, Christ will not take his own bride to his Father's court.

For a complete and excellent understanding of the accounting that Christians will give to Jesus, see the small booklet *Judgment Seat of Christ* by L. Sale-Harrison, written in the 1930s.[2] It is still relevant today.

The verses above, about the life of the saved after death, pretty clearly say that we as NT church-age Christians (I'm slightly dispensational) will upon death enter heaven to be with Christ, our espoused husband. As Paul says, we would prefer to be away from the body and at home with the Lord. The Spirit gives life. The soul of the saved is quickened back to life. Upon bodily death, the Christian's soul is immediately translated to heaven to be in the presence of Jesus. I do not accept soul sleep for the grace-age Christian.

FULL AGREEMENT

My theory is in full agreement with the traditional theory that upon death the believer's living soul goes to heaven. The "goes to heaven" part gets more complicated, and we discuss it in further detail in part 2. But for the "living soul" part, hallelujah, what a blessing of Himalayan proportions that God has bestowed upon us.

Wayne Jackson—an oft-published Church of Christ minister from Stockton, California, with a strong Internet following—has pointed out in his defense of the immortal soul of all humans:

> In his first epistle, Peter, by *implication*, suggests that the human "spirit" is "incorruptible" (1 Peter 3:4). ["But let it be the hidden man of the heart, in that which is not *corruptible*, even the ornament of a meek and quiet spirit, which is in the sight of God of great price."] Why would a person need "incorruptible" apparel for a "corruptible" spirit? Thus, the human spirit, by deduction, is suggested as being incorruptible. This appears to be confirmed by Paul's interchangeable usage of *athanasia* ("immortal") and *aphtharsia* ("incorruptible") in his discourse concerning the resurrected body (see 1 Corinthians 15:42, 50, 53–54).
>
> In his second Corinthian letter, Paul speaks of the "outward" man and the "inward" man (2 Corinthians 4:16). ["For which cause we faint not; but though our outward man perish, yet the inward (man) is renewed day by day."] These two expressions contrast the body with the soul. But in the same context, the apostle distinguishes between that which is temporal and that which is "eternal." The implication clearly seems to suggest that the "inward man," i.e., the soul, is eternal. Not that it has existed forever; rather, from the commencement of its creation, it partakes of the nature of an everlasting entity (cf. 2 Corinthians 5:1; 2 Thessalonians 2:16).[3] (emphasis in original)

I agree with Brother Jackson. The aforementioned passages do imply an eternal, incorruptible nature for the *believer's* soul. When read in context, these passages all refer to the soul/spirit of the born-again, believing Christian. Jackson has fortified my faith, as his website newsletter aims to do. I do not think that there are any such similar verses that speak of the incorruptible nature, the eternal life, the vibrant inner man, or any other dualistic terminology in the context of unbelieving non-Christians. In my opinion, this collaborates the Dead Soul Syndrome theory.

WE HAVE A NEW LIFE IN CHRIST

Jesus said that believers have life numerous times. See, for example, John 3:36: "Whoever believes in the Son has eternal life, but whoever rejects the Son will not see life, for God's wrath remains on him." A very similar verse is found in John 5:24; 6:47; 6:54; and 10:28. Note also the following passages:

Ephesians 2:1-2: "As for you, you were dead in your transgressions and sins, in which you used to live when you followed the ways of this world."

Ephesians 2:4-5: "But because of his great love for us, God, who is rich in mercy, made us alive with Christ even when we were dead in transgressions."

First John 5:11-13: "And this is the testimony: God has given us eternal life, and this life is in his Son. He who has the Son has life; he who does not have the Son of God does not have life. I write these things to you who believe in the name of the Son of God so that you may know that you have eternal life."

First Corinthians 6:17: "For it is said, 'The two will become one flesh.' But he who unites himself with the Lord is one with him in spirit." In this verse, Paul is using the marriage between a man and wife as an analogy to the union of God and believer. If we have a living spirit, as I have suggested, then this verse seems to mean that our spirit is "married" to God's spirit. Certainly, at the death of the body, the spiritual bond will not be broken. God will not leave his bride in the grave.

Romans 8:1-17 also speaks of life in the Spirit. Traditionally, these verses have been understood as a spiritual quality of life, not a reality of existence. The deadness in sin has traditionally been understood as a separation or alienation from God, but not something really dead. I take these verses literally, though. I do not think these passages and others are metaphorical language for increased spiritual awareness within our existing mind and life. I think they very simply mean that we are either dead or alive. How can an unsaved person who has a job, is rearing children, and clearly lives a socially productive life be classified as dead? Because they suffer from Dead Soul Syndrome, and with this disease they are incapable of communing with God. I believe that these references to being dead in sin and being alive in Christ refer to the animation of our human soul. The soul is the spirit, the third essence of humans that was created in the image of God.

Robert Morey, in his book *Death and Afterlife*, is a strong supporter of the traditional eternal-torment-and-immortal-soul theory. Even though he is far more learned and eloquent than I am, I respectfully disagree with his conclusions. I humbly take issue with much of what he claims. However, he touches on my point above in his refutation of soul sleep. He points out that "when one turns to the Greek New Testament, one discovers numerous instances where believers are grammatically said to have everlasting life as a present possession. Thus in 1 John 5:11–13, the Apostle uses the present indicative tense in the Greek which means that the believer has everlasting life now because he possesses Jesus Christ now."[4] Praise God for our life in Christ, I fully agree. However, this does not apply to the unregenerate sinners.

WE ARE PROMISED TO SEE HIS GLORY

Proponents of soul sleep explain the "being with Christ" verses written by Paul by analogizing them with a sleeping child held in his loving parents' arms. Certainly the child is with his parents, even though he is asleep.

In John 17, Jesus prays for his disciples and for future disciples. He knows that he is going to die soon. In verse 11a, Jesus says, "I will remain in the world no longer," and in verse 13a, speaking to the Father, he says, "I am coming to you now." There is no dispute among Bible-believing Christians about what happened to Jesus. At the ascension, Christ went to be in heaven with the Father, and he now sits at the right hand of God. Verse 24 in this prayer, which takes place immediately after the Last Supper on Jesus' last night on Earth, is the verse of significant interest to my theory.

John 17:24: "Father, I want those you have given me to be with me where I am, and to see my glory, the glory you have given me because you loved me before the creation of the world." Jesus is going to heaven, and his saints are requested to be with him. Do soul sleepers suppose that the Father refused to grant Jesus his request? If his saints were dead, sleeping in his arms, then they could not see his glory. Some level of consciousness is required for them to see and recognize his glory.

John 12:26a: "Whoever serves me must follow me; and where I am, my servant also will be." Praise God! He will never leave us, even during this two-millennia age between his advents. We shall always be with him, either through the Holy Spirit in life or spiritually in death. Not even the grave can separate us from God.

HE SLEPT WITH AND WAS GATHERED TO HIS FATHERS

The phrase "he slept with his fathers" appears about forty times in the Old Testament. The similar concept of people sleeping is additionally used about ten times in the New Testament. It is a euphemism for death. Soul sleepers love to point out that sleep is a state of unconsciousness. It cannot be denied that "sleep" continues to happen after Ascension/Pentecost, when my theory states that souls of the chosen have been resurrected, made alive, quickened, born again, re-created, and made new, all to see the glory of Christ.

Here are several NT cases of "sleeping." For these verses I have used the more literal KJV as it retains the "slept" from the Greek (*koimao*).

Stephen falls asleep as he is stoned in Acts 7:60 (KJV): "And he kneeled down, and cried with a loud voice, Lord, lay not this sin to their charge. And when he had said this, he fell asleep."

Paul says in 1 Cor 11:30 (KJV): "For this cause many are weak and sickly among you, and many sleep."

First Thessalonians 4:14 (KJV): "For if we believe that Jesus died and rose again, even so them also which sleep in Jesus will God bring with him."

Soul sleepers claim that these verses offer evidence for their theory. I find these verses to speak of the condition of the body; otherwise they would contradict all of the earlier quoted passages. Again, sleep here is a euphemism for physical bodily death.

Another figure of speech about death that should not be taken literally is the phrase "to go to one's fathers." The phrase has been received in by the immortal-soul camp as language that speaks of the immediate conscious existence of the soul after death. The ancient Hebrew method of burial was typically a two-stage process. The body was wrapped in linen clothes and laid upon a long, flat shelf inside the tomb cave. After about a year, when all of the flesh had sufficiently decomposed (bodies were typically not embalmed), relatives would collect the remaining bones and scraps and ceremonially place them in a large pit toward the rear of the sepulchre. This makes room for a new interment upon the shelf. Burial caves were expensive to hew out of solid rock, so one tomb would remain in the family for many generations. After several decades, with the fairly high death rate of the time, many fathers, uncles, and brothers would have their bones piled on top of each other within the gathering pit. This is the context and the allusion for the saying "gathered to his fathers."

However, Abraham's nuclear family had died in Haran. His ancestral fathers had died in Ur of the Chaldees. He was the first male to be buried in the cave of Machpelah near Mamre, yet God told Abraham that he "shall go to your fathers," and later Scripture says that he "was gathered to his people."[5]

Moses and Aaron are also excellent examples, according to immortal-soul theorists. They were buried somewhere in the wilderness—Mount Pisgah and Mount Hor, respectively—in private graves that were never utilized by anyone else. Harry Buis states, "It is often descriptive of death in the Old Testament, and meant more than simply burial in an ancestral tomb, for in several instances the phrase is used where no such common burial took place. Gerlach, commenting on Genesis 15:15 says that this phrase is 'the gracious expression for a life after death.' Baumgarten says 'a continuance after death is assuredly expressed therein.' Delitzsch commenting on Genesis 25:8 says 'The union with the fathers is not a mere union of corpses, but of persons.'"[6]

If these examples are meant to prove a disembodied spirit's ascent to another world, then it poses difficulties with John 3:13 (KJV): "No man ascendeth to heaven." Unfortunately, we are thousands of years and miles removed from the biblical culture. We don't always quickly identify a figure of speech, even though we use them ourselves every day. Being "gathered to his fathers" is another euphemism for death. It substitutes a more polite and favorable expression for a socially delicate topic. We still do this today with "he passed away," in lieu of "he died." Euphemisms are also used, even in the Bible, for bathroom and bedroom business. We must be careful not to literalize overtly every word of the biblical text.[7]

MORE OBJECTIONS

Proponents of particular judgment have pointed to Jesus' words concerning marriage after the resurrection. The passage in Matt 22 appears to lend support to the idea that Abraham and other patriarchs were at that very point already in heaven. My theory is that their soul/spirit would be raised and translated to heaven after the resurrection of Christ, but before his resurrection, all humans would be fully dead (that is, not alive in any dimension).

Matthew 22:31–32 states, "But about the resurrection of the dead—have you not read what God said to you, 'I am the God of Abraham, the God of Isaac, and the God of Jacob'? He is not the God of the dead but of the living."

If, however, we read the same story from Luke's and/or Mark's Gospel, I think the idea vanishes; the righteous patriarchs were actually dead, because although saved, they had not yet been justified. See Luke 20:37–38: "But in the account of the bush, even Moses showed that the dead rise, for he calls the Lord 'the God of Abraham, and the God of Isaac, and the God of Jacob.' He is not the God of the dead, but of the living, for to him all are alive."

Mark 12:26–27 (KJV): "And as touching the dead, that they rise: have ye not read in the book of Moses, how in the bush God spake unto him, saying, I am the God of Abraham, and the God of Isaac, and the God of Jacob? He is not the God of the dead, but the God of the living: ye therefore do greatly err."

This statement of Jesus was directed to the Sadducees, a Jewish sect that did not believe in the resurrection. His point is that God's covenant extends beyond death. Even though the patriarchs are in the grave today, they shall rise in that great day. Jesus' affirmation is in the resurrection (the topic of this discussion), not in the heavenly destination of the saved.

Another objection frequently put up by Bible Students, Seventh-day Adventists, or others who accept universal soul sleep is the case of David as spoken by Peter in his Pentecost discourse:

Acts 2:32–35: "God has raised this Jesus to life, and we are all witnesses of the fact. Exalted to the right hand of God, he has received from the Father the promised Holy Spirit and has poured out what you now see and hear. For *David did not ascend to heaven*, and yet he said, 'The Lord said to my Lord: "Sit at my right hand until I make your enemies a footstool for your feet"'" (emphasis added). In this passage Peter is proving the physical bodily resurrection of Jesus. In Ps 16, David had prophesied that the Messiah would rise from the dead and not rot in the grave. Some Jews apparently thought that this psalm referred to David himself. Peter refutes that idea by telling them that David's grave persists to that day (v. 29) and that David did not ascend into heaven (v. 34). The topic of discussion is bodily physical resurrection. David's fleshly body is still dead in the sepulchre. Christ alone is the firstfruits of physical resurrection. However, by the time of Pentecost when Peter is speaking this message, I think David's soul/spirit would have been now recalled to heaven by his Master, as we shall see later in an upcoming study.

A HOPE FOR THE RESURRECTION

A long-standing objection to immediate translation of the Christian's soul to heaven has been the pro–soul sleep argument that conscious felicity in heaven renders the resurrection pointless. If the saints are already conscious and enjoying their reward, then what is the point of resurrection? It is clear from Scripture that the resurrection is the hope and reward of the righteous.

David wrote, "As for me, I will behold thy face in righteousness: I shall be satisfied when I awake with thy likeness" (Ps 17:15 KJV).

Daniel said, "Many of them that sleep in the dust of the earth shall awake, some to everlasting life" (Dan 12:2a KJV).

Isaiah spoke, "Awake and sing, ye that dwell in dust, for the earth shall cast out the dead" (Isa 26:19b KJV).

Martha, the sister of Lazarus, remarked, "I know that he shall rise again in the resurrection at the last day" (John 11:24b KJV).

The elder promised, "We know that when he [Jesus] shall appear, we shall be like him for we shall see him as he is" (1 John 3:2b KJV).

Paul also looked ahead to the resurrection: "If by any means I might attain unto the resurrection of the dead" (Phil 3:11 KJV).

Peter looked forward to the return of Christ as the time when he and others would receive their reward: "When the chief Shepherd shall appear, ye shall receive a crown of glory that fadeth not away" (1 Pet 5:4 KJV).

This is an excellent point and should be well noted. My understanding of the intermediate condition of the saved is that they are spiritually alive, with Christ, in security and comfort, but not yet complete. They still are lacking. They do not yet know as they are known. They have not yet received their reward. We discuss this line of thought further in part 2 of the study.

ENDNOTES

1. Thayer, *Thayer's Greek-English Lexicon*, 598.
2. Sale-Harrison, *Judgment Seat of Christ*.
3. Jackson, "Do Human Beings Have an Immortal Soul?"

4. Morey, *Death and Afterlife*, 27.
5. Gen 15:15; 25:8.
6. Buis, *Doctrine of Eternal Punishment*, 9.
7. For more information about figures of speech, rhetoric, and locution, see E. W. Bullinger's classic work, *Figures of Speech Used in the Bible Explained and Illustrated* (1898; repr. Grand Rapids: Baker Books House, 1968).

4

"Well, Then, How Do You Explain . . . ?"

Where Was Jesus for Those Three Days?

JOHN 20:17A (KJV) STATES, "Jesus saith unto her, Touch me not; for I am not yet ascended to my Father."

This was spoken to Mary Magdalene on the Sunday morning after the crucifixion (which was the Feast of Firstfruits), after Jesus Christ arose from the grave. At this point, after having been dead for three days, Jesus according to his own proclamation had not yet been to heaven. Where was he?

Jesus Christ was dead. He was in the grave, Sheol, the common fate of all men. Yeshua, the anointed one, was a man. Solomon tells us that the rich and poor; the powerful and weak; the good, the bad, and the ugly all have a joint destiny in death. Since Jesus never sinned, and he did not inherit the original sin of Adam passed down by the male father, the spirit/soul of Christ was alive during his life. For thirty-plus years, Jesus was a whole body, soul, and spirit in full communion with his Father. However, upon the cross, "He was pierced for our transgressions, he was crushed for our iniquities; the punishment that brought us peace was upon him" (Isa 53:5a).

Let me be clear, lest someone confuse me with a member of the Jehovah's Witnesses. Jesus of Nazareth was divine. Christ has always been eternally coexistent with the Father. He and the Father and the Spirit are all One. They together are uncaused and unbegun. I am confident that Scripture is very clear that Jesus was God incarnate. One of my favorite proofs for the divinity of Christ is a comparison of John 1 and Gen 1 and 2. John 1 clearly says that the Word—that is, Jesus—created everything that exists in the universe. Even Jehovah's Witnesses will agree to this. Genesis 1 says that God created everything. Genesis 2, in repeating the story, even calls God by the ineffable name Yahweh. There is no contradiction, they are equal. Jesus was a man; yet He was Yahweh in bodily form.

The eternal Son of God was, however, separated from his Father. The Savior cried out from underneath the burden of sin and death, "My God, my God, why hast thou forsaken me?" (Ps 22:1 KJV; Matt 27:46 KJV). This is the point, the very moment, when I suspect the soul of Jesus Christ died. The spirit of Jesus, God himself, died on Calvary. The hand of God was laid upon the head of Jesus to transfer the sins from humanity to the sacrificial offering. Jesus was the offering without blemish. The laying on of hands was the Levitical custom of the priests when offering a lamb as substitutionary atonement for the sins of Israel (Lev 1:4). Just as Adam's spirit died when he sinned, Christ's spirit—that third part of humans which is the image of God—died when he received our sin. This is the only way that a truly vicarious sacrifice can be made. First Peter 3:18 (KJV) calls it "the just for the unjust." His substitution is our acquittal. If the spirit of Jesus did not die, then our sins have not been paid for and our soul/spirit shall not be granted life.

For some people, this point presents a serious problem. After all, how can God die? He must have had some level of existence. That is a good question, and I don't know how it works. However, in Mark 13:32 Jesus says about his own second coming, "No one knows about that day or hour, not even the angels in heaven, nor the Son, but only the Father." Jesus himself affirms that he doesn't know the timing. How can God not know something? Weird, huh? It must have something to do with his giving up (at least partially) part of his Godhead to become man.

If you are familiar with the feasts of Israel, Sukkot/Booths is representative of God, in Christ, tabernacling among people by leaving heaven and taking up residence in a frail human body. I don't celebrate the ancient biblical festivals ritually, but I do partake of them occasionally to deepen my understanding of our Hebraic roots. I remember the first time that I celebrated Sukkot; I was a college student living in Jerusalem and studying ancient history, languages, and archaeology. We had several pomegranate trees nearby, so our sukka roof was more woody than leafy. We were well within the rabbinic rule of being able to see the stars through the roof; except we could see no stars due to the clouds. The latter rains of October as promised by Deut 11:14 came upon us, and—as is usual for me—I was all wet. It is a small thing for me to give up a dry sleeping bag in order to receive the object lesson of what God gave up when Jesus was born as a fragile, helpless human baby.

Somehow he limited his divine aurora and powers when he entered a flesh-and-blood body. I admit, it's strange, and I certainly don't know the mechanics of how God could be dead, but I do believe that Christ died and didn't exist for three days. If Adam died spiritually when he sinned, then Christ died spiritually when he accepted the burden of our sin. For an even-Steven fair swap, his life for my life was required. If he didn't really die spiritually, physically, and every other way that a man can die, then I'm not off the hook yet.

Please note that I am definitely not advocating any of the crazy and unbiblical theories that have been put forward about the spiritual death of Christ and his suffering in hell. E. W. Kenyon taught that Jesus was imputed with Satan's nature on the cross, died spiritually, and went to hell to suffer in our place.[1] Christ's soul was allegedly dragged to hell by Satan, where Christ suffered the torments for the damned for three days and nights. He was three days later re-created in hell and thus become the first born-again man. The theories go on to include many transcendental and metaphysical ideas. Such ideas are unequivocally unbiblical. Yes, the spirit/soul of Christ died, the same way that the spirit/soul of Adam died the very day that he sinned. But that is it. He certainly did not go to any place of torment, because as we have already studied, such a mythological place does not exist.

Extreme Charismatics of the positive confession movement—such as Kenneth Hagin, Kenneth Copeland, Benny Hinn, and others—have adopted many of these unbiblical ideas.[2] This is certainly not what I am teaching.

As Jesus died on the cross, he declared, "It is finished!" The blood of Christ had been shed. All of the work for atonement and all of the Messiah's sufferings were over and finished. Reconciliation between God and man would not be complete until the resurrection, because Paul says that without the resurrection, Christ's death was in vain. These last words of Jesus as he hung on the tree exclude the possibility of any additional suffering that some speculate he should endure.

Most Evangelical believers think that even though Jesus died physically on the cross, he never died spiritually. They imagine fanciful adventures that the living Christ while dead (oxymoronic?) undertook during those three days. This is tantamount to rejecting the resurrection. Some people claim that Jesus' body never really died on the cross. They claim that he was only in a coma with very shallow breathing and a nearly undetectable heart rate. Later he resuscitated in the peace and quiet of the tomb. They claim that he was medically lucky, but never really dead. If Jesus cheated death and was either physically alive or spiritually alive, then he was no sacrifice at all. God would have failed at his redemption effort. I affirm the absolute death of Jesus, both physically and spiritually. His resurrection was a miracle of God.

Scripture repeatedly tells us that, on the third day, the Spirit of God *raised* Jesus from the dead. This is the beauty and power of the miracle. The righteousness of Christ Jesus was so perfect that God could not allow death, the grave, and the tomb to hold him. Jesus was not already alive. He did not never die spiritually. Jesus was raised from the dead by God the Father/Holy Spirit. He had been truly dead.

In his letter to the Ephesians, Paul writes a curious passage (4:8–10) that has long been debated: "This is why it says: 'When he ascended on high, he led captives in his train and gave gifts to men.' (What does 'he ascended' mean except that he also descended to the depths of the Earth? He who descended is the very one who ascended higher than all the heavens, in order to fill the whole universe.)" Paul is quoting from Ps 68:18.

I read this passage to mean that when Christ died, he descended to the depths of the earth or the lower, earthly regions—which simply means the grave, not some mythical abode of disembodied spirits. Christ went to Sheol, the grave, just like every other dead man since the creation of the world. Sacrificing himself as a vicarious act of love allowed him after his resurrection then to lead the captives (that is, dead saints stuck in the grave) to heaven, and to give the gift of immortality to justified people. In accordance with an OT understanding of Sheol and death, when Jesus died, he was spiritually unconscious and truly dead. Thus, this leading of captives in Ephesians must have happened during the ascension or shortly thereafter, maybe at Pentecost, ten days after the ascension. Remember, when he was speaking to Mary Magdalene in John 20, Jesus himself had not yet been to heaven. I think upon his redemptive purchase of humanity, he took the spirits of Abraham, David, and righteous OT figures back to heaven.

See also Isa 42:7 (KJV): "To open the blind eyes, to bring out the prisoners from the prison, and them that sit in darkness out of the prison house"; and Isaiah 61:1: "The Spirit of the Sovereign Lord is on me, because the Lord has anointed me to preach good news to the poor. He has sent me to bind up the brokenhearted, to proclaim freedom for the captives and release from darkness for the prisoners."

We know that these are messianic prophecies, because in Luke 4:18, Jesus reads this passage in the Nazareth synagogue, and tells them in 4:21, "Today this scripture is fulfilled in your hearing." Christ has opened the prison house. The prison house is the tomb, which holds millions of dead righteous saints. The tomb is the greatest prison of all time. It could not, however, hold Jesus Christ. He burst forth on the third day. At his ascension, probably with a shout and a shofar blow, release from the dark prison of the grave was proclaimed by Christ Jesus for those who hear his voice.

John 5:25–29 states, "I tell you the truth, a time is coming and has now come when the dead will hear the voice of the Son of God and those who hear will live. For as the Father has life in himself, so he has granted the Son to have life in himself. And he has given him authority to judge because he is the Son of Man. Do not be amazed at this, for a time is coming when all who are in their graves will hear his voice and come out—those who have done good will rise to live, and those who have done evil will rise to be condemned."

John 5:25 is commonly thought to be the resurrection of the dead at the second coming/Final Judgment, but I think that is found three verses later in 5:28–29. Those who have done good rise at the rapture/second coming (this is rising of the physical body, because my hypothesis is that the spirit/soul is already in heaven), and those who have done evil will rise to be condemned (both physical and soul) at the Final Judgment. Since I'm premillennial, I think the second resurrection will happen about one thousand years after the first resurrection. The earlier verse in 5:25, I believe, relates back to the Ephesians passage, when Jesus recalls the souls of saints during his ascension. When the OT saints died in their own day, hundreds or thousands of years before Christ, they had been promised redemption. However, it had not yet been fulfilled. Their salvation was no different than ours today, except for the tense of the verb and the details. They believed that God would provide a messiah/salvation if they humbly repented of sins and trusted in him.

Since the redemption had not yet happened, sin-stained OT saints could not enter God's presence in heaven. The outpouring of the Holy Spirit, the translocation of God's temple from a building in Jerusalem to the heart of believers, did not happen until after Christ's mission on Earth was complete and Pentecost saw the full expression of the Spirit. Their souls slept in the grave, awaiting Christ's glorious proclamation of their redemption.

ANOMALIES AND SUPPOSED ANOMALIES

What about Elijah and Enoch? They were preredemption saints, and Scripture implies that they bypassed death and went straight to heaven in spirit or possibly even bodily form. They seem to be the exception to the rule. I think the two witnesses of Rev 11 are probably Elijah and Enoch. As they have, so far, also bypassed Heb 9:27 (KJV): "And as it is appointed unto men once to die, but after this the judgment." All men must die. Elijah and Enoch will have their chance soon. "Very oddly, and often escaping notice, is that these occurrences do not elicit a reaction or theological comment in OT literature. Nowhere in the Hebrew Bible is there an explanation of their significance or a prayer for a similar destiny," as Philip Johnston observes.[3]

Some more anomalies: Moses' appearance at the mount of transfiguration seems to show a coconscious existence after death. Matthew 17:1–8; Mark 9:2–13; and Luke 9:28–36 are the passages on the transfiguration where we find Moses and Elijah appearing on the mountain with Jesus. Moses, who died and was buried, has his spirit speaking to Christ along with Elijah, who never died. Also, in 1 Sam 28, Saul enquired of the witch of Endor to conjure up the spirit of Samuel. In both of these cases, Moses and Samuel were dead. They certainly did not yet have physical glorified bodies, as Christ the firstfruits had not yet finished his mission. Their soul was, however, awake. This was, I believe, a short special session, an anomaly to the general rule. I can offer no further explanation.

Interestingly, at the transfiguration, Jesus, Moses, and Elijah spoke of the "exodus" that Christ was about to fulfill. In Luke 9:31, "[Moses and Elijah] appeared in glorious splendor, talking with Jesus. They spoke about his departure, which he was about to bring to fulfillment at Jerusalem."

The Greek word "exodus" is translated in the NIV as "departure" and in the KJV as "decease." "Decease" is a bad translation, as it makes an assumption about what was meant. The word "exodus," as all Bible students know, means to leave or depart. It is possible for it to figuratively mean death, as in 2 Pet 1:15, but more commonly means departure. It is difficult to use "exodus" without thinking of a mass horde of millions of people departing into freedom from a place of bondage. I propose that Christ and these two anomalously alive prophets were discussing the great release from Dead Soul Syndrome of all the saints.

Jesus' comment to the good thief while on the cross has often been used to support the immediate translation of OT saints to paradise even before their redemption. Luke 23:43 states, "Jesus answered him, 'I tell you the truth, today you will be with me in paradise.'" But I think this is mistaken. Using my chronology, the repentant criminal would have to wait either forty-three or fifty-three days until he got into heaven, because Christ himself did not immediately go to heaven. Remember his comment to Mary Magdalene on Sunday morning and his appearances to many in Judea for forty days before his ascension. Possibly we should add an extra ten days until Pentecost. The answer, I believe, is that the punctuation was added centuries later, somewhere around the twelfth century, by medieval translators. Ancient Hebrew and Greek manuscripts have no quote marks, commas, periods, paragraphs, or verse numbering. Maybe the verse should read, "I tell you the truth today, (This day that I'm dying on the cross, this day with the crown of thorns upon my head, this day with blood running down my face, this day when I'm saving humanity, this day that it looks like I'm a criminal); you will be with me in paradise." It all depends where you put that comma![4]

RICH MAN AND LAZARUS

The only other passage I find favoring a literal contemporary hell is the parable of the Rich Man and Lazarus in Luke 16. I'm sure you know the story, but here it is anyway:

> There was a certain rich man, which was clothed in purple and fine linen and fared sumptuously every day; and there was a certain beggar named Lazarus, which was laid at his gate, full of sores, and desiring to be fed with the crumbs which fell from the rich man's table; moreover, the dogs came and licked his sores. And it came to pass, that the beggar died, and was carried by

the angels into Abraham's bosom. The rich man also died, and was buried; and in hell [*hades*] he lifted up his eyes, being in torments, and seeth Abraham afar off, and Lazarus in his bosom. And he cried, and said, Father Abraham, have mercy on me and send Lazarus, that he may dip the tip of his finger in water, and cool my tongue; for I am tormented in this flame. But Abraham said, Son, remember that thou in thy lifetime receivedst thy good things, and likewise Lazarus evil things; but now he is comforted and thou art tormented. And besides all this, between us and you there is a great gulf fixed; so that they which would pass from hence to you, cannot; neither can they pass to us, that would come from thence. Then he said, I pray thee therefore, father, that thou wouldest send him to my father's house: for I have five brethren; that he may testify unto them, lest they also come into this place of torment. Abraham saith unto him, They have Moses and the prophets; let them hear them. And he said, Nay, father Abraham; but if one went unto them from the dead, they will repent. And he said unto him, If they hear not Moses and the prophets, neither will they be persuaded, though one rose from the dead. (Luke 16:19–31 KJV)

Should this be taken as a real-life case study or as a parable? If looked at in the context of the Gospel of Luke, note that seven parables appear immediately before this passage, almost without break. There are several after it. This is the last of a three-chapter run of parables. We know that Jesus spoke in parables deliberately to confound the wise (Matt 13:10–15). From verses 14 and 15, we see that this passage was clearly addressed to the Pharisees and crowds while in public, most likely the porches of the temple. We read in Mark 4:33–34 (KJV), "And with many such parables spake he the word unto them [the Pharisees and general public], as they were able to hear it. But without a parable spake he not unto them: and when they were alone, he expounded all things to his disciples." According to Mark 4:33, he *only* spoke to the crowds in parable. He would then carefully explain everything to his disciples when they were alone in private. The disciples were quite ignorant, and almost everything required a detailed explanation. (That makes me feel better, because frequently I need jokes explained to me.) However, the only thing the Pharisees and general public received were these enigmatic parables. Mark's comment that "without a parable spake he not unto them" is virtually proof, at least for me, that this passage is in fact a parable.

After all, why would Jesus be teaching the Pharisees doctrine? Did he give to them, not only the clearest, but the *only* passage of Scripture that details the concept of a two-compartmented hell between death and the resurrection? Is he unveiling to them this mysterious "truth," which is never explained elsewhere to his disciples, and is even apparently contradicted by OT passages? Do you really think Jesus gave this revelation to the Pharisees, his archenemies? In Matt 7:6, Christ himself advises against such action: "Do not give dogs what is sacred; do not throw your pearls to pigs. If you do, they may trample them under their feet, and then turn and tear you to pieces."

Again in Matt 13:11, Jesus replied to the disciples, "The knowledge of the secrets of the kingdom of heaven has been given to you, but not to them." He is referring to the people and the Pharisees, to whom he has not revealed any secrets.

Another reason that some suppose that this must be a literal account is that it refers to a "certain rich man" and a "certain beggar named Lazarus." Being a certain person implies to such readers that this must be speaking of a real-life case study with which Jesus is familiar.

The inference about the word "certain," however, is incorrect. This is the standard format with which parables commence. In the KJV translation of many Lukan parables, Jesus speaks of certain people. He mentions a certain creditor who had two debtors (7:41); a certain man passed over by a certain priest, but then helped by a certain Samaritan (10:30–33); the ground of a certain rich man brought forth plentifully (12:16); a certain man who had a fig tree (13:6); a certain man who made a great supper (14:16); a certain man with two sons, one of whom was prodigal (15:11); a certain rich man who had a steward (16:1); a certain nobleman who went into a far country (19:12); and finally a certain man who planted a vineyard (20:9). If anything, we might argue that starting off with a "certain rich man" is a verbal and literary clue to the listener that the following *is* a parable.

Literalists also point out that Lazarus is specifically and properly named. The name Lazarus means "whom God helps." It is closely related to the Hebrew name Elezear. They claim that parables never have proper names. However, in Ezek 23, the Lord gives Ezekiel a parable about the two adulterous sisters, Oholah and Oholibah. They are fictional characters in a story that metaphorically represent the nations of Samaria and Judah. Even though they are clearly parabolic, they have real, personal, individual names. Jesus certainly read and was familiar with the prophecies and dirges of Ezekiel. The personal name of Lazarus has precedent and does not necessarily make the story a literal account.

In a parable, what is intended is not spoken and what is spoken is not intended. Jesus used fictitious stories—a common practice in his day—to relate a moral or to make a point. Storytelling is not much of an art in the modern West. In our literal, logical, analytical society today, we consider this tantamount to lying. However, the intent was never to deceive. In the culture in which Christ lived, teaching through storytelling was considered an acceptable and highly revered practice of rabbis.

A valid point to consider has been made:

> If this account is literal and describes actual conditions of the netherworld then a number of problems arise. Will those in heaven be able to hold conversations with those in Hell? Is there prayer in Hell? Do citizens of Hell have compassion and sympathy for those still alive? Does Abraham speak for God? If this is a factual account of life after death then people will be able to look across the impassable gulf and see their loved ones in indescribable torment. Fathers will see daughters, mothers will see sons, husbands and wives see relatives all uttering ceaseless pleadings for cool water to assuage their thirst. Continual torment as such being witnessed by loved ones, seeing and hearing such screaming and hopeless despair would hardly give one in paradise a sense of comfort! Such a harrowing situation in no way would grant peace to the Godly occupants of a literal Hades.[5]

If this story is literal, then how could we believe that one drop of water on the tip of one finger could alleviate those who are incarcerated in such a fiery torment? For that matter, how could a drop of water exist in such a place, without being immediately evaporated, in this imaginary flaming hades? Again, if this story is literal, then how does one who has died and is buried possess a tongue to speak? Do the disembodied souls in the spirit realm have a tongue?

The literalist must explain these problems if this Scripture is not regarded as a parable. Doctrines have been formulated from it—such as particular judgment without a fair trial for wretched sinners. I believe this is a misapplication of the parable and a misunderstanding of its message. I don't claim to have all the answers, but I think Jesus was making one of two points with this parable:

Option #1—That Jews and Gentiles will shortly swap positions of God's favor. By this interpretation it is noted that the rich man was clothed in purple and fine linen. Purple was the color of kings, and linen was the raiment of priests. This rich man represents Judah, the southern kingdom of the Jews, and more personally the Pharisees themselves.

Lazarus was a poor beggar, neglected, and full of sores. Dogs showed more mercy and kindness than the rich man. Jewry considered everyone and every nation outside of themselves as dogs and heathen. Lazarus represents the Gentiles, those outside of the blessings of the covenants, not having received the riches and oracles bestowed upon the Israelites. Lazarus is the heathen world: lost, diseased, poverty stricken, an outcast, spiritually dead.

They both died. The death of these two is symbolic, representing a basic switch in their positions. Jesus prophesies that the Jews would become the outcasts and be separated from their God. A reading of Deut 28 aptly describes the incredible suffering of a disobedient people. Conversely, abundant grace would be given to any humble, repentant Gentile, and they may be grafted into the family of Abraham. Lazarus represents the heathen nations of the world, who by natural birth are outside Israel, but now are brought in by faith to apprehend and receive the blessings of Abraham. Paul speaks of the Age of Gentiles and this switching of positions in Rom 9–11. Romans 11:11b states, "Salvation has come to the Gentiles to make Israel envious." Likewise, in Song of Songs 5, Solomon (parabolically God) attempts to make his beloved (parabolically Israel) jealous by visiting other gardens, metaphorically other wives (parabolically Gentiles), and his beloved ardently searches the city for her lover Solomon.

In this interpretation of the Lazarus parable, Jesus is prophesying about the soon-to-be switch in the favored positions between Jew and Gentile. This option is more symbolic and complicated, and I think less likely. Many pages are written on this interpretation,[6] but it sometimes smacks of anti-Semitism and replacement theology.

Option #2—This is my favored interpretation. It is very simple: money and prosperity are not indicators of righteousness. Read verses 13 and 14, just a few sentences before this parable starts. The Pharisees loved money. Jesus told them, "You cannot serve God and mammon" (Luke 16:13 KJV). The Pharisees, who were covetous and greedy, sneered at him. Then Jesus moved into this parable in full hearing of the ever-present crowds that rubbernecked around him waiting for a really cool miracle. The Jews of this period believed that God blessed you financially directly in accordance with your righteousness. Jesus told them this story to show them that their belief system was upside down. We have a couple of other similar lessons in the Gospels, too. See Matt 19:30 and Luke 13:30.

These are the two leading interpretations that I find for this parable which concur with the rest of my thesis. The idea of accepting this as a literal story I do not find convincing. To believe that Christ was teaching his adversaries, the Pharisees, about a deep and not well understood doctrine, the afterlife, I find inconceivable.

Many preachers use this particular parable as an illustration of heaven and hell, but Scripture don't seem to warrant this interpretation. Besides, what happened to the righteous who predeceased Abraham? Where did Noah reside? Abraham's bosom is not heaven. This figurative expression originates from the custom of Christ's day. It speaks of an honored guest who sat next to the host. This was referred to as "reclining on his bosom." In the Eastern countries you reclined when eating, and one's head would be near the chest or bosom of the one next to him. The word is used forty-one times in the Bible, and anything anyone embraces is referred to as "in the bosom." It indicates a close, personal, and honored relationship.

I wrestle with many things in the Bible, though. As Jacob wrestled with God, I, too (and I hope you), struggle with understanding deep and difficult passages. We are blessed and come out stronger if we are persistent. I openly admit that the clear language in this passage of torment in hades and consciousness after death is confusing and problematic. An objection frequently advanced to this parable is: Why would Jesus utilize a Greek fable (hades being Greek mythology)? Titus 1:14a tells us to "pay no attention to Jewish myths."

The bosom of Abraham, the torments of hades, and the other strange things that appear in this Scripture are unique to this passage. These elements do not appear anywhere else in the Bible. They have no parallel, and they even seem to contradict other references in the Bible. All of these elements, however, do appear in the traditions that the Pharisees themselves believed.

Josephus Flavius was a historian of the first century who was born around A.D. 37 or 38. He lived very close to the time of Christ's ministry. He claims in his autobiography to be a Pharisee, and among others he wrote the following work: *Josephus's Discourse to the Greeks Concerning Hades*. There we read the Pharisees' beliefs about hades and the afterlife. The complete text can be found on the Internet.[7]

The images that Jesus used in this story, speaking to the Pharisees, were what the Pharisees themselves believed happened after death. He apparently used their own story to pass along his own message. To tell them the message, Jesus used one of the most effective methods—their own language. A Greek scholar observes:

> Jesus didn't intend to give a sermon on what happens in the afterlife, as many have taken His words to mean. What the Lord did, when addressing the Pharisees, was to refer to their very own beliefs about the afterlife to tell them that what matters is not riches but keeping the Word of God. He used their own framework, their own beliefs about afterlife, to add his own conclusion. He could have chosen another framework to say the same thing. But few will doubt that the most effective way to speak to somebody is using a language that is familiar to him. This is what the Lord did: he spoke to them using their picture of the afterlife as a framework, adding to it the message He wanted.[8]

At the very least, I find it dangerous to base an entire doctrine of hell on a single parable. I really don't think Jesus' intent was to satisfy our itching curiosity about the nature of the afterlife. That is my job.

NOT UNIVERSALISM OR SECOND CHANCE

I am in no way a universalist, believing that in the end all people will be saved. Some Christians say that God does not judge, since he finds all to be precious. Universalism teaches that God so loves of all his children that he would never send anyone to hell. Sometimes universalists teach that God may send people to hell for a period of time, but the experience will purify them and eventually they may be granted acceptance into God's kingdom.

There is no hint in Scripture that the purpose of hell/Gehenna is redemptive or rehabilitative (like the concept of purgatory). Hell is punitive—for the purpose of punishment.

See 2 Thess 1:8–9: "He will punish those who do not know God and do not obey the gospel of our Lord Jesus. They will be punished with everlasting destruction and shut out from the presence of the Lord and from the majesty of his power."

If hell could serve a redemptive or rehabilitative purpose, then the crucifixion, death, burial, resurrection, and even the atonement of Christ were not necessary! Unrighteous souls would be able to work off or burn off their sin, and then, at a later time, eventually enter God's presence. Universalism amounts to salvation by works.

God is love. However, God also is jealous of worship and takes vengeance on his enemies. Nahum 1:2–3a states, "The LORD is a jealous and avenging God; the LORD takes vengeance and is filled with wrath. The LORD takes vengeance on his foes and maintains his wrath against his enemies. The LORD is slow to anger and great in power; the LORD will not leave the guilty unpunished." A great many other verses mention Yahweh's wrath and coming punishment. Bible believers must reject universalism. The wicked will be punished. All unsaved humans, no matter how good they may seem in our human eyes, are wicked. In Isa 64:6 (KJV), we read, "But we are all as an unclean thing, and all our righteousnesses are as filthy rags; and we all do fade as a leaf; and our iniquities, like the wind, have taken us away." Only through Christ may a person become innocent of sin.

The hope of restoration from the lake of fire is impossible within the context of my theory. As we shall see, my proposed doctrine requires a judgment by fire that will be all consuming. The sinner will be exterminated; there will be nothing left; there is absolutely *no* hope for restoration or universal salvation.

Sinners in Gehenna may be sorry, but it will be too late. It is human nature to be sorry when caught and confronted with your sin. This is not true repentance but a form of self-preservation. Almost anyone who owns a television could cite a dozen cases of modern American politicians, movie stars, and televangelists who have been caught with their sin, and all of a sudden they are extremely sorry. However, the powerful difference is that these exposed sinners are still alive.

Mercy is available only to the living, for on Judgment Day there will be no more time for mercy. James 2:13 (KJV) states, "for he shall have judgment without mercy." Praise his name, for I am a benefactor of that mercy.

I also do not accept the millennial second-chance theory as taught by Bible Students, Worldwide Church of God, Mormons, and probably some others. Other names for the concept are postmortem evangelization, future probation, or divine perseverance. This theory teaches that the unsaved who never had a good obvious chance to hear or accept the gospel would be raised to live a second life during the millennium or be evangelized somewhere after death, and thereby have an opportunity to receive Christ. This is supposed to apply to the majority of B.C. Gentiles, premissionary Indians, Chinese, Aborigines, Africans, and so on. It would also possibly include aborted babies, dead children, mentally handicapped people, or others who could not make a decision for Christ because they did not have the necessary mental and emotional judgment.[9] Consider the following verses:

Psalms 78:39: "He remembered that they were but flesh, a passing breeze that does not return."

Hebrews 9:27–28a (kjv): "And as it is appointed unto men *once to die*, but after this the judgment: So Christ was *once offered* to bear the sins of many" (emphasis added).

Everyone must die a regular human death, so these verses seem to indicate that humans only die naturally once. Notice that the pair of verses in Hebrews says that as man once dies, so Christ once died. The Greek word used for "once" both times is the same word: *hapax*. It clearly means only one time, without repetition. The singular death of humans is tied to the singular death of Christ. Much of Heb 9 discusses that the death of Jesus Christ was a unique incident, never to recur. It has perpetual validity. This makes it unlike the Levitical priests who were constantly sacrificing animals over and over again. Hebrews 9:27–28a includes correlative conjunctions. These are the paired conjunctions "as" and "so." They link the balanced clauses of man's one-time death with the unique sacrifice of Jesus. On the other hand, if humans were to reincarnate into another earthly life, then Christ would have to suffer crucifixion again.

These verses teach that there is no reincarnation, which is basically what I find the second-chance theory to be. Reincarnation is a system that, in effect, believes that our salvation comes from our own works of righteousness. Eastern religious reincarnation teaches that you must live your life cyclically, over and over again, until you have attained a level of goodness that frees you from the rounds of human existence. When reincarnation is applied to a Christian framework, including the second-chance theory, it eliminates the grace and election of God. Reincarnation makes salvation conditional upon human action.

God's grace and mercy are available only to the living—not to the dead during the afterlife (universalism) and not to the reincarnated/resurrected during the millennium or some future forum. This makes it evident that *today* is the day of salvation. The gospel's offer of pardon must be taken urgently in this life, not as a vain hope for the next life.

See Heb 3:13: "But encourage one another daily, as long as it is called Today, so that none of you may be hardened by sin's deceitfulness."

Scripture clearly says the wicked will be destroyed and will die. There are numerous references to resurrection of the dead. Revelation 20 tells us that after the great white throne, the lost are cast into the lake of fire. So here is the next part of this theory and biblical question: are they eternally preserved with perpetual pain, or do they cease to exist after an equitable punishment has been meted out for their sin?

Trying to be fair, I desire to study especially well the verses and passages that appear to support my opposition's theory. I always find it particularly annoying when authors point out all of the reasons and verses supporting them and their own crazy ideas, but totally ignore reasons and verses that appear to contradict their teaching. So, first, let us look at some problematic verses.

ENDNOTES

1. Kenyon, *Identification*, 15.
2. Moriarty, *New Charismatics*, 79.
3. Johnston, *Shades of Sheol*, 200.
4. Finley, *Real Truth*.
5. Patching, "Rich Man and Lazarus."
6. In antiquity, it has been suggested that Augustine and Gregory the Great supported this view. In the nineteenth century, it was advocated by Richard Trench, *Notes on the Parables of our Lord* (New York: Appleton, 1867), 369–70, and by George Homer Emerson, *Doctrine of the Probation Examined* (Boston: Universalist Publishing House, 1883), 61–63. More modern scholars of this school include the Church of Christ author Cecil Hook, *Free to Change* (New Braunfels, TX: Freedom's Ring, 1990), .110–13.
7. "An Extract out of Josephus's Discourse to the Greeks Concerning Hades," http://wesley.nnu.edu/biblical_studies/josephus/hades.htm (accessed February 9, 2008).
8. Kioulachoglou, "Lazarus and Rich Man."
9. This topic is fascinating, but way beyond the scope of my study. For further reading about the fate of the unevangelized, see John Sanders, ed., *What about Those Who Never Heard? Three Views on the Fate of the Unevangelized* (Downer's Grove, IL: InterVarsity Press, 1995).

5

Problematic Passages

Open Problems in Revelation

I HAVE NOT BEEN able to discover a complementary and convincing interpretation for only two passages in the entire Bible that appear to favor the eternal torment theory. Both passages come from John's words in the last book of the New Testament. First is Rev 14:9–11 (KJV):

> And the third angel followed them, saying with a loud voice, If any man worship the beast and his image, and receive his mark in his forehead, or in his hand, The same shall drink of the wine of the wrath of God, which is poured out without mixture into the cup of his indignation; and he shall be tormented with fire and brimstone in the presence of the holy angels, and in the presence of the Lamb: And the smoke of their torment ascendeth up for ever and ever: and they have no rest day nor night, who worship the beast and his image, and whosoever receiveth the mark of his name.

The most solemn, fiery threat in all of Scripture applies to anyone who receives the mark of the beast. Accepting this mark is equivalent to worshiping the beast. You must give it your allegiance. By so doing, you will be worshiping Satan. You will be breaking the first of the Ten Commandments, as found in Exod 20. Second Thessalonians 2:11–12 (KJV) speaks about the time of tribulation when the "Wicked be revealed": "And for this cause God shall send them strong delusion, that they should believe a lie: That they all might be damned who believed not the truth, but had pleasure in unrighteousness."

If you accept the mark, there is no hope for you. By divine will, you will believe the lie. You will swallow the deceit—hook, line, and sinker. Beastly marked people will receive the full wrath of God. His wrath will not have any mercy mixed in with it. The measure of wrath will be undiluted. The people who receive the mark of the beast will lose the opportunity to live forever. They will be tormented with fire and brimstone instead.

Please note that Rev 14:11 never actually says that beast worshipers will burn forever—only that the smoke (remembrance?) is forever and ever. Not having rest clearly means that they are moving, wiggling, and squirming around. They must be conscious to do this, at least while they are yet burning.

The second example is Rev 20:10 (KJV): "And the devil that deceived them was cast into the lake of fire and brimstone, where the beast and the false prophet are, and shall be tormented day and night for ever and ever."

I have to admit these two verses seem problematic to my hypothesis. The Greek word for "for ever and ever" in both Revelation verses is *aeon aeon*—literally, "ages unto ages." This appears to mean infinite and eternal; however, it could be taken as an age or epoch with a finite beginning and end. Only God himself is infinite and eternal. I concur that the best interpretation of a verse is the obvious point-blank meaning. I dislike it when people cook up clever explanations to avoid admitting that they don't know an answer. I don't know how to take these verses. As no honest scholar has the answer to everything, I must admit that these two verses seem to mean eternally forever.

However, look at Jer 25:9: "'I will summon all the peoples of the north and my servant Nebuchadnezzar king of Babylon,' declares the LORD, 'and I will bring them against this land and its inhabitants and against all the surrounding nations. I will completely destroy them and make them an object of horror and scorn, and an everlasting ruin.'"

The Hebrew word is *olam*; it means forever, everlasting, perpetual, a long, long time. The word is used many times in relation to God's everlasting covenant, everlasting glory, and everlasting kingdom. In the case of Jer 25:9, it means seventy years, not really everlasting. The terms "everlasting" and "for ever," as used in the Bible, can simply mean a period of time, limited or unlimited.

In Jonah 2:6 (KJV), "for ever" means three days and nights: "I went down to the bottoms of the mountains; the earth with her bars was about me for ever: yet hast thou brought up my life from corruption, O LORD my God."

Understanding the context is critical to a solid interpretation. According to Fudge, "The word means 'forever' but within the limits of the possibility inherent in the person or thing it modifies. When God is said to be 'eternal' (eg: Deut 33:27) that is truly forever. When the mountains are said to be 'everlasting' (eg: Hab 3:6), that means that they last ever so long as they can last."[1]

I believe the words *aeon aeon* in these problematic Revelation verses must be an idiomatic phrase. From the ages to the ages must mean a long time, totally consuming, and most important, with eternal consequences.

Our understanding of these verses needs to be canonically in synchronization with the rest of the Bible's teaching. If the Revelation verses really do mean eternally forever, then this poses a contradiction within Scripture. See the many, many verses following in chapter 6 showing destruction, ashes, and cessation of being. Something has to give. At least one of these meanings (or possibly both) must be a figure of speech. They cannot both be literal interpretations. Revelation is well known for its figurative and symbolic language. These two verses are within a few pages of each other. To make figurative the verses speaking of fiery consumption and cessation of being would require spiritualizing Psalms, Isaiah, Jeremiah, Nahum, Malachi, 2 Thessalonians, 2 Peter, and others. Many Evangelicals tend to just flat-out ignore the Old Testament, figuring that it has been supplanted by the New Testament. This is very unfortunate. The OT writings were the cornerstone of understanding for the NT authors.

So the wicked burn in the fire as long as they live, or until death. This fiery punishment for sin varies according to the degree of sins (quantity of chaff or culpability) for each individual. During its rage, it torments without rest, but after the punishment, the wicked go extinct and the fire goes out.

FATE OF THE BEAST AND FALSE PROPHET

According to Rev 19:19–21, "Then I saw the beast and the kings of the earth and their armies gathered together to make war against the rider on the horse and his army. But the beast was captured, and with him the false prophet who had performed the miraculous signs on his behalf. . . . The two of them were thrown alive into the fiery lake of burning sulfur. The rest of them were killed with the sword that came out of the mouth of the rider on the horse, and all the birds gorged themselves on their flesh."

The second coming of the Messiah interrupts the beast's tribulation persecution of Israel and the saints. The whole world makes war with the great king on a white horse. In verse 20, the beast and the false prophet are cast alive into the lake of fire. One minute they are standing on the battlefield cursing their enemy; the next minute they are engulfed with flames. They bypass bodily human death, they bypass the second resurrection of the wicked, and they bypass the great white throne judgment. Instead, these two are hurled directly into Gehenna's lake. How can this be? Does God not obey the rules of fair trial in Num 35? Does God skip the Last Judgment of Rom 2:5 for these particular individuals? No, certainly not. Since Heb 13:8 tells us that "Jesus Christ is the same yesterday and today and forever," there must be another explanation. I agree with Froom, Fudge, and others who believe that these two are not individual people at all, but personified systems of wicked civil government and an apostate world religion of beguilement.[2] Of course, as institutions they could not suffer conscious, sensible pain. The language is visionary and symbolic. It signifies the total destruction, the final and complete end, at the hand of Christ, of an ungodly human system, never to rise again.

This understanding further helps to interpret Rev 20:10, which appears to say that when Satan is cast into the lake of fire, the beast and the false prophet are still there. This occurs about one thousand years later, after the millennium and after the great white throne judgment. This observation is frequently used by eternal-torment advocates showing that the lake of fire does not destroy.

Scripture provides further evidence that the beast is not a human: Rev 17:8 (KJV) states, "The beast that thou sawest was, and is not; and shall ascend out of the bottomless pit, and go into perdition." See also Rev 11:7; both verses tell us that the beast came up out of the bottomless pit. Human beings do not originate in the bottomless pit, and they do not come out of the bottomless pit. The beast is a demonic system, the empire of antichrist. It is the government of world rule. It cannot be simplified as a single man. The bottomless pit, I believe, equals the abyss and Tartarus that we spoke of in chapter 1.

Additionally, recognizing these images of John's vision as sociopolitical institutions anthropomorphized as creatures lends new understanding when reading Rev 13—17.

For the interpretation of this passage, I owe a debt of scholarship to Edward Fudge and his book *The Fire That Consumes*, whose lead I have been following throughout this section. My friend, Brother Edward has developed and postulated the conditional immortality doctrine for thirty years, making him the senior elder in its school. His clear intellect entitles him to that position.

UNDYING WORMS

Another passage uses a poetic phrase on which many people stumble. It is considered a proof-text for students of conscious eternal torment. However, once understood and explained, it clearly fits within my hypothesis. This passage is not found in the other Gospels, only in Mark 9:48. The KJV repeats the last key phrase in verses 44 and 46, but the repetition is not found in the oldest manuscripts. The entire passage of Mark 9:42–48 is as follows:

> And if anyone causes one of these little ones who believe in me to sin, it would be better for him to be thrown into the sea with a large millstone tied around his neck. If your hand causes you to sin, cut it off. It is better for you to enter life maimed than with two hands to go into hell [*gehenna*], where the fire never goes out. And if your foot causes you to sin, cut it off. It is better for you to enter life crippled than to have two feet and be thrown into hell [*gehenna*]. And if your eye causes you to sin, pluck it out. It is better for you to enter the kingdom of God with one eye than to have two eyes and be thrown into hell [*gehenna*], where "their worm does not die, and the fire is not quenched."

The traditional understanding of this passage among advocates of eternal torment is that the "worm" (Gr = *skolex*) is figurative of the soul of the doomed individual who has been cast into Gehenna for causing one of the little ones to sin. They correctly note that Jesus says "their" worm, as if it belongs to them. Since we are told by Christ himself that their worm never dies, it must mean that their soul is consciously aware of their fiery surroundings, which do not cease. Advocates believe that this is plain language of eternal torment. However, before we attempt to bring meaning to the words of Christ, we must earn that interpretational privilege by first reading and understanding the Hebrew prophets.

When Jesus says of Gehenna (literally a valley outside Jerusalem; symbolically probably the lake of fire), "Where their worm dieth not, and the fire is not quenched," he is clearly quoting Isa 66:22–24: "'As the new heavens and the new earth that I make will endure before me,' declares the LORD, 'so will your name and descendants endure. From one New Moon to another and from one Sabbath to another, all mankind will come and bow down before me,' says the LORD. 'And they will go out and look upon the dead bodies of those who rebelled against me; their worm will not die, nor will their fire be quenched, and they will be loathsome to all mankind.'"

In Hebrew the worm is *towla*. It is most commonly translated as "scarlet," referring to the dark carmine color used in dying fabric that comes from these insects. The scarlet *towla* is not a worm at all as we would define such. It is actually a scale insect, related to cochineals and mealy bugs. They are a sessile, plant-sucking parasite known to most gardeners. The type harvested in the ancient Mediterranean was of the specie *Kermes ilicis* (previously named *Coccus ilicis*). Natural insect-based crimson dyes are still available today; a related species has been farmed in Mexico since ancient Mayan time.

The Israelites did not have a detailed taxonomic description of various biological life forms. The same word *towla* is also used in reference to various types of maggots, grubs, and caterpillars. In Exod 16:20, worms cause decay and stink in day-old manna. In Deut 28:39, worms destroy the grapes of a vineyard. In Isa 14:11, worms eat corpses in a grave. In Jonah 4:7, a worm kills the disgruntled prophet's beloved shade-giving gourd. In all of these instances, as well as in Isa 66:24 above, the worm of putrefaction is *towla*.

In the Isaiah passage, and also in Jesus' use of *skolex*, the worm represents destruction and consumption from the inside out. Isaiah says that *their* worm will not die, and that *their* fire will not be quenched. Observers are correct to note that the worm belongs to the wicked, but so does the fire. Jesus only uses the added force of the demonstrative pronoun "their" (Gr. = *autos*) one time at the beginning along with the worm. I'm afraid he paraphrased, or maybe Mark paraphrased what Jesus actually said.

The worm should not be equated with the human soul. It should be equated with the fire. This is an example of Hebrew parallel poetry. The worm destroys from the inside out, and the fire destroys from the outside in. They are both views of punishment. The fact that the worm does not die is the same fact that the fire will not be quenched. In other words, that punishment will not cease prematurely. It will be complete, absolute, and thorough. The worm's work is to skeletonize the corpse. The fire's work is to reduce the contents of the furnace to ashes.

Our modern Western minds like to make lists. We organize our thoughts in a bulleted list of tasks to accomplish. However, in this case—and so many times in parallel poetry—this is not a list of different actions but rather repetition for emphasis. The purpose of the poetic redundancy is to show significance.

In conclusion, this passage has nothing to do with the immortality of the human soul, as it is so often forced to say. It does, however, bring up a good question about the fire being quenched. Numerous verses say that the fire of Gehenna is everlasting or cannot be quenched. A point to note, except for the parable in Luke 16 of Lazarus and the *Dives* (*dives* is Latin for rich or splendid), no verse ever mentions fire in hades/Sheol, which is the grave. Fiery punishment is always to be found in Gehenna.

EVERLASTING FIRE AND SMOKE, BUT NO COMMENT ABOUT PEOPLE IN THE FIRE

Several biblical passages use the image of burning sulfur, or brimstone, to represent divine wrath. The KJV often renders such imagery with the phrase "fire and brimstone." In Gen 19, God destroys Sodom and Gomorrah via a rain of fire and brimstone, and in Deut 29, the Israelites are threatened with the same punishment should they abandon their covenant with God. Elsewhere, divine judgments involving fire and sulfur are prophesied against Assyria (Isa 30), Edom (Isa 34), Gog (Ezek 38), and all the wicked (Ps 11). Notably, brimstone appears in Rev 19—21 in God's wrath and judgment upon the earth.

Note the text of Isa 33:14 (KJV): "The sinners in Zion are afraid; fearfulness hath surprised the hypocrites. Who among us shall dwell with the devouring fire? Who among us shall dwell with *everlasting burnings*?" (emphasis added).

The Hebrew word for "everlasting" is *olam*—forever, always, everlasting, perpetual. It is used many times of God's everlasting covenant, everlasting glory, and everlasting kingdom; in that context, I think it really does mean eternal. Notice in Isa 33 however, that the people cannot stay there very long, but the fire is forever.

Matthew 25:41 (KJV) states, "Then shall he say also unto them on the left hand, Depart from me, ye cursed, into *everlasting fire*, prepared for the devil and his angels" (emphasis added).

Matthew 18:8–9 (KJV): "Wherefore if thy hand or thy foot offend thee, cut them off, and cast them from thee: it is better for thee to enter into life halt or maimed, rather than having two hands or two feet to be cast into *everlasting* fire. And if thine eye offend thee, pluck it out, and cast it from thee: it is better for thee to enter into life with one eye, rather than having two eyes to be cast into hell [*gehenna*] fire" (emphasis added). Similar also is Mark 9:43, which we recently studied.

Jude 1:7: "In a similar way, Sodom and Gomorrah and the surrounding towns gave themselves up to sexual immorality and perversion. They serve as an example of those who suffer the punishment of *eternal fire*" (emphasis added).

The Greek word used in all of these verses for "everlasting/eternal" is *aeon*. Even if the fire really is everlasting, it does not say the people live forever. Most likely, though, the "eternal" is figurative for "bigger then they are," "no turning around or stopping." The "fire" is figurative for God's judgment being eternal and irrevocable.

Compare this with 2 Pet 2:6: "If he condemned the cities of Sodom and Gomorrah by burning them to ashes, and made them an example of what is going to happen to the ungodly."

These cities on the Dead Sea are not burning today. The fire went out after everything was burned up. Likewise, everlasting fire will go out after it has turned the wicked to ashes. The same thing that happened to Sodom and Gomorrah will happen to the ungodly; they will be turned to ashes and totally destroyed.

When God destroys the great harlot/Babylon during the tribulation, her smoke rises forever and ever, too. See Rev 19:2–3: "For true and just are his judgments. He has condemned the great prostitute who corrupted the earth by her adulteries. He has avenged on her the blood of his servants. And again they shouted: 'Hallelujah!' The smoke from her goes up for ever and ever."

I doubt this is literal. Babylon is not literally the Iraqi city of Babylon. It is an arrogant worldly system that exalts itself analogously to the ancient city. The harlot is not literally a street prostitute. It is a religious system that has flagrantly broken its covenant with God by mixing with pagan doctrines and practices. So, too, I doubt the smoke is literal or eternal. The poetic point being made with passages involving everlasting fire and smoke is the absolute, irreversible judgment and justice of God.

UNQUENCHABLE FIRE

Consider the following verses:

Isaiah 1:31: "The mighty man will become tinder and his work a spark; both will burn together, with no one to quench the fire."

Jeremiah 17:27 (KJV): "But if ye will not hearken unto me to hallow the sabbath day, and not to bear a burden, even entering in at the gates of Jerusalem on the sabbath day; then will I kindle a fire in the gates thereof, and it shall devour the palaces of Jerusalem, and it shall not be quenched."

Ezekiel 20:47 (KJV): "And say to the forest of the south, Hear the word of the LORD; Thus saith the Lord GOD; Behold, I will kindle a fire in thee, and it shall devour every green tree in thee, and every dry tree: the flaming flame shall not be quenched, and all faces from the south to the north shall be burned therein."

Matthew 3:12 (KJV): "Whose fan is in his hand, and he will thoroughly purge his floor, and gather his wheat into the garner; but he will burn up the chaff with unquenchable fire." See also Luke 3:17.

In the New Testament, the Greek word used for "unquenchable" is probably familiar to everybody. It is *asbestos*, the adjective meaning inextinguishable. When we think of asbestos, we think of a material that does not burn. Nonflammable and noncombustible are the main characteristics of the mineral asbestos. But in Greek *asbestos* is an adjective meaning "never put out." Notice it is never applied or modified to a person, but only to the judgment of fire.

Does "unquenchable" mean "everlasting"? Or does it simply mean what it says—the fire cannot be quenched? According to Webster's dictionary, to quench means to snuff out, dampen, or extinguish. To quench the flames means to actively extinguish prior to the complete consumption of the fuel. A fire that totally consumes its fuel source is never quenched. Note all the above examples of fires that naturally ceased burning after accomplishing the purpose of the Lord. Today, the army of Israel, the gates of Jerusalem, the forests of Judea, and threshing mills of the land are not still on fire.

Second Kings 22:17: "Because they have forsaken me and burned incense to other gods and provoked me to anger by all the idols their hands have made, my anger will burn against this place and will not be quenched." See also 2 Chr 34:25 for a very similar verse. God's unquenchable anger is not eternally burning against Israel. His unquenchable wrath ran its course and was completed. The anger subsided of its own accord after it had accomplished its goal. However, God's wrath was never diverted or put out by men.

When unquenchable fire is viewed in Gehenna's punishment, it means that the sentence of death is irreversible, without mitigation. It is an eternal consequence.

PUNISHMENT OF THE WICKED IS ETERNAL

No dispute here. There shall be no resurrection from Gehenna. Many people shall be utterly destroyed.

Daniel 12:2 (KJV): "And many of them that sleep in the dust of the earth shall awake, some to everlasting life, and some to shame and everlasting contempt."

Mathew 25:46 (KJV): "And these shall go away into everlasting punishment: but the righteous into life eternal."

Second Thessalonians 1:8–9: "He will punish those who do not know God and do not obey the gospel of our Lord Jesus. They will be punished with everlasting destruction and shut out from the presence of the Lord and from the majesty of his power."

The verse in Matt 25:46 is a much controverted passage. People supporting the eternal-torment perspective have employed it heavily as a proof verse. In the Greek it uses exactly the same adjective (*aionios*) to modify each prepositional noun (punishment and life). In the KJV, the word for "everlasting" and the word for "eternal" are the same word, *aionios*. Most modern translations have corrected this inconsistency in the English. Notice, however, that the above verse does not say that the *punishing* goes on eternally, but that the *punishment* is eternal. God's capital punishment is forever.

John Wesley's classic commentary on the Bible written in the mid-1700s states, "Either therefore the punishment is strictly eternal, or the reward is not: the very same expression being applied to the former as to the latter.... It is not only particularly observable here, That the punishment lasts as long as the reward; but, That this punishment is so far from ceasing at the end of the world, that it does not begin till then."[3]

Similarly, Robert Peterson's book *Hell on Trial* is a noble attempt to uphold the eternal-torment theory. He figures along with Augustine, quite logically and with an algebraic mind, that if our eternal life is everlasting without end and gloriously abundant forever, then the fate of the doomed, based on the twin usage of "eternal" or "aionios," must be equally eternal as our life.[4] His opinion appears to be a yin/yang relationship, claiming that if the wicked do not exist forever, then we cannot (grammatically according to this verse in his opinion) exist forever. They are complementary opposites within a greater whole as required by the double use of the same word.

I agree that this verse does amount to an inequality within the use of "eternal." But whoever said that they have to be equal? I praise God that he is treating us with eternal favor. I praise God that I am given eternal life of far greater value than I am worth. They receive the "eternal" for which they are worth, while we receive the "eternal" for which Jesus is worth. The cloned "eternals" in Matt 25:46 are not equal.

The fallacy in thought is that Wesley, Peterson. and other eternal tormentors appear to believe that the punishment and the reward must be equal and opposite in all characters. That is not true; the reward is far greater than the punishment. When we get to our section on the equal and just judgment of God, we learn that the punishment is required to be equal and opposite, perfectly reciprocal, to one's own crime, but never to someone else's reward. Paul assures us in Rom 5:15, "But the gift is not like the trespass." They are both eternal in consequence, but they are not reciprocally equal.

This chapter shows the half dozen genres of what I believe to be misinterpreted verses. Verses containing "aion aion" in Revelation, fate of the beast, undying worms, everlasting fire, fire that is never quenched, and eternal punishment are easily misconstrued by the earnest Bible reader. I understand how someone can honestly come to the conclusion of eternal conscious torment, especially when they grow up in our culture, which is soaked with that theory. But when reviewed next to the volume of verses that the next chapter provides, I think a better theory—more fitting to the biblical evidence—is possible.

So, my hypothesis is that the wicked will burn in the fire as long as they live, or until death. This fiery punishment for sin will vary according to the degree of sins (quantity of chaff) for each individual. This includes Satan and his demons. Obviously, they will cook longer than the average human. During its rage, the fire will be a torment without rest, but after the punishment, the wicked will go extinct and the fire will go out. The universe will then be at peace.

ENDNOTES

1 Fudge, *Fire That Consumes*, 39.
2 Ibid., 303.
3 Wesley, *Explanatory Notes upon the New Testament*, 249.
4 Peterson, *Hell on Trial*, 46, 107.

6

Death of All the Wicked

THE TIME HAS COME to address the verses that I think support the death and destruction, both spiritually and physically, of the wicked. There are many such verses, especially in the Old Testament. The long lists of Bible verses in this chapter are more extensive than in other sections of the book because my study started here. Bumping into all of these verses is what first started my thinking about this subject. The weight of Scripture is undeniable. I do not draw this doctrine from one or two verses, and I doubtlessly have missed some passages. I do not promise absolute comprehensive coverage of all similar verses.

The punishment of death for sinners is repeated dozens of times in Scripture. God gave this warning over and over, starting in the garden of Eden. See Gen 2:17 (KJV): "But of the tree of the knowledge of good and evil, thou shalt not eat of it: for in the day that thou eatest thereof thou shalt surely die."

God gives a time deadline: that day. Since Adam and Eve did not fall over dead physically that very day, God must have meant some other type of death. This was the death of Adam's soul and the start of Dead Soul Syndrome that has adversely affected everyone ever since. The following citations depict the death of the wicked. (All italics in the citations throughout this chapter were added for emphasis.)

Deuteronomy 6:15b (KJV): "Lest the anger of the LORD thy God be kindled against thee, and *destroy thee from off the face of the earth*."

Job 18:5 (KJV): "Yea, the light of the *wicked shall be put out*, and the spark of his fire shall not shine."

Job 36:6 (KJV): "He preserveth not the life of the wicked: but giveth right to the poor."

In this six-chapter monologue, Elihu proclaims that God will not keep the wicked alive. Ironically, this is exactly the opposite of what the eternal soul teaching claims.

All commentators who deal with the fate of the impenitent must eventually do business with the psalms. The psalms are strong on the destruction of the wicked. How can we ignore them?

Psalm 1:6: "For the LORD watches over the way of the righteous, but the way of the *wicked will perish.*"

Psalm 2:9: "You will rule them with an iron scepter; you will *dash them to pieces* like pottery."

Psalm 9:5: "You have rebuked the nations and destroyed the wicked; you have *blotted out their name* for ever and ever." If they do not suffer extinction, will the wicked have a name in hell?

Psalm 11:6: "On the wicked he will *rain fiery coals* and burning sulfur; a scorching wind will be their lot."

Psalm 21:9 (KJV): "Thou shalt make them as a fiery oven in the time of thine anger: the LORD shall swallow them up in his wrath, and the *fire shall devour them.*"

See also many references in Ps 37 (all KJV):

Psalm 37:2: "For they shall soon be *cut down like the grass*, and wither as the green herb."

Psalm 37:9: "For *evildoers shall be cut off*: but those that wait upon the LORD, they shall inherit the earth."

Psalm 37:10: "For yet a little while, and the *wicked shall not be*: yea, thou shalt diligently consider his place, and it shall not be."

Psalm 37:20: But the *wicked shall perish*, and the enemies of the LORD shall be as the fat of lambs: they shall consume; *into smoke shall they consume away.*"

Psalm 37:38: "But the transgressors shall be destroyed together: the end of the *wicked shall be cut off.*"

Psalm 49:20: "A man who has riches without understanding is *like the beasts that perish.*"

Psalm 50:22: "Consider this, you who forget God, or I will *tear you to pieces*, with none to rescue."

Psalm 58:7a: "Let them *vanish like water that flows away.*"

Psalm 59:13: "Consume them in wrath, *consume them till they are no more*. Then it will be known to the ends of the earth that God rules over Jacob. Selah."

Psalm 68:2 (KJV): "As smoke is driven away, so drive them away: *as wax melteth before the fire*, so let the wicked perish at the presence of God."

Psalm 73:18–20: Referring to the wicked, "Surely you place them on slippery ground; you cast them down to ruin. How suddenly are they destroyed, *completely swept away* by terrors! As a dream when one awakes, so when you arise, O Lord, you will despise them as fantasies." The wicked are like a bad dream, gone in the morning.

Psalm 104:35a (KJV): "Let the sinners be consumed out of the earth, and *let the wicked be no more*."

Psalm 119:119: "All the wicked of the earth you *discard like dross*; therefore I love your statutes."

Psalm 139:19 (KJV): "Surely thou wilt *slay the wicked*, O God: depart from me therefore, ye bloody men."

Psalm 145:20 (KJV): "The LORD preserveth all them that love him: but all the *wicked will he destroy*."

A rebuttal that I've heard to all of the Psalms verses is that these verses refer to the millennium, when there will be no wicked in the earth, because they will all be in hell. That is definitely not the impression that you get from reading these verses with an open mind and no agenda. But you can't argue with people who know everything.

Solomon, one of the wisest men who ever lived, had the following to say about the fate of the wicked:

Proverbs 2:22 (KJV): "But the wicked shall be *cut off* from the earth, and the transgressors shall be *rooted out* of it."

Proverbs 10:7: "The memory of the righteous will be a blessing, but the name of the *wicked will rot*."

Proverbs 10:25: "When the storm has swept by, the *wicked are gone*, but the righteous stand firm forever."

Proverbs 10:30: "The righteous will never be uprooted, but the *wicked will not remain* in the land."

Proverbs 11:19: "The truly righteous man attains life, but he who pursues evil *goes to his death*."

Proverbs 12:7: "Wicked men are overthrown and *are no more*, but the house of the righteous stands firm."

Proverbs 13:9: "The light of the righteous shines brightly, but the lamp of the wicked is *snuffed out*."

Proverbs 24:20: "For the evil man has no future hope, and the lamp of the wicked will be *snuffed out*."

Similar to the argument against the psalms, those who prescribe to the concept of eternal torments claim that these curses upon the wicked are to occur in this life. They will be rooted up like a weed, snuffed out like a candle wick, and rot like roadkill. When the wicked go "to his death" and "are no more" must refer to this life, because these interpreters assume the human soul to be immortal and eternal. Where I live, unrepentant, unsaved, and wicked sinners still thrive. These verses are prophetic toward the Day of Judgment, when God will execute all arrogant, unjustified people.

PROPHETS ALSO TELL ABOUT THE POSTMORTEM FATE OF SINNERS

Consider the following verses from the prophetic tradition:

Isaiah 1:28: "But rebels and sinners will both *be broken*, and those who forsake the LORD will perish."

Isaiah 1:31: "The mighty man will become tinder and his work a spark; both will burn together, with no one to quench the fire."

Isaiah 5:24: "Therefore, as tongues of fire lick up straw and as dry grass sinks down in the flames, so their roots will decay and their flowers blow away like dust; for they have rejected the law of the LORD Almighty and spurned the word of the Holy One of Israel."

Isaiah 29:20: "The ruthless will vanish, the mockers will disappear, and all who have an eye for evil will be cut down." Vanish and disappear—similar to the dodo birds or dinosaurs. They become extinct.

Isaiah 33:12 (KJV): "And the people shall be as the burnings of lime: as thorns cut up shall they be burned in the fire."

Isaiah 43:17: Referring literally to Babylon's mighty military that tried to control the world, but allegorically applying to anyone who arrogantly exalts him- or herself above God's dominion: "Who drew out the chariots and horses, the army and reinforcements together, and they lay there, never to rise again, extinguished [KJV = extinct], snuffed out like a wick."

Isaiah 47:14 (KJV): "Behold, they shall be as stubble; the fire shall burn them; they shall not deliver themselves from the power of the flame: there shall not be a coal to warm at, nor fire to sit before it."

Isaiah 51:8a (KJV): "For the moth shall eat them up like a garment, and the worm shall eat them like wool." This refers to the revilers and those full of reproach for the saints.

Ezekiel 18:4 (KJV): "Behold, all souls are mine; as the soul of the father, so also the soul of the son is mine: the soul that sinneth, it shall die." The "soul" here is *nephesh*; remember that it means "life." To die simply means not to live. It does not have the meaning of living in ruin. That interpretational definition is not supported by the original language.

Ezekiel 33:11 (KJV): "Say unto them, As I live, saith the Lord GOD, I have no pleasure in the death of the wicked; but that the wicked turn from his way and live: turn ye, turn ye from your evil ways; for why will ye die, O house of Israel?" Again "death" does not mean living in remorse or living removed from pleasure. Death means death. This verse and others specifically contrasts death to life.

Obadiah 1:16: "Just as you drank on my holy hill, so all the nations will drink continually; they will drink and drink and *be as if they had never been*."

Nahum 1:9–10 (KJV): "What do ye imagine against the LORD? *He will make an utter end*: affliction shall not rise up the second time. For while they be folden together as thorns, and while they are drunken as drunkards, *they shall be devoured as stubble fully dry*."

Malachi 4:1–3: "'Surely the day is coming; it will *burn like a furnace*. All the arrogant and every evildoer will be stubble, and that day that is coming will *set them on fire*,' says the LORD Almighty. 'Not a root or a branch will be left to them. But for you who revere my name, the sun of righteousness will rise with healing in its wings. And you will go out and leap like calves released from the stall. Then you will trample down the wicked; *they will be ashes under the soles of your feet* on the day when I do these things,' says the LORD Almighty."

Another rebuttal I've heard to Malachi 4:3 and others involving fire, ashes, and lime: the ashes are from the postmillennium final war after Satan is released from the abyss for a short season. This is described in Revelation 20:9 (KJV): "And they went up on the breadth of the earth, and compassed the camp of the saints about, and the beloved city: and fire came down from God out of heaven, and devoured them." They claim that this refers to regular human ashes on Earth, not the ashes of souls in Gehenna. This interpretation limits the focus and target audience of many verses. The rebellious men in that final revolt have not even been born yet, whereas I believe that such verses are broad warnings to all of humanity.

Using a reversed allusion to the notable Presbyterian evangelist of the early twentieth century, William Biederwolf, it might be said that a man who can read eternal torment into Scriptures like these can discover a Beethoven symphony in a frog pond.[1]

Many verses in the Old Testament appear to be warning people that if they do not repent, then they will die, be cut off, be consumed into smoke, destroyed, devoured, and perish. They will be rooted out, cut up, broken to pieces, extinct, snuffed out, and burned to ash. Their names shall be blotted out forever. They shall not be anymore. It will be as if they had never been. They will be devoured as stubble, fully dry. How clear can God make it? The Bible exhausts the vocabulary of death when explaining the fate of the wicked. We must be confident that God will faithfully bring his word to fruition. The wicked shall surely go extinct, and righteousness will reign unanimously. In the Old Testament, I don't see the notion of evil men without God being made deathless to receive unending conscious torment. What about the New Testament?

NEW TESTAMENT VERSES SAYING THE WICKED WILL DIE

Jesus speaks frequently of death and destruction:

Matthew 7:13 (KJV): "Enter ye in at the strait gate: for wide is the gate, and *broad is the way, that leadeth to destruction*, and many there be which go in thereat."

Matthew 10:28 (KJV): "And fear not them which kill the body, but are not able to kill the soul: but rather fear Him which is able to *destroy both soul and body* in hell (Gehenna)." See also Luke 12:5.

The word "destroy" is the Greek *apollumi*. It means to put out of the way entirely, abolish, put an end to, ruin, render useless, kill, loose, declare that one must be put to death, and perish.

Matthew 13:40–43: "As the weeds are pulled up and burned in the fire, so it will be at the end of the age [*aeon*]. The Son of Man will send out his angels, and they will weed out of his kingdom everything that causes sin and all who do evil. They will throw them into the fiery furnace, where there will be weeping and gnashing of teeth. Then the righteous will shine like the sun in the kingdom of their Father. He who has ears, let him hear." Notice, they do not die immediately; there will be enough time to cry and gnash teeth. More on this later.

John 3:15–16 (KJV): "That whosoever believeth in him should not perish, but have eternal life. For God so loved the world, that he gave his only begotten Son, that whosoever believeth in him should not perish, but have everlasting life." Perish = *apollumi* (same as above). Notice the contrast between life and death. The contrast is never made between a really good life and a ruined life.

The words of Jesus himself are those most frequently misunderstood by those who propound eternal torment. They hear severe language of eternal fire and great torment. They assume, without further research, that this means sinners eternally existing within a fire that tortures but does not kill.

Paul believed in death of the sinner. Paul was immersed in the Old Testament. It was his foundation. He probably had vast portions of it memorized. His message repeatedly harkens back to the Old Testament:

Romans 2:12 (KJV): "For as many as have sinned without law shall also perish without law: and as many as have sinned in the law shall be judged by the law."

Romans 5:12: "Therefore, just as sin entered the world through one man, and death through sin, and in this way death came to all men, because all sinned."

Romans 6:23 (KJV): "For the wages of sin is death; but the gift of God is eternal life through Jesus Christ our Lord."

Peter too knew the Hebrew Scriptures, with which he was well read and extremely familiar:

2 Peter 2:12b: Bold and arrogant men "are like brute beasts, creatures of instinct, born only to be caught and destroyed, and like beasts they too will perish." Do beasts suffer eternal life in torment? Or does this word "perish" simply mean to die?

2 Peter 3:7: "By the same Word the present heavens and earth are reserved for fire, being kept for the day of judgment and destruction of ungodly men." That day has not yet come. Maranatha, Lord Jesus!

2 Peter 3:9 (KJV): "The Lord is not slack concerning his promise, as some men count slackness; but is longsuffering to us-ward, not willing that any should perish, but that all should come to repentance." It is not God's hope and desire for any person to die; however, many people will die, perish, and be destroyed due to their lack of repentance.

John, who received the Revelation while on Patmos, speaks of death of the ungodly:

Revelation 21:8 (KJV): "But the fearful, and unbelieving, and the abominable, and murderers, and whoremongers, and sorcerers, and idolaters, and all liars, shall have their part in the lake which burneth with fire and brimstone: which is the second death." If this involved eternal existence in hell, why did John use the Greek word *thanatos*, clearly meaning "death" or lack of being?

Finally in Rev 20:14, "Death and Hades were thrown into the lake of fire. The lake of fire is the second death." If death itself is destroyed, how can people still be alive in hell?

AGRICULTURAL METAPHORS

The society of ancient Israel during biblical times was agrarian. From the Bronze and Iron ages of the Old Testament, all the way through and even including the Greco-Roman world of the New Testament, the economy and social structure were oriented around farming, ranching, fishing, and similar activities. So it makes perfect sense that God in his inspired word would use figures of speech from the land and from farming to convey his message to these people. Here is a sampling of such verses:

Daniel 2:35: "Then the iron, the clay, the bronze, the silver and the gold were broken to pieces at the same time and became like chaff on a threshing floor in the summer. The wind swept them away without leaving a trace. But the rock that struck the statue became a huge mountain and filled the whole earth."

Matthew 3:10: "The ax is already at the root of the trees, and every tree that does not produce good fruit will be cut down and thrown into the fire."

Matthew 7:19: "Every tree that does not bear good fruit is cut down and thrown into the fire."

Matthew 13:40: "As the weeds are pulled up and burned in the fire, so it will be at the end of the age."

Luke 13:6–7: "Then he told this parable: 'A man had a fig tree, planted in his vineyard, and he went to look for fruit on it, but did not find any. So he said to the man who took care of the vineyard, "For three years now I've been coming to look for fruit on this fig tree and haven't found any. Cut it down! Why should it use up the soil?"'"

John 15:5–6: "I am the vine; you are the branches. If a man remains in me and I in him, he will bear much fruit; apart from me you can do nothing. If anyone does not remain in me, he is like a branch that is thrown away and withers; such branches are picked up, thrown into the fire and burned."

The above list is by no means complete; there are many others. The simple, clearly understood meaning is the absolute destruction of the rebellious.

WHAT IS IN A NAME?

The name of an individual was considered by the ancients to be that person's character, life-blood and identity. To be without a name was to be expunged, forgotten and erased from history. Numerous examples exist within history of an incoming kingdom erasing the names and memory of the previous dynasty. Consider the following prophecies:

Job 18:17 (KJV): "His remembrance shall perish from the earth, and he shall have no *name* in the street."

Psalm 9:5 (KJV): "Thou hast rebuked the heathen, thou hast destroyed the wicked, thou hast put out their *name* for ever and ever."

Psalm 34:16: "The face of the LORD is against those who do evil, to cut off the *memory* of them from the earth."

Psalm 41:5 (KJV): "Mine enemies speak evil of me, When shall he die, and his name perish?"

Psalm 109:13 (KJV): "Let his posterity be cut off; and in the generation following let their name be blotted out."

Psalm 109:15: "May their sins always remain before the LORD, that he may cut off the memory of them from the earth."

Proverbs 10:7 (KJV): "The memory of the just is blessed: but the name of the wicked shall rot."

Ecclesiastes 6:4 (KJV): "For he cometh in with vanity, and departeth in darkness, and his *name* shall be covered with darkness."

Isaiah 26:14 (KJV): "They are dead, they shall not live; they are deceased, they shall not rise: therefore hast thou visited and destroyed them, and made all their *memory* to perish."

If the wicked sinners are eternally alive and conscious, undergoing the torments of Gehenna, then at least one must concede that they will be nameless. We, as the redeemed, living gloriously in the new earth (see part 2 for details) will not remember them as individuals. God himself will forget their names and their identities. The lost sinner, who is himself consciously boiling in brimstone-laden fire, will not be able to remember who he is or why he is there. God promises to wipe away every tear (Isa 25:8; Rev 21:4), including those tears shed for the lost.

For a punishment to be meaningful and just, there must be a recollection of what the crime had been. For a punishment to be meaningful and just, there must be an accounting of who is being punished for what. Prisons keep very accurate records of who is incarcerated and for what crimes they are being punished. I believe these verses are further evidence that the wicked themselves will be expunged. It will be as if they had never been (Obad 1:16).

By contrast the saved are promised as follows:

Isaiah 56:5 (KJV): "Even unto them will I give in mine house and within my walls a place and a name better than of sons and of daughters: I will give them an everlasting *name*, that shall not be cut off."

Isaiah 66:22 (KJV): "For as the new heavens and the new earth, which I will make, shall remain before me, saith the LORD, so shall your seed and your *name* remain."

Revelation 3:5 (KJV): "He that overcometh, the same shall be clothed in white raiment; and I will not blot out his *name* out of the book of life, but I will confess his name before my Father, and before his angels."

BLOTTING OUT THE AMALEKITES

The Amalekites were a nation that Israel encountered shortly after they left Egypt on the exodus. Deuteronomy 25 tells the story of how the Amalekites attacked the hind flanks of the wandering Israelite nation shortly after they crossed the Red/Reed Sea, and slaughtered those who were too weak or young to keep pace in the desert with the main group. They fought a famous battle with Joshua, where Aaron and Hur supported the outstretched arms of the aged and tired Moses to ensure victory. God was extremely upset with Amalek for their ungodliness and rebellion and pronounced this cursing prophecy in Exod 17:14 (KJV): "And the LORD said unto Moses: Write this for a memorial in the book, and rehearse it in the ears of Joshua: for I will utterly blot out the remembrance of Amalek from under heaven." Balaam, too, prophesied about Amalek in Num 24:20b (KJV), when he said, "His latter end shall be that he perish forever."

Israel had a long and violent struggle with Amalek. In the book of Esther, we are told that Haman, the evil vizier who tried to exterminate the Jews, was an Agagite. He was probably a descendant of King Agag, the hereditary name of the Amalekite chiefdom (see 1 Sam 15).

The Jewish festival of Purim celebrates the victory of Mordecai and Esther over Haman (see Esth 9:20–28). Many synagogues today still honor God's decree to blot out his name with an amusing and undignified tradition. Whenever the name "Haman" comes up during the reading of the scroll of Esther (fifty-four times), the entire congregation shouts, hums, whistles, and stomps their feet so that the spoken name of the Amalekite is drowned out to the ear. A Jewish object lesson during Purim for children and adults alike is to write the name "Haman" (in Hebrew, of course) on the soles of the shoes with chalk, and when the name is pronounced everyone stamps his feet. The chalky name is blotted out very quickly. A renowned Jewish professor at UCLA, Mark Kleiman, has commented, "But of course all of that shouting and stamping calls attention to Haman and preserves his name, rather than effacing it. Surely there are many Jews who couldn't tell you quite who Melchizedek was or what Josiah did, but to whom Haman is a familiar name."[2] He also notes that today, however, there is no longer any Amalekite population anywhere in the world—no Amalekite literature, no Amalekite language, no Amalekite cities or ruins, no Amalekite flag, and certainly no Amalekite delegation to the Olympics.

There is, of course, an obvious problem, as noted by Kleiman. As I write this and as you read it, there is still a memory of the Amalekites. The more we talk about erasing their memory, the more they are remembered. It is like telling a child *not* to picture in his mind an elephant. It will be impossible for the Jews celebrating Purim to ever erase this memory, no matter how loud they whistle. If you believe that God will literally fulfill all words of his prophecies, then this blotting out of the remembrance of Amalek must still take place at some future time, and God must do it himself.

It cannot be done during this world time; it must happen in the new world. We are told numerous places in Scripture that the nation of Israel is symbolic of all God's people. Yes, they were and still are literally God's people; however, there is also a metaphor wherein they represent the redeemed of all time. For a study of this concept, if you are in doubt, refer to Gal 6:16 or anywhere in the book of Hebrews.

In the same vein, I believe Amalek is a metaphor for all of the wicked who reject God. This curse will very literally come true, in due time, at the lake of fire by the second death, when the name and the memory of all Amalekites will be blotted out from under heaven.

SATAN, TOO, IS ANNIHILATED

Satan was a created being. Originally, he was a powerful angel who covered the throne of God. We are not told what his name used to be in those early days. His name is not Lucifer; that is a mistranslation. "Lucifer" is a Latin compound word meaning light bearer. In the KJV it appears only once, in Isa 14:12, as a translation of the Hebrew "morning star." Lucifer does not appear in the original Hebrew or Greek languages. Jerome introduced it about A.D. 405 in the Latin Vulgate. The Hebrew Scriptures call him the Satan, which is actually a title. "The Satan" means the accuser or the adversary. He accuses the saints, as he did to Job, who was a righteous man. Satan stands as an adversary against God. His extreme sin will have equal reciprocity in punishment. In the end, however, Satan himself will cease to exist, and finally the universe will be clean of all ungodliness. We know this from Ezek 28:12–19 (KJV):

> Son of man, take up a lamentation upon the king of Tyrus, and say unto him, Thus saith the Lord GOD; Thou sealest up the sum, full of wisdom, and perfect in beauty. [Although addressed to the king of Tyre, I think even a literalist will agree that this is really talking about Satan himself.]
>
> Thou hast been in Eden the garden of God; every precious stone was thy covering, the sardius, topaz, and the diamond, the beryl, the onyx, and the jasper, the sapphire, the emerald, and the carbuncle, and gold: the workmanship of thy tabrets and of thy pipes was prepared in thee in the day that thou wast created. [I think the stones are part of his wardrobe or clothing. Tabrets appear to be brass bells, like a timbrel, set into a costume. "Pipes" are a technical jeweler's term, relating to sockets for the setting of a gem, or maybe of the tabret. This is the apparel of a high king. He is a created being, not eternal and not born.]
>
> Thou art the anointed cherub that covereth; and I have set thee so: thou wast upon the holy mountain of God; thou hast walked up and down in the midst of the stones of fire. [Satan used to be one of the cherubim who covered the throne of God. Stones of fire represents God's presence in heaven.]
>
> Thou wast perfect in thy ways from the day that thou wast created, till iniquity was found in thee.
>
> By the multitude of thy merchandise they have filled the midst of thee with violence, and thou hast sinned: therefore I will cast thee as profane out of the mountain of God: and I will destroy thee, O covering cherub, from the midst of the stones of fire. [Satan is destroyed. He is permanently removed from earth and heaven.]

> Thine heart was lifted up because of thy beauty, thou hast corrupted thy wisdom by reason of thy brightness: I will cast thee to the ground, I will lay thee before kings, that they may behold thee. [Satan will be humiliatingly prostrated before human observers.]
>
> Thou hast defiled thy sanctuaries by the multitude of thine iniquities, by the iniquity of thy traffick; therefore will I bring forth a fire from the midst of thee, it shall devour thee, and I will bring thee to ashes upon the earth in the sight of all them that behold thee. [He is devoured and destroyed. He is turned to ashes. There are witnesses that watch this execution. Maybe the lake of fire will be within view of the redeemed. There are other verses that seem to say that the righteous will view and be horrified by the doom of the wicked. Executions do not last forever. It is gruesome for a period, but then it is over. Justice will have prevailed, and every tear will then be wiped away. At least in the beginning, there will be tears in heaven.]
>
> All they that know thee among the people shall be astonished at thee: thou shalt be a terror, and never shalt thou be any more. [Cessation of existence is the obvious meaning; any other interpretation is exaggerating and twisting the meaning to fit a biased theology.]

The author of Hebrews also believed that someday soon the devil would be destroyed:

Hebrews 2:14–15: "Since the children have flesh and blood, he too shared in their humanity so that by [Christ's] death he might destroy him who holds the power of death—that is, the devil—and free those who all their lives were held in slavery by their fear of death."

A RESURRECTION FOR DAMNATION?

A number of verses support two resurrections. The first resurrection will be at the rapture/second coming of Christ for the saved who have died with faith. The second resurrection occurs after the millennium. It is a resurrection of the unjust. Among Evangelicals, there is not much debate or disagreement on this topic, except in relation to the timing. See Dan 12:2; Rev 20:12; John 5:29. My opinions concerning the sequencing of events during the Parousia (rapture, millennium, or not) are nondogmatic, except that none of it has happened yet. This is not the forum for its discussion.

Most notably, Jehovah's Witnesses deny the second resurrection entirely. They teach that the unredeemed wicked simply remain dead forever. A common question or objection to a resurrection for the wicked, however, is why? Why bother to raise the evil, only for the very purpose of putting them down again? Doesn't the resurrection of the wicked imply their endless existence?

The question is answered with an understanding of justice. The entire book of Habakkuk, my personal favorite among the Minor Prophets, deals with the question of unresolved justice. Habakkuk, a righteous Jew during the time of the Babylonian persecution, asks God why the evil people in the world get away with murder, literally and figuratively. They seem to be rich and in powerful positions. They live in luxury and eat the choicest foods (Hab 1:16). They crush the honest people, expose their nakedness, and build their realm on unjust gain (Hab 2:9). They live their entire life in the safety of their walled castles. Finally, the evil and ruthless are buried with honor and distinction. Evil seems to triumph, so Habakkuk complains to God. His complaining directly to God about the unfairness of life is what makes this book my favorite. This guy has courage and boldness. He has a really good point, too.

Leo Durocher, manager of the Brooklyn Dodgers, New York Giants, Chicago Cubs, and Houston Astros in the mid-twentieth century, famously commented, "Nice guys finish last." It was true in Habakkuk's day, it was true at the Polo Grounds and Wrigley Field, and it is still true today. Good guys do seem to come up short in life. I'm sure you've noticed that people who do *not* serve God do quite well. On average, they are probably richer than those who do serve God. If you want to get ahead in this world—if you want lots of money, prestige, and power—it helps if you step on somebody. If you brag about your achievements, or you ridicule and cut down other people, it will help to promote yourself. If you lie and cheat at the right opportunity, you really can get ahead. Now I'm not saying that all rich people are cheaters, nor is the inverse true—that all poor people are honest. It is still possible to make an honest fortune without crushing others. But if you are totally honest, merciful, and generous, it will probably cost you some opportunities.

Habakkuk notices this injustice. He has an intimacy and personal comfort level with God, so he is not intimidated to speak candidly with the Master of the Universe.

God eloquently replies to Habakkuk, promising that sin will be punished and evildoers will be repaid. The language is figurative and the style poetic, but the meaning is clear and the message is true. He tells Habakkuk to do what is very difficult for people with courage and boldness: Wait. Be patient. It may appear that the bad guys are winning from our perspective of a short lifespan, but it is only the beginning. In God's perfect timing, righteousness will prevail.

The reason that those who mock God are raised to temporary life again in the second resurrection is for them to be punished to the extent that they sinned. This is the infallible fulfillment of God's judgment and justice.

Do they have eternal life in hell? To support that, I've even heard that Paul's resurrection chapter in 1 Cor 15 applies to the wicked as well. This preposterous theory claims that the unsaved will be given antiglorified resurrection bodies of a worm—bodies that are immune to death and fire, bodies that are immortal and eternal, bodies that require no food, water, or sleep. Yet they are fully corrupted and fiendishly designed for an everlasting life of pain, anguish, and torture.

Please reread Paul's glorious passage of resurrection in context; such a theory is not acceptable and is an affront to eternal life. First Corinthians 15:20–23 states, "But Christ has indeed been raised from the dead, the firstfruits of those who have fallen asleep. For since death came through a man, the resurrection of the dead comes also through a man. For as in Adam all die, so in Christ all will be made alive. But each in his own turn: Christ the firstfruits; then, when he comes, those who belong to him." Notice, the only ones who receive this resurrection are they whom are Christ's at his coming.

YOU HAVE BEEN WARNED

My next point in this hypothesis is that God is upfront and forthright. He gives people ample warning. His declarations are clear and unambiguous.

Isaiah 45:19: "I have not spoken in secret, from somewhere in a land of darkness; I have not said to Jacob's descendants, 'Seek me in vain.' I, the LORD, speak the truth; I declare what is right."

Ezekiel 3:17–21: "Son of man, I have made you a watchman for the house of Israel; so hear the word I speak and give them warning from me. When I say to a wicked man, 'You will surely die,' and you do not warn him or speak out to dissuade him from his evil ways in order to save his life, that wicked man will die for his sin, and I will hold you accountable for his blood. But if you do warn the wicked man and he does not turn from his wickedness or from his evil ways, he will die for his sin; but you will have saved yourself. Again, when a righteous man turns from his righteousness and does evil, and I put a stumbling block before him, he will die. Since you did not warn him, he will die for his sin. The righteous things he did will not be remembered, and I will hold you accountable for his blood. But if you do warn the righteous man not to sin and he does not sin, he will surely live because he took warning, and you will have saved yourself."

Amos 3:7 (KJV): "Surely the Lord GOD will do nothing, but he revealeth his secret unto his servants the prophets."

God gives people fair warning. As already shown, dozens of verses say that the wicked will die and that their name will perish. Beginning in Genesis with Adam and Eve, people have been warned that sin leads to death. I believe this refers to both physical, temporal death and spiritual, eternal death.

In Gen 9, God tells Noah to implement capital punishment. The murderer shall die. God, too, obeys these rules that he set for people. Capital punishment of the wicked is divine justice for the soul. Then, continuing from Exodus through Malachi, Moses and the prophets warned us, time and time again, that the unrepentant will die. Godless sinners will be burned to chaff and ash. But it is not until Revelation (A.D. 95, written by John on Patmos) that we are told they would be eternally tormented in anguish without rest. These are the two *Aeon aeon* verses for which I admit interpretational difficulties. Wow, such a serious consequence—you would hope God would tell somebody before A.D. 95. How many millions of people went to their doom before the Revelation was written, never having been warned of the eternal-torment clause? Since this is uncharacteristic of God, then those two verses in Revelation must be interpreted differently.

GOD IS JUST

Isaiah 28:17a: "I will make justice the measuring line and righteousness the plumb line."

Deuteronomy 32:4 (KJV): "He is the Rock, his work is perfect: for all his ways are judgment: a God of truth and without iniquity, just and right is he." The Hebrew word for "just" is *tzaddik*.

Jesus claims justice; see John 5:30b (KJV): "I judge: and my judgment is just; because I seek not mine own will, but the will of the Father which hath sent me." The Greek word for "just" is *dikaios*.

Christ is called the Just One in Acts 7:52, and again Acts 22:14. In Rev 15:3b, the martyred saints in heaven sing praises to God, proclaiming, "Lord God Almighty; just and true are thy ways." There can be no doubt; God is just.

According to *Webster's*, "just" means "exactly, precisely, no more—no less," as in the phrase, "just below my knee." When applied to moral character, it means (again according to *Webster's*) "reasonable, proper, deserved, equal, fair, lawful." The concept is clear: justice demands equality. In Lev 19:36 (KJV), God commands Israel to use "just balances, just weights, a just *ephah*, and a just *hin*." This is the same Hebrew word, *tzaddik* as applied to God himself. The measuring for commercial sale must be no more—no less. In Exod 21:24—"eye for an eye, tooth for a tooth"—God tells Moses that punishment for crimes should be reciprocal. It was illegal to put to death a noncapital criminal, and it was equally illegal to excuse a death sentence. Even in this age of grace, our sins are not freely excused. They were paid, 100 percent, substitutionally by Christ Jesus. God's judgment on sin is just. No more, no less. Christ's vicarious death, because he is God himself, is of *infinite* redemption value. His death and payment are enough for ten universes full of human beings. People, Satan and fallen angels are finite. As bad as our sins may be, they are finite, with a beginning and an end. Satan, too, is a created being and is only finite. Human sin justly deserves a finite punishment big enough to fit the crime.

If human sin was infinite, then Christ would have to die again every time for every person. Infinite equals infinite. Eternal torment is infinite punishment, and is unjust for a finite quantity of sin. This is an impossible act for God. It degrades the infinite and unparalleled atonement of Christ. Basically, it promotes human nature to God's own nature-deserving infinity. This is a very Greek idea, but not taught in the Scripture.

God's justice is an evenhanded assessment, without favoritism and without respect of persons. God will not overlook sin or be liberal on Judgment Day, but likewise he will not be vindictive, capricious, or cruel. We know that God's punishment will be equal, fair, reciprocal, and just. He cannot deny himself. Notice again why our Lord *died* for our redemption. This is another evidence of the punishment penalty. If the penalty against us had been eternal torment, our redemption from it would have cost Jesus that price. He would have been obliged to suffer eternal torment, the just for the unjust. But eternal torment was not the penalty; hence, Jesus did not pay that penalty for us. Death was the penalty, and, thus, Christ *died for our sin*. "He by the grace of God should taste *death* for every man" (Heb 2:9 KJV). Remember, my hypothesis requires that Christ fully die in body, soul, and spirit. He was completely dead.

HOW LONG DO THEY COOK?

Some people believe that the fire of Gehenna is so intense that the lost souls cast into it are incinerated almost immediately. I don't think so. I have no idea how long they will cook. That judgment is left up to God, but it will be just. It will be equally opposite and reciprocal to the quantity and severity of their sin. It will be an eye for an eye, a tooth for a tooth, as in Exod 21. Because of that, I am certain that there are degrees of punishment.

Some sins are actually worse than other sins. Moses' law given by God at Sinai made this distinction. In Exod 21:14–16, murderers, those who curse their parents, and kidnappers are to be put to death. Immediately juxtaposed, the balance of Exod 21 tells of other, less serious crimes, such as assault and battery, personal injury without death, liability for open pits, and stealing livestock—all of which require payment and restoration of the loss. Capital punishment for these minor crimes is not mandated; as a matter of fact, elsewhere it is prohibited.

Some things are simply more important than others. Matthew 23:23a (KJV) states, "Woe unto you, scribes and Pharisees, hypocrites! for ye pay tithe of mint and anise and cummin, and have omitted the weightier matters of the law, judgment, mercy, and faith." The lack of love is a greater sin than the lack of paying tithe on mint.

Mark 12:38–40: "As he taught, Jesus said, 'Watch out for the teachers of the law. They like to walk around in flowing robes and be greeted in the marketplaces, and have the most important seats in the synagogues and the places of honor at banquets. They devour widows' houses and for a show make lengthy prayers. Such men will be punished most severely.'" See also nearly the exact same verse at Luke 20:45–47.

Second Timothy 3:13: "While evil men and impostors will go from bad to worse, deceiving and being deceived."

The exact same sinful act performed by different individuals under different circumstances will receive weighted penalty.

Proverbs 24:12: "If you say, 'But we knew nothing about this,' does not he who weighs the heart perceive it? Does not he who guards your life know it? Will he not repay each person according to what he has done?"

Hebrews 10:28–29: "Anyone who rejected the law of Moses died without mercy on the testimony of two or three witnesses. *How much more severely* do you think a man deserves to be punished who has trampled the Son of God under foot, who has treated as an unholy thing the blood of the covenant that sanctified him, and who has insulted the Spirit of grace?"

Second Peter 2:20–21: "If they have escaped the corruption of the world by knowing our Lord and Savior Jesus Christ and are again entangled in it and overcome, they are worse off at the end than they were at the beginning. It would have been better for them not to have known the way of righteousness, than to have known it and then to turn their backs on the sacred command that was passed on to them."

Matthew 11:22–24: "But I tell you, it will be more bearable for Tyre and Sidon on the day of judgment than for you. And you, Capernaum, will you be lifted up to the skies? No, you will go down to the depths [*hades*]. If the miracles that were performed in you had been performed in Sodom, it would have remained to this day. But I tell you that it will be more bearable for Sodom on the Day of Judgment than for you."

Luke 12:47-48: "That servant who knows his master's will and does not get ready or does not do what his master wants will be beaten with many blows. But the one who does not know and does things deserving punishment will be beaten with few blows. From everyone who has been given much, much will be demanded; and from the one who has been entrusted with much, much more will be asked."

John 19:11b: "Therefore the one who handed me over to you is guilty of a greater sin."

Christ's statement to Pilate verifies that there are greater and lesser sins based on personal knowledge. Christ means that the high priest and Jewish leaders had the Hebrew Scriptures and prophets at their fingertips. They should have known better.

Wayne Jackson of *Christian Courier* explains this well: "Caiaphas, of all people, should have known the testimony of Israel's Bible, and thus have been familiar with many of the more than 300 Old Testament prophecies that detailed the identifying qualities of the Messiah. There was no excuse for his role in the death of the Son of God; his heart simply was encrusted with rebellion (cf. 2 Corinthians 3:14). Without question Pilate sinned by weakly caving in to political pressure. He knew that the motive of the Jewish leaders was ungodly (Matthew 27:18), and likely that their evidence was jaded (cf. Matthew 26:59), but for fear of falling out of favor with Caesar (John 19:12), he dismissed Christ to the Jews for execution. As bad as Pilate's sin of weakness and self-motivated political correctness was, it was not depraved to the degree of the calculated rebellion that saturated the soul of Caiaphas. Thus, because of the high priest's broader knowledge, and his opportunity to believe and yield to what was right, the spiritual leader's responsibility was greater."[3]

This concept of proportionate punishment is related to the demand for justice. A more serious sin requires a more serious punishment. Furthermore, sinning against a greater light will receive a more serious punishment then the exact same sin committed under less well-understood circumstances. The legal principle of proportionate punishment is called *lex talionis*. It is a Latin phrase meaning "law of retaliation." It has been considered a foundation of ethical government since the dawn of human civilization. I believe it is morally just and scripturally supported. I am certain that God will impose degrees of punishment that are morally just, scripturally supported, and ethically measured against his evil adversaries.

The duration of Gehenna will be enough time for extreme agony and pain, at least for some. This requires that the anguish of Gehenna will be shorter and softer for some, while lengthy and torrentially intense for the most hardened. Although a fluctuation of the intensity of Gehenna's fire is certainly probable, I believe the main mechanism to achieve parity of retaliation will be by duration. All sinners in Gehenna will be in utter despair and torment. Even the light-duty sinners will be totally miserable. So I perceive that intensity of flame will be a minor infliction. I suspect that duration of agony will be the main force of justice. Of course, this is pure speculation. God will do as he does and judge justly.

Christ and the angels will witness the execution, so I doubt that it will last too long. Angels are not omnipresent. Christ will not enjoy this. I hope we are not there to watch; however, there is some evidence that we may be with our Husband. First Thessalonians 4:17 promises that, from our resurrection onward, "So shall we ever be with the Lord."

Psalm 91:8 additionally promises that for those who dwell in the secret places of God, "You will only observe with your eyes and see the punishment of the wicked."

While Rev 14:9–10 warns, "If anyone worships the beast and his image and receives his mark on the forehead . . . he will be tormented with burning sulfur in the presence of the holy angels and of the Lamb. " If the Lamb is witnessing the execution and we are with the Lord, then it would appear to follow that we are present at the tormenting and burning of the wicked.

Within the framework of eternal torment, degrees of punishment are lost. This is the Achilles heel of that doctrine. For example, hypothetically, let's suppose a twenty-two-year-old unsaved girl dies in a car accident. She has lived a sheltered life and has never committed any major sins. She is not a Christian; however, she is clearly lost. By the traditional eternal-torment doctrine, she goes to hell and suffers eternally. Adolf Hitler receives the same duration of punishment, although probably hotter and more intense pain. Maybe he has the fifteen-hundred-degree furnace, instead of her only six-hundred-degree furnace. Proponents of eternal torment and conditionalists alike envision the fire crackling and the smoke belching from the chasm of Gehenna. I suppose the inhabitants are full of blisters and fifth-degree burns (only four degrees are medically recognized; I invent a fifth degree for this application). I suppose the skin falls away, exposing raw meat and sinews. Do you have any idea how intensely hot a furnace like this is? See Isa 33:14b (KJV): "Who among us shall dwell with the devouring fire? who among us shall dwell with everlasting burnings?"

Eternal tormentors agree that both the lost young girl and Adolf Hitler are absolutely miserable, with no hope, outside of the presence of God. If she is absolutely miserable, how can Hitler be *more* absolutely miserable? Do some more intolerable corners of the pit exist, so that the truly wicked can have it worse? Since infinity is endless and inexhaustible, their punishments are really quite equal. This is not eye-for-an-eye, tooth-for-a-tooth justice. It appears more akin to a potato for a million dollars, a truckload of potatoes for a million dollars. These would hardly be called just scales.

The same hypothetical situation with the twenty-two-year-old girl is further evidence for Dead Soul Syndrome (wicked's soul sleep), as previously presented in this book. What if the girl did not die in a car wreck, but rather she died from leprosy three thousand years ago during the reign of King David? If particular judgment is correct, then she has already been abased with the torments of hell for three thousand years—possibly already over the top of what her just judgment would be.

Additionally, if an unsaved person had a long, hard life, full of many calamities and misfortunes, possibly God will take this into account as he measures out the exact portion of punishment due. Punishment garnered during this life may very possibly count toward the quota due.

Yes, God's judgment by fire will be scripturally accurate per the eye-for-an-eye law of Moses. No, individuals will not suffer until after they have been condemned by God's court. Retributive justice will be precisely accurate and fair-handedly administered. Surely, those who are cast into the lake of fire will suffer a second death. They will be repaid. Those wicked people who lived their entire life and seemingly never got caught will pay exactly what they owe. Those unsaved wretches who never benefited from the free blood of Christ, even if they were overall "good" people, will die. The measure of suffering will exactly match the measure of sin. The righteous will be fully satisfied with the retribution inflicted on the unjust. The second resurrection is only temporary. The ungodly rise to appear before the great white throne judgment and receive a judicially administered sentence of death. They rise to shame and rejection and are subjected to differences in the duration and intensity of suffering as justice may demand—after which they suffer the second death and their existence is obliterated from the presence of the Lord. Their name is forgotten. They perish and are no more.

GNASHING OF TEETH

Many people assume that the image of gnashing teeth refers to physical torment; however, that is not the meaning of this biblical idiom. Here are a couple of typical passages where the figure of speech is used in the context of God's judgment:

Matthew 13:42: "They will throw them into the fiery furnace, where there will be weeping and gnashing of teeth." Matthew 13:50 in this same chapter is nearly identical.

Luke 13:28: "There will be weeping there, and gnashing of teeth, when you see Abraham, Isaac and Jacob and all the prophets in the kingdom of God, but you yourselves thrown out."

Weeping and gnashing of teeth are found in a total of six Gospel passages; all are quotes of Jesus. See also Matt 8:12; 22:13; 24:51; 25:30. Additionally, foaming at the mouth with gnashing or grinding of the teeth is found at Mark 9:18 in a demon-possessed mute boy.

Gnashing of teeth is a fairly common Hebrew idiom used throughout the Old Testament as well.

God figuratively gnashes his teeth in the OT, so the image certainly doesn't refer to physical pain. Job 16:9: "God assails me and tears me in his anger and gnashes his teeth at me; my opponent fastens on me his piercing eyes."

Elsewhere, this action is usually performed by hypocrites, the wicked and enemies as they observe the righteous with envy.

Psalm 35:16 (KJV): "With hypocritical mockers in feasts, they gnashed upon me with their teeth."

Psalm 37:12 (KJV): "The wicked plotteth against the just, and gnasheth upon him with his teeth."

Psalm 112:10 (KJV): "The wicked shall see it, and be grieved; he shall gnash with his teeth, and melt away: the desire of the wicked shall perish."

Lamentations 2:16 (KJV): "All thine enemies have opened their mouth against thee: they hiss and gnash the teeth: they say, We have swallowed her up: certainly this is the day that we looked for; we have found, we have seen it."

In the New Testament, when Steven gave a stirring message, the Jews became furious and stoned him. Acts 7:54 (KJV): "When they heard these things, they were cut to the heart, and they gnashed on him with their teeth." The Pharisees hated Steven and wanted to kill him.

The gnashing of teeth, whether in Gehenna or on earth, is done because of hatred and rage, not because of physical pain. Sinners gnash their teeth at God's people or at God as a sign of ridicule and contempt. It is probably accompanied by growling and aggressive behavior. They do it to mock and show disrespect. The wicked do not quietly fade away. It has been noted that the weeping and gnashing of teeth seem "to express the bitter rage and acrimony they feel toward God, who sentenced them, and toward the redeemed, who will forever be blessed . . . But even while he grinds his teeth in fury, he wastes away and comes to nothing."[4]

A DOUBLE PORTION FOR THE WHORE

Revelation 18:6: "Give back to her as she has given; pay her back double for what she has done. Mix her a double portion from her own cup."

With the destruction of the whore of Babylon, an angel decries for God's judgment to include a double portion of punishment for her sin. If God is just and if the payment of sin should be equal and opposite to the sin itself, as I have suggested, then why does she get a double whammy?

First, recall our section on the beast of Revelation. It was not human, but represented an evil sociopolitical system anthropomorphized as a creature. This section is similar. The whore is not an evil female. She is the idolatrous church. She claims to be Christian in name, but she prostitutes herself with other gods. The whore of Babylon represents apostate Christianity. So, first of all, religious systems are not literally punished with torture and grief (Rev 18:7); they are destroyed.

But more significant to the meaning of the passage, in biblical times the firstborn received a double portion. Paul Caram, vice chancellor of Zion Ministerial Institute, explains,

> In scripture the eldest or firstborn son inherited special *privileges*. The position was one of great honor and responsibility. In the absence of the father he had authority over his brethren. For example, in the Book of Genesis it was Reuben, the firstborn, who saved Joseph from being killed by his brothers, Gen. 37:21–22. The firstborn also had special *responsibilities*, for he was accountable to the father for the welfare of his younger brothers and sisters. Reuben was very distressed when he failed to rescue Joseph from the pit. He tore his clothes and was ashamed to face his father, Gen. 37:29–30. At the death of the father, the firstborn became the head of the home and received a *double portion* as his share of the inheritance, Deut. 21:15–17. If a man with four sons divided up his inheritance, he divided the inheritance into five equal shares, giving two shares to the firstborn and one share to each of the other three sons. In Bible times there was a great *distinction* between a younger son and a firstborn son.[5]

The organization of the church is supposed to guide and shepherd the flock. John is saying that she has the responsibilities of the firstborn, although she has miserably failed. She has lost her privileges of the birthright due to her immorality (see Reuben in Gen 35:22), her profanity (see Esau in Heb 12:16), her idolatry and rebellion (see Israel in Exod 32).

I think (or at least I hope) that it was a little bit tongue-in-cheek about taking up the lectern, when James said (3:1), "Not many of you should presume to be teachers, my brothers, because you know that we who teach will be judged more strictly." The truth of this point, I have already attempted to make. Rebellion against a greater light will receive a more serious consequence than that which is undertaken in the fog.

For her grievous sins, the whore of Babylon, and all personal individuals who abide in her, will pay with agony, suffering, and death. Their punishment will be reciprocal to their sin, their knowledge, and their position of authority and teaching.

TORTURE IS AGAINST THE CHARACTER OF GOD

My next point is that I don't think God is into torture. Unfortunately, I can find no Bible verses prohibiting torture. Mishnaic law based on Deut 25:3 was to give no more than thirty-nine lashes (forty save one) for a noncapital crime. It seems out of God's loving and merciful character to eternally torment his enemies. Make your point, punish your enemies, and get on with eternity. God certainly demands justice and righteousness. That is why the wicked will not live. That is why they must suffer tit for tat. The God of the universe eternally tormenting helpless sinners reminds me of a sadistic boy pulling legs off a spider, or a redneck in a pickup truck deliberately swerving to hit a snake on the road. It is the strong dominating the weak. My internal moral conscience tells me there is something wrong with it, although I'm having trouble pinpointing biblical references against cruelty and torture. If you can think of any, please let me know. My contact information is at the back of this book.

Clark Pinnock, a theologian from Toronto, has wittily noted that if eternal torment is true, then "not only is it God's pleasure so to torture the wicked everlastingly, but it will be the happiness of the saints to see and know this is being faithfully done. It would not be unfair to picture the traditional doctrine in this way: just as one can imagine certain people watching a cat trapped in a microwave oven squirming in agony and taking delight in it, so the saints in heaven will, according to [Jonathan] Edwards [colonial American preacher, who delivered a famous damnation sermon titled 'Sinners in the Hands of an Angry God'], experience the torments of the damned with pleasure and satisfaction."[6]

I do find some biblical support for God being humane. Deuteronomy 21:23 commands Israel to bury the accursed criminal who hangs upon a tree. Even the horrible criminal is human and deserves some respect through burial. This concept has come down to our modern legal system, with humane treatment of all people. Torture is not ethical. Leviticus 22:28 says not to slaughter a mother and its young on the same day. Deuteronomy 22:6 also says not to take a mother bird and her eggs or young chicks simultaneously, and in Deut 14:21 not to boil a calf in its mother's milk. Isaiah 66:3 compares breaking a dog's neck to the actions of murderers and pig eaters.

Rabbinic understanding has long been in favor of respect for life. Even though it is just a dog, bird, or cow, all animals are alive, beautiful creatures created by God. We should respect the sanctity of life and not be greedy in our harvesting of it. We should not relish with blood lust the death of even an animal. These concepts point toward an ethical and humane treatment of people, even your enemies, and sway me against the eternal torment theory.

However, without solid biblical references, I admittedly find this to be the weakest of my reasonings.

GOD SUSTAINS THE UNIVERSE

Muslims believe that Allah creates and re-creates the entire universe every moment. The sun, the stars, the sea, the birds—every atom of the world and cosmos is so finite, so small and fickle, that it would disintegrate into nothingness without the constant creative energy flowing moment by moment from Allah. That is Islamic doctrine.

The Bible does not make that statement about the true God of Israel and the cosmos that God created. The Islamic idea and those details are a little over the top, but the attitude is scripturally justified. God is totally sovereign. He sustains the whole world. Nothing happens without his consent. Consider these verses with emphasis added:

Colossians 1:16–17: "For by him all things were created: things in heaven and on earth, visible and invisible, whether thrones or powers or rulers or authorities; all things were created by him and for him. He is before all things, *and in him all things hold together.*"

Hebrews 1:3a: "The Son is the radiance of God's glory and the exact representation of his being, *sustaining all things by his powerful word.*"

Revelation 4:11: "You are worthy, our Lord and God, to receive glory and honor and power, for you created all things, and *by your will they were created and have their being.*"

Will Christ "hold together" sinners in Gehenna? Will the powerful Word of God "sustain" them in the pit? Is it the will of the Lord for them to "have their being"? I think not. God will not sustain evil to continue existing in some remote corner of the new world order of the cosmos. Scripture declares that the new heaven and the new earth will be free of sin, sinners, evil, and unrighteousness. Such will not exist.

THE FINAL VICTORY OF GOOD OVER EVIL

My closing point on this subject is found at Rev 21:4: the new Jerusalem appears coming down out of heaven (more of that anon), and John hears a loud voice from the throne, saying, "He will wipe every tear from their eyes. There will be no more death or mourning or crying or pain, for the old order of things has passed away." No more death, crying, or pain. Is this only for the bride of Christ and only applicable to those within the new earth? Will there still be a part of the universe where crying and pain exist? Will evil be eternal? I don't think so. I cannot reconcile that with this entire book full of Bible verses.

Isaiah 25:7–8a: "On this mountain he will destroy the shroud that enfolds all peoples, the sheet that covers all nations; he will swallow up death forever. The Sovereign LORD will wipe away the tears from all faces."

The shroud and the sheet that cover all people is death. Death will cease to exist. God will be victorious in the end.

Paul sums it up nicely in 1 Cor 15:26: "The last enemy to be destroyed is death."

And 1 Cor 15:54 borrows from Isa 25:8: "Death has been swallowed up in victory."

In the end, God will have the victory. Evil and those who practice it will be extinct. Ephesians 1:9–10 states, "And he made known to us the mystery of his will according to his good pleasure, which he purposed in Christ, to be put into effect when the times will have reached their fulfillment—to bring all things in heaven and on earth together under one head, even Christ." The universe will be unified in Christly joy. For this verse and others to be logically true leaves no ontological room for the existence of sinners, evil, or suffering in hell.

Colossians 1:19–20 states, "For God was pleased to have all his fullness dwell in him, and through him to reconcile to himself all things, whether things on earth or things in heaven, by making peace through his blood, shed on the cross." All things in earth and heaven shall be at peace in Christ.

Finally, 1 Cor 15:28 says that in the end, God will be "all in all" or "everything to everybody." How can God meaningfully make this claim while an unspecified number (in the billions, I suppose) of people still continue in rebellion against him and are currently under his judgment? God's victory will be final and absolute. His justice will be finished and fully vindicated. The universe will be clean at last. Hallelujah!

ENDNOTES

1. Biederwolf, *Seventh-day Adventism*, 20.
2. Kleiman, "Remembering Amalek."
3. Jackson, "Are Some Sins 'Greater' than Others?"
4. Fudge, *Fire That Consumes*, 172.
5. Caram, "Double Portion of the Firstborn."
6. Pinnock, "Destruction of the Finally Impenitent."

Appendix to Part One

Afterlife Chart

THE FOLLOWING CHART DEPICTS the afterlife condition during the all ages of time since the creation of the world. There have only been two classes of people—"righteous" or saved, and "wicked" or unsaved. Of course, we are not righteous by ourselves but by belief, then the righteousness of Christ is accounted to us (Gal 3:6). The wicked is everyone else not redeemed by Jesus, because the imagination of man's heart is evil from his youth (Gen 8:21). There are three epochs of time ever since creation. The first is the period before Christ (B.C.), from Adam until the finished redemptive work of Jesus at the resurrection, shortly after the cross. The second is the A.D. period, from the redemption until the Last Judgment, or the beginning of eternity. We are now living in this period. The final epoch follows the Last Judgment. It is eternity future.

Everyone who has ever lived, is currently alive, or will ever be born to live on earth falls into one of the six permutations of two categories and three epochs shown in this table. This book attempts to address all six situations.

	B.C.	A.D.	Eternity
Saved	Body and spirit dead awaiting redemption.	Body dead awaiting resurrection. Spirit with Christ in heaven.	Body and spirit whole with life eternal upon Earth.
Unsaved	Body and spirit dead awaiting judgment.	Body and spirit dead awaiting judgment.	Body and spirit tormented until utter extinction.

Part Two

Heaven

7

The Vocabulary of Heaven

What about Heaven?

I HAVE SPENT A fair amount of time reading book after book about death, hell, and punishment. I have bounced ideas off of my wife and told her my own thoughts. She has heard all of my theories probably a couple of times through as I have refined my outline of the afterlife for the wicked. She has expressed concern over my spending too much time thinking about something that I myself claim will shortly not even exist anymore: the wicked. In her female wisdom, she suggested that I endeavor to meditate instead on the future of the saved. "What about heaven?" she asked.

The Apostle Paul in Phil 4:8 also recommends that we dwell on that which is true, honest, just, pure, and lovely. Focus upon items of good report, with virtue and praise. Think on these things.

That's pretty good advice. Why didn't I think of that? So with my epistle nearly finished about the doom of the lost, the soul sleep of the pregospel Jewish saints, and the conscious but incomplete state of those during the grace age who are obedient to the faith, I set out to explore the eternal life of those in Christ.

I soon realized that I had bitten off what could easily be an entire book just in this one state. By reviewing the afterlife chart following chapter 6, we see that thus far we have addressed five of the six possible permutations of the afterlife.

I also soon realized that the standard Evangelical born-again believer is usually as wrong about "heaven" as I had come to believe that they were wrong about "hell." Again I found an infiltration of Greek mythology into our concept about our own eternal destiny—my own theological concepts included.

In the first section of this book—the study of destruction, popularly known as hell—we started off reviewing all the biblical words translated into English as "hell." We additionally considered similar word concepts such as *abaddon*, lake of fire, and outer darkness. I would like to start this section with a similar exercise, reviewing all of the words containing the notion of heaven.

HEAVEN AS THE ABODE OF GOD

We are not given much to work with in the Hebrew Scriptures when discussing heaven. As discussed earlier in the Sheol section, the focus for Jews was on this life, not on the afterlife.

The only Hebrew word for heaven or heavens is *shamayim*, which is always a plural noun. It is a common word and appears about 420 times in the OT. It *never* is used to say that people go to heaven. The majority of the time that the word "heaven" is used in Scripture, it is merely referring to the atmosphere, or outer space. Three examples are the fowls of the heaven (Gen 7:23), rain of heaven (Deut 11:11), and stars of the heaven (Exod 32:13).

There can be no doubt that God dwells in heaven. Since God is a spirit, I think that there must be a spiritual nature of heaven that is not within our three-dimensional universe. I do not think that the heaven of God is on a planet somewhere in deep outer space. I tend to think that this spiritual dimension is like a fourth dimension; it is all around us, yet unseen. Wherever it is, God can see us and hear us from there.

Some scriptural citations including "heaven" are as follows:

Second Chronicles 2:6a: "But who is able to build a temple for him, since the heavens, even the highest heavens, cannot contain him?"

Second Chronicles 6:27a (KJV): "Then hear thou from heaven, and forgive the sin of thy servants, and of thy people Israel."

First Kings 8:43a (KJV): "Hear thou in heaven thy dwelling place, and do according to all that the stranger calleth to thee for: that all people of the earth may know thy name."

Deuteronomy 26:15: "Look down from heaven, your holy dwelling place, and bless your people Israel."

Psalm 14:2 (KJV): "The LORD looked down from heaven upon the children of men, to see if there were any that did understand, and seek

God." God frequently looks down from heaven—in Ps 53:2; 33:13; 80:14, among other places.

Isaiah 66:1a (KJV): "Thus saith the LORD, The heaven is my throne, and the earth is my footstool."

That God dwells in heaven is again confirmed in the New Testament. See Matt 5:16: "Let your light shine before men, that they may see your good deeds, and praise your Father in heaven." "Father in heaven" is a phrase that Jesus used in the gospels eighteen times.

There are angels in heaven, along with God, as the following verses show:

Mark 12:25 (KJV): "For when they shall rise from the dead, they neither marry, nor are given in marriage; but are as the angels which are in heaven."

After the resurrection, Jesus returned to heaven and now sits at the right hand of God.

Mark 16:19 (KJV): "So then after the Lord had spoken unto them, he was received up into heaven, and sat on the right hand of God." See also 1 Pet 3:22.

Acts 1:11 (KJV): The angel "which also said, Ye men of Galilee, why stand ye gazing up into heaven? This same Jesus, which is taken up from you into heaven, shall so come in like manner as ye have seen him go into heaven."

So heaven is the abode of God. Angels live there. Jesus Christ is currently in heaven with a real, tangible resurrected body. Heaven is a real, literal place, but of a dimension that we are incapable of perceiving. The literalness of heaven is an important point, although seemingly oxymoronic. Since it is in a spiritual dimension, we cannot travel there in bodily form, but it is still real. The same theologians who claim that the lake of fire is not a real literal place but merely a state of extreme mental anguish usually claim that heaven is likewise to each one's own blissful state of mind. Heaven is never portrayed in Scripture as a fancy dream or an abstract idea. It is an actual place.

URANOS—GREEK DEITY AND GOD'S HOME

The only Greek word for heaven used in the New Testament is *uranos*. In classic Greek mythology, Uranos was the god of the sky. From this same word, we derive the name of the seventh planet from the sun, Uranus.

Uranos was a primordial god, serving as part of the creation story within Greek mythology. Uranos spontaneously sprung from the cosmic chaos at the creation of the world, as did his female consort Gaia. Uranos was the sky. He was married to the earth, Gaia. They are revered as Father Heaven and Mother Earth. The twelve Titans were their children, six male and six female. Uranos was not a very good father. He imprisoned all of his children in Tartarus (hell), where they could not see any light. His wife, Gaia, contrived a plan to free one of their sons, Kronos, the youngest and her favorite, out of the pit. Kronos envied the power of his father, who was the ruler of the world. One day, when Uranos approached Gaia to make love, Kronos attacked and castrated his father. He cut off Uranos's genitals with a sickle and threw the still-erect phallus into the ocean. Uranos's blood that was dropping to the earth produced the Erinyes, giants and nymphs. The phallus prowled on the sea and finally arrived at Paphos on the island of Cyprus. Out of the sperm-filled foam that was upon the floating penis, Aphrodite, the love/sex/fertility goddess, was born.

After Kronos had emasculated his father, he took the throne, released his sibling Titans, and married his sister Rhea. Together they reigned during the so-called Golden Age, a period of incessant joy, where people lived carefree without any laws, wars, and discord. However, a nagging prophecy predicted that Kronos would be overthrown by one of his own children, a sort of karma for what he had done to his father. Kronos sired by Rhea numerous gods, including Demeter, Hera, Hades, Hestia, Poseidon, and Zeus. To preempt the prophecy, Kronos ate his children immediately after their birth. Rhea, however, was able to preserve her sixth child, Zeus, from the fate of his brothers and sisters by outwitting Kronos. She gave her ravenous husband a stone wrapped in swaddling clothes to swallow instead of the newborn child. Kronos greedily devoured the rock, believing it to be the boy. Zeus grew up hidden in a cave on the island of Crete. He was raised and suckled by a goat—a deific surrogate mother named Amalthea.

Zeus grew to manhood. Soon, the prophecy that Kronos so feared came true. Zeus returned to Greece and overthrew his father. Zeus compelled Kronos to vomit up all of the children he had swallowed. There precipitated a great battle between Zeus with the Olympian gods on his side and Kronos with the Titans in allegiance. The Olympians were victorious. Zeus imprisoned all of the Titans into Tartarus once again (their father, Uranos, had once impounded them there, too). Zeus then ruled from Mount Olympus as the head of the Greek pantheon.

From that point, Uranos played a tangential role in Greek mythology. The Greeks did not pay him adoration. He had no temples dedicated to him—no festivals, offerings, or clergy. I'm recounting a little bit of this Greek mythology for you here because these stories were certainly very well known and probably studied by the Greek constituents of the churches in the cities of Corinth, Galatia, Ephesus, Philippi, Colossae, and by other Hellenistic Gentiles to whom Paul wrote letters. We call it "mythology," but that very word is somewhat discounting. To the ancient Greek, this is theology, not mythology. This creation account is their religion, and they thoroughly believed it to be true.

These Greek creation myths were likely familiar to Paul, maybe even to Jesus and the Jewish apostles. I doubt that these men of Judea would have studied or even read the Homeric tales, but it seems probable that in a world steeped in pagan worship, they would have heard the story. They probably listened to the tale and then retorted with their own understanding of creation as described by Moses in the book of Genesis.

In the Greek language, *uranos* is the word for heaven. It has the meanings of "sky," "outer space," "universe," and "celestial abode of God." It is used in the Greek New Testament text 284 times. Referring back to the section on the parable of the Rich Man and Lazarus found in Luke 16, one of the traditional arguments against that being merely a fictitious story to deliver a moral message is that it is supposed Jesus would not rely on Greek myth and fable to make his point. Hence, the account must be a literal, real-life situation. However, the multiple uses of the word *uranos* in the Greek text shows that inspired authors freely used a word laden with heavy pagan religious meaning. Jesus probably spoke Aramaic most of the time, so I'm not claiming that he used this Greek word in his daily language. Paul, the Beloved Disciple (author of the Fourth Gospel), and John of Patmos (author of Revelation) were all fluent in Greek. Their mastery of the language is clearly shown in their writings. They appear to have no qualms about using a word to describe the very abode of God that has the heavy baggage of mythological pagan etymology.

(Discussing the proper Christian attitude toward Christmas and Easter is beyond the scope of this text. I will, however, mention in passing that if the authors of holy writ can utilize a pagan word for their own devices and give to it an entirely new meaning apart from its original, then so, too, can I celebrate a once-pagan festival with a clear conscience, for my own device of honoring the birth and resurrection of the true Messiah, Jesus Christ.)

KINGDOM OF HEAVEN/KINGDOM OF GOD

In the Gospel of Matthew, Jesus repeatedly refers to the kingdom of heaven. In Mark and Luke, the same references are made with the kingdom of God. They are the same thing. Matthew was written primarily for a Jewish audience. Rabbis have an aversion to speaking the name of God or even using the word "God" out of a reverence for his holiness. Matthew thus refers to the kingdom of heaven (*uranos* in Greek). Luke's Gospel was written to Gentiles who do not have this quirky hang-up about the name of God, so his writing more directly calls it the kingdom of God.

Jesus told a dozen or so parables about the kingdom of heaven/God. The Lord likened the kingdom of heaven to a man sowing good seed (Matt 13:24), a grain of mustard seed (Matt 13:31), leaven (Matt 13:33), treasure hid in a field (Matt 13:44), a merchant seeking goodly pearls (Matt 13:45), a net that gathers fish of every kind (Matt 13:47), a householder with new and old treasure (Matt 13:52), a king who forgives a debt (Matt 18:23), a landowner paying early and late workers all the same wage (Matt 20:1), a king who throws a wedding feast (Matt 22:2), ten virgins (Matt 25:1), and a rich man giving talents of money in escrow to his servants (Matt 25:14).

Note that the kingdom of heaven is different from heaven itself. "This is the kingdom 'of' heaven—not kingdom 'in' heaven. 'Of' does not mean 'in.' It is the kingdom of, or owned and ruled by, heaven in the same sense that 'kingdom of God' does not mean a kingdom in God. But it does mean a kingdom owned and ruled by God whose throne and dwelling place is in heaven."[1] Similarly, in Acts 21:39, the Apostle Paul says that he is a citizen of Rome, which does not mean that he lives in Rome or that he has ever even been to Rome. Paul was born in Tarsus. He spent much of his career in Antioch and Corinth, frequently visiting Jerusalem. He is a citizen of Rome because Rome is an empire with far-flung holdings throughout the known world. This explanation also applies to Phil 3:20, which states that we are "citizens of heaven."

The kingdom of heaven is on earth, governed by heaven's rules. Just as the mustard seed grows into a tree (Matt 13:31–32), the kingdom of heaven starts small at Pentecost during the spirit-filled Christian age of the church. Jesus said on more than one occasion that the kingdom of heaven/God is at hand (Matt 4:17; Mark 1:15). In other words, it is about to begin quickly.

Mark 9:1 states, "And he said to them, 'I tell you the truth, some who are standing here will not taste death before they see the kingdom of God come with power.'" See also Luke 9:27.

The day that Jesus spoke these words, the kingdom of God was not yet in existence. The righteous dead were still dead in their graves (*sheol*). Mankind, including repentant Jews, had not yet been redeemed and was still suffering from Dead Soul Syndrome.

In Mark 12:28–34, a scribe speaks wisely to Jesus. Christ replies in verse 34 (KJV), "Thou art not far from the kingdom of God." The wise scribe was still thousands of years away from the literal, messianic, millennial kingdom of God that the Jews were expecting. This shows that the blossoming of the kingdom was not real and literal upon earth, but spiritual in the heart of the believer. Jesus sums it up himself in Luke 17:20–21: "Once, having been asked by the Pharisees when the kingdom of God would come, Jesus replied, 'The kingdom of God does not come with your careful observation, nor will people say, "Here it is," or "There it is," because the kingdom of God is within you.'"

Today, the kingdom of heaven has already begun. It is still growing and is manifested daily in the spirit and grace that have been poured upon the world during the church period. The rebirth of the human soul, that spiritual nature of man, is the beginning of the kingdom of God. This spiritual kingdom is vibrant and alive. Jesus told his disciples in Luke 10:19 that they had been given power to tread on serpents and scorpions and over all the power of the enemy, and nothing would injure them. There is an "incomparably great power for us who believe" (Eph 1:19) that is available by the Holy Spirit. I thank God that a small part of it, generously, resides with me.

However, in some references the kingdom of heaven/God also includes the fullness of eternity. It cannot be exclusively set within our current world, because Matt 5:20 (KJV) says, "For I say unto you, That except your righteousness shall exceed the righteousness of the scribes and Pharisees, ye shall in no case enter into the kingdom of heaven."

Matthew 8:11 states, "I say to you that many will come from the east and the west, and will take their places at the feast with Abraham, Isaac and Jacob in the kingdom of heaven."

We have not yet feasted with the patriarchs. This is the fully grown mustard tree, the ultimate kingdom of heaven, which would correspond to the millennium/eternity after the resurrection. First Corinthians 15:28 proclaims that, in the end, God will become "all in all." In order for God to be successful in his accomplishment of this statement, he must be absolute Lord of both the spiritual, fourth-dimensional kingdom of God in our hearts *and* in the physical temporal reality in which we live. This is where the preterists and some amillennialists make a gnostic decision that the temporal earth is insignificant.

I propose that the kingdom of heaven/God, of which Jesus so frequently speaks, commenced at his ascension or at Pentecost, when the redeemed dead were recalled to heaven and the redeemed living were regenerated in their soul, so as to have a living, fourth-dimensional being. We currently live in the spiritual kingdom and have great power in it. However, that is only the firstfruits of glory. The kingdom of heaven/God will be fully manifested upon earth after the glorious second coming. Ultimately and for all eternity, the great kingdom of heaven will be upon earth and ruled by God. But I'm getting ahead of myself; we have one more heavenly word to consider.

PARADISE

The Greek word *paradeisos* is used only three times. The word comes from the Persian language and was Hellenized into Greek after Alexander's conquest. It means a beautiful garden or a peaceful oasis. From Paul's comment in 2 Cor 12:2–4, I think paradise is equivalent to the third heaven, or spiritual abode of God: "I know a man in Christ who fourteen years ago was caught up to the third heaven. Whether it was in the body or out of the body I do not know—God knows. And I know that this man—whether in the body or apart from the body I do not know, but God knows—was caught up to paradise. He heard inexpressible things, things that man is not permitted to tell."

Notice that Paul calls this place "third heaven" and "paradise" interchangeably. The third heaven is an ordinal numeration of the heavens, and it is a customary term of the NT period that meant the spiritual realm of God. The first heaven refers to the atmosphere, or what we would call sky. This is where the birds fly, the clouds waft, and from which the rain falls. The second heaven is outer space. This is where the stars, moon, and sun are hung. The second heaven is black and, like a curtain, envelops all creation. The third heaven is beyond all that. In the third heaven God has his throne and dwells there.

The second usage is in Rev 2:7: "He who has an ear, let him hear what the Spirit says to the churches. To him who overcomes, I will give the right to eat from the tree of life, which is in the paradise of God."

The tree of life is a metaphor for Jesus Christ. It has nothing to do with actually eating from some magical species of fruit tree. As he is the Living Water, he is also the Tree of Life. By eating of the tree, we gain eternal life. The notion of eating Jesus is also, of course, symbolic. It is the exact same symbolism used at the Last Supper in Matt 26:26b, when Jesus said to his disciples about the bread, "Take and eat, this is my body."

Where is Jesus right now? The tree of life, Jesus the Messiah, is in the paradise of God. He sits at the right hand of God. He is in the third heaven, which is exactly what this verse claims.

The third and last time Jesus uses this word is in Luke 23:43b, while hanging on the cross and speaking to the repentant thief: "You will be with me in paradise." So, apparently, humans do get to go to paradise, or third heaven, eventually at some point. My thesis, as has been explained, is that the dead sleeping soul of the righteous was delivered from the grave (*sheol*) to the third heaven, paradise, upon the ascension of Christ, or possibly ten days later at Pentecost. Currently, in this church age after the pouring out of the Pentecostal spirit but before the great resurrection, the repentant thief and all others redeemed by the Lamb are in paradise with their master, the Tree of Life.

ENDNOTES

1. *Ambassador College Correspondence Course*, Lesson 7, "Will You Go To Heaven When You Die?"

8

Going to Heaven

LET'S PICK UP WHERE we left off at chapter 3. To gain a fuller understanding of the triune nature of man and that spiritual component that suffers from Dead Soul Syndrome, I spilled the beans early. We have already started the discussion of the contemporary condition of the deceased Christian and all OT saints. They go to heaven, in my theory. This is, of course, not news to most traditional Evangelicals; however, it may be upsetting to my soul-sleep friends, with whom I share a lot in common.

There are additional passages of Scripture that lead me to a belief in the saint's current heavenly presence with Jesus.

MY FATHER'S HOUSE

John 13:33, 36: "'My children, I will be with you only a little longer. You will look for me, and just as I told the Jews, so I tell you now: Where I am going, you cannot come'... Simon Peter asked him, 'Lord, where are you going?' Jesus replied, 'Where I am going, you cannot follow now, but you will follow later.'"

John 14:2–6: "'In my Father's house are many rooms; if it were not so, I would have told you. I am going there to prepare a place for you. And if I go and prepare a place for you, I will come back and take you to be with me that you also may be where I am. You know the way to the place where I am going.' Thomas said to him, 'Lord, we don't know where you are going, so how can we know the way?' Jesus answered, 'I am the way and the truth and the life. No one comes to the Father except through me.'"

During the Last Supper, right after the prediction of the betrayal by Judas, Jesus speaks about his Father's house. Unfortunately the last few verses of chapter 13 have been disjoined from the first few verses of chapter 14. Jesus said that he was going away. Peter asks him where he is going. Then early in chapter 14, Jesus answers the question. He is going to his Father's house.

Some people have noted that the expression "my Father's house" elsewhere in Scripture always refers to the temple. Some examples:

Luke 2:49: "'Why were you searching for me?' he asked. 'Didn't you know I had to be in my Father's house?'"

John 2:16: "To those who sold doves he said, 'Get these out of here! How dare you turn my Father's house into a market!'"

Matthew 21:13: "'It is written,' he said to them, 'My house will be called a house of prayer,' but you are making it a 'den of robbers.'"

Soul sleepers sometimes claim that this reference found in John 14 is also toward the physical temple building in Jerusalem. However, it makes no sense that Jesus would physically and literally go to the temple of the Sadducees in order to prepare a place for his disciples. Jesus was not a popular figure among the Sadducees. They would not appreciate him preparing any places within their compound. Anyway, he clearly told Pilate in John 18:33 that his kingdom was not of this world. Such a physical temple/building interpretation is weak and lacking in common sense.

Others believe that "my Father's house" refers to my Father's family, household, dynasty—not a specific place or geographic location at all. This interpretation is most popularly found among soul sleepers who deny Christians in heaven before the resurrection. The word translated as "house" is *oikea*. It is used ninety-two times in the Greek New Testament, and can mean a literal house or a collective family household or dynasty. For verses clearly containing the family/household idea, see Matt 10:12–13; 13:5–7; 19:29; Mark 3:25; and John 4:53. This is a more feasible rendering, but it still appears forced. If everyone in the family of God is co-heirs with Christ, why are separate rooms required? Why does Christ tell his disciples that they cannot follow him to this location, but will gain access later? If this is not referring to an actual abode or dwelling, but metaphorically speaking of the family of God, then why are there many rooms? Will there be partitioning and separation within the dynasty of the Father?

I do not think so. We are promised intimate fellowship in the resurrection. The veil at the Holy of Holies is torn down. The bond with Christ in our spiritual organism is likened to the union of marriage. Metaphorical language of "many rooms" is counterproductive to the mental image of our eternal harmonious destiny. Jesus made this statement right after the Last Supper, on the eve of his crucifixion. The Lord knew that these men would be very distraught and confused. His intent was clearly to comfort them with words of unity. Putting up metaphorical walls between them and himself would not lessen the troubling of their heart.

Another problem with the dynasty or family theory is that Jesus says that he is going there. It is the present tense—right now he goes, which implies that he is not there already. The word "go" (Gr. = *poreuō*) means to lead over, carry over, or transfer. Was Jesus Christ at the Last Supper not already within the family or dynasty of his Father? Must he transfer over into it?

Pretribulationists view this passage as a reference to the rapture of the church. Verse 3 "I will come back" is clearly a reference to the second coming. However, Jesus spoke these words to his disciples at the Last Supper. Peter, John, Matthew, Simon the Zealot and all the rest were the referent to the pronoun "you." Jesus said that *you* cannot follow him, that *you* will come later, and that he will prepare a place for *you*. These promises must first and foremost apply to the individuals to whom he was speaking. Of course, the words also apply to Christians of all ages, but it is originally a word to the disciples. Since the twelve disciples were not caught up in the rapture, a different meaning must be sought.

The multiple interpretations of this passage have more lives than a cat. Felines only survive nine lives, but the John 14:2 passage has many more possible views of its true meaning. Tunneling down through the hard rock to discover this meaning is much like the miners of King Hezekiah's time who dug his famous water tunnel. As they hammered with their pickaxes, they followed a small stream of water naturally percolating through the stone.[1] This karstic dissolution channel led the tunnelers toward the spring of Gihon, similarly to how we must follow small threads, individual words, and phrases in the interpretation of Scripture. It is hard work. Our path is frequently blocked by copious amounts of flowstone—hard mineral deposits carried by the water that have accreted through the centuries. But our diligence and hard work will be rewarded by God. The threat of the siege by our enemies can be mitigated if we secure the spring as a perpetual water source for the city. Hezekiah did not give up. I encourage all Bible students to continue through their life studying and digging toward the Eternal Spring.

The simplest, most direct meaning of this passage, without bias or predetermined theology, is that Jesus is going to the third heaven, the highest *shamayim*, the *uranos* of God. Paradise is his Father's house, the abode of God. He tells his disciples that they cannot follow immediately due to Dead Soul Syndrome. During the period before the resurrection, the spirit of all men was still dead. However, the Lord reassures them that soon they will have access to the same location to which he will be going—that is, heaven. He tells them that the way to get to heaven (the place where he is going) is through himself, for he is the Way, the Truth, and the Life. The place that Christ prepares for Christians is a place for dead saints after death, but before the resurrection. We affirm that truth unequivocally. The traditional view of this verse seems the most convincing and natural, especially when considered in context with the closing verses of chapter 13. Other positions have to juggle and balance the words in an awkward fashion.

However, Christ doesn't stop there, and at this point the traditional interpretation falls short. Christ makes no claim that these "many rooms" or "mansions" in the KJV are the final disposition of the saved. Jesus says that he will come back. Come back where? To earth, of course. Then he says that he will take us to be with him (the KJV says to "receive us unto himself," which is probably a better translation). The verb *paralambano* is future tense, middle-deponent voice, indicative mood. According to *Thayer's Greek Lexicon*, it is not a takeaway sort of action, but a take-with-oneself or join-to-oneself sort of action.[2] Instead of Christ whisking us off the earth toward heaven where he had been, the text is saying that we will be united with Christ, so we will forevermore be physically and inseparably together. This is speaking of the first resurrection and the preparation for the marriage of the Lamb, which occurs at the glorious second coming of Christ, or possibly at the rapture (if you insist on such).

I believe that traditionalists are correct that the first part of this verse speaks of Christians going to heaven, but other theologians are also correct that this verse speaks of eternal life on earth when the Lord of glory returns to us. Death immediately ushers the believer into a higher (but not fuller) realm in the very presence of the Lord. Not until the resurrection will our mortality be swallowed up in a more abundant life. In the meantime, we wait eagerly for our adoption as sons (Rom 8:23).

TWENTY-FOUR ELDERS, A MULTITUDE IN WHITE ROBES

Further evidence for a conscious existence of redeemed humans in heaven before the resurrection is to be found in Revelation. In the beginning of Rev 4, Christ says to John, "Come up here, and I will show you what must take place after this." This statement of John's immediate teleporting into the invisible realm is frequently (by pretribulation dispensationalists at least) paralleled with the rapture of the church just before the start of the great tribulation. For those who hold such a doctrine of the rapture, it would not be at all out of place to see humans in heaven. After all, the rapture would have just happened. The first phase of the second coming is by that doctrine concurrent with the resurrection of the dead saints and catching up of those still alive, according to 1 Thess 4:15–17. Eschatology of the rapture is, however, out of the scope of this study.

Many good Christians, and even myself, are not convinced about a pretribulation or even a pre-wrath rapture. They anticipate a single second coming at the end of this age. Almost always, believers in soul sleep are amillennial or at least a-rapture. To this audience I wish to point out the twenty-four elders and the multitude in white robes. Revelation 4—19 in all contains twelve verses mentioning the elders. More important, these same chapters contain the "multitude in white robes," the 144,000 martyrs, and "them that dwell in heaven." Amillenarian Christians frequently believe that the church/Gentile age in which we now live is the spiritual millennium, with a figurative thousand years before the second coming of Christ. These chapters are undeniably detailing a vision in heaven before the great Parousia of Christ. Hence, these verses are a glimpse of heaven before the resurrection of the saints.

Revelation 4:4: "Surrounding the throne were twenty-four other thrones, and seated on them were twenty-four elders. They were dressed in white and had crowns of gold on their heads." The elders fall on their face to worship God, and they also enjoy singing in verses 4:10; 5:8; 7:11; 11:16; and 19:4. They lay their crowns at the throne of God while they worship and sing praises to the Lamb.

Are the elders men or angels? Personally, I lean toward their being human, but the evidence is inconclusive. Some apologists point out that men wear white robes to symbolize the righteousness of Christ imputed toward humans through faith. But angels are also seen regularly in white. Angels at the tomb of Christ (Matt 28:3) and at the ascension on Olivet (Acts 1:10) are in white robes. White simply shows purity.

Some believe that the golden crown (Gr. = *stephanos*) proves that they are men. The *stephanos* crown is a victor's crown traditionally made from a laurel wreath. At the ancient Olympics, it was awarded to the victors of the race, those who overcame all adversaries. However, drawing too much from this analogy is inappropriate. Christ had a *stephanos* of thorns while being crucified (Mark 15:17). The demon locusts emerging from the pit wear something like a *stephanos* crown (Rev 9:7). The woman with a child wears a *stephanos* crown in Rev 12:1. The antichrist on a white horse at the opening of the first seal also wears a *stephanos* crown (Rev 6:2). I agree that the crown is mild evidence for the humanity of the elders, because nowhere in Scripture are holy angels seen wearing one. However, it hardly proves the case.

The fact that they sit on thrones is also slight, but soft, evidence for humanity. In Matt 19:28, Jesus promises that the apostles will sit on twelve thrones, judging the twelve tribes of Israel. However, Rev 2:13 mentions Satan's throne. Since Satan is an angelic-type being, it is not impossible for holy angels in heaven to have thrones. We are just not given enough information about the elders to make a conclusive determination about their nature.

I am lightly persuaded that they are human, but a much more solid case can be built for the existence of people in heaven before the second coming/resurrection by observing the "multitude in white" and the 144,000 martyrs.

Revelation 7:9, 13–14: "After this I looked and there before me was a great multitude that no one could count, from every nation, tribe, people and language, standing before the throne and in front of the Lamb. They were wearing white robes and were holding palm branches in their hands. . . . Then one of the elders asked me, 'These in white robes—who are they, and where did they come from?' I answered, 'Sir, you know.' And he said, 'These are they who have come out of the great tribulation; they have washed their robes and made them white in the blood of the Lamb.'"

There can be no doubt that the great multitude is human. The elder specifically identifies them as such. The scene is also surely in heaven, and the multitude are sentient and conscious. They sing praises to God and serve the Lamb. There can be little contention that this occurs before the second coming with majesty and glory. It is viewed after the sixth seal but before the seventh seal. The insurmountable difficulties of denying their conscious existence lie on the surface and are clearly visible to all. In my opinion, although this point is much debated by godly believers, the scene is a literal view of what John observes. Reducing the scene to a symbolic vision is the last resort for an apologist who does not want to admit to the existence of people in heaven before the second coming.

Revelation 14:3–4: The 144,000 "sang a new song before the throne and before the four living creatures and the elders. No one could learn the song except the 144,000 who had been redeemed from the earth. These are those who did not defile themselves with women, for they kept themselves pure. They follow the Lamb wherever he goes. They were purchased from among men and offered as firstfruits to God and the Lamb."

Again humans are viewed in heaven. At the beginning of chapter 14, these 144,000 are seen at Mount Zion, which is, of course, on earth. A couple of verses later, they are seen in heaven singing before the throne of God. Apparently they have been martyred. In Rev 7, we are told that these 144,000 come 12,000 from each of the tribes of Israel (shy only of Dan). These are Jewish Christians. These are genetically Hebrew descendants of Abraham who have received Moschiah (Messiah). Being the firstfruits of their nation is a nod toward the prophecy of Paul in Rom 11:26—that after the fullness of the Gentiles, all Israel will be saved. Earlier in this chapter, Paul reveals that Israel's rejection became the Gentiles opportunity for salvation and upon the ultimate salvation of Israel the Christ will return and the resurrection will occur. Rom 11:15: "For if their rejection is the reconciliation of the world, what will their acceptance be but life from the dead?" The "life from the dead" is the first resurrection. It occurs shortly after all Israel is saved. Hence, our view in Rev 14 of the 144,000 martyred firstfruits is before the resurrection. They sing, learn secret names, and follow Jesus. They are awake and they are present in heaven, yet before the resurrection.

That the 144,000 men are not defiling themselves with women is metaphorical of not adulterating themselves with pagan idols and worldly values. Frequently the Bible expresses spiritual purity in terms of sexual purity. I do not think that this phrase could be literal, because it would directly contradict 1 Cor 7:28 and Heb 13:4, which specifically say that marriage is pure and without sin. I try to always take a verse literally at its simplest and most basic meaning. There are, however, two instances where a literal reading is not preferred: first, as in this case, if a literal and simple reading would cause direct contradictions to other

Bible verses and teachings, and second, if a simple understanding is ridiculous and not logically possible. In those cases, and only in those cases, I accept a figurative meaning.

More people are said to be in heaven when the beast makes mischief on earth for his brief period. Revelation 13:6 (KJV) states, "And he opened his mouth in blasphemy against God, to blaspheme his name, and his tabernacle, and them that dwell in heaven."

Who are "them that dwell in heaven"? Angels? More likely this is referring to the entire multitude of saints that the beast just massacred.

Unfortunately, many people attempt to mold the interpretation of Bible verses around a predefined doctrine with which they have already become thoroughly ossified. We saw this phenomenon with the eternal-torment doctrine, and now here again it occurs for some soul-sleep people with the admission of the redeemed into heaven before the end of time and general resurrection.

A healthier approach is just the opposite. We must mold our doctrine around Bible verses. As for myself, if I am confronted with Scripture passages that I have inadvertently not noticed in the past, I hope to change my doctrine humbly to conform to the perfect word of God.

A CLOUD OF WITNESSES

Hebrews 11 is well known as the hall of fame for righteous men of faith who have born testimony of God and trusted in him. Abraham, Moses, Elijah, and Sampson are listed as individuals who obeyed the calling of God and who will receive their reward in the resurrection. The very first verse of chapter 12 alludes to this antecedent of saints, but because the chapter breaks have isolated it from its context, the verse is sometimes misunderstood as referring to angels or some other witness, such as the Scriptures. Hebrews 12:1 (KJV) states, "Wherefore seeing we also are compassed about with so great a cloud of witnesses, let us lay aside every weight, and the sin which doth so easily beset us, and let us run with patience the race that is set before us."

The book of Hebrews was written during the later half of the first century by an unknown author. I have no clue what his name was; however, I do not think it was Paul. When seen in context that the cloud is referencing the Jewish saints of Heb 11, then I hope it lends credence to my theory that believers upon death pass into the presence of God, into a spiritual realm. Notice that the cloud is all around us. These saints are not far away in an outer-space heaven. They surround us in the invisible realm just beyond the veil. (We learn more of this close proximity in chapter 10 of this book.) Another point to consider: these witnesses (*martyr* in Greek) are not witnesses of us, as if they are observing our behavior; they are witnesses of Christ.

RESURRECTION SEEN IN THE FESTIVALS

Rabbis and pastors both recognize that the seven festivals of Israel as mandated by Moses in Lev 23 are representative of God's working on earth. To put it in Christian terms, these ancient holidays are symbolic of Jesus. Almost everything in Jewish law and tradition is reflective of the coming of messiah. The old covenant and the new covenant are mirror images, shadows, types of each other. By studying the ancient rituals of the Israelites, we can learn much about our own relationship with God, and prophecies of his advents to earth.

I don't have space to explain fully the meaning of the festivals. Alfred Edersheim did the classic work, and several excellent modern books have appeared on the topic.[3] In order to make my point, I give a very brief introduction.

Leviticus 23 is where God tells Moses about the seasons and the festivals. Israel has seven major holidays. There are four in the spring: Passover, Unleavened Bread, Firstfruits, and Pentecost. Then in the fall, after the harvest, there are three more: Trumpets, Day of Atonement, and Tabernacles.

Israel was an agrarian society. Not very many modern people are involved in the primary sector of actually growing food, but everyone was in antiquity. Society revolved around farming. Today, much to our loss, we have become deaf to the rhythm of planting and harvesting. Usually in early April, the first Sunday after Passover is called the Festival of Firstfruits. The priests would make a wave offering of a sheaf of grain, the very first of the barley harvest. Agriculturally, it is a thanksgiving to God for the upcoming anticipated harvest. It is also symbolic. The unleavened sheaf that is waved in the temple represents something. In Gen 37, Joseph had a vision of his sheaf rising up and lording over the other sheaves in the field. Sheaves can represent people. Our sheaf being waved in the temple represents a person too. It is symbolic of Christ, who rose from the dead on the day of firstfruits. In that year, it was three days after Passover. Jesus is the unleavened firstfruit sheaf. He is a big plump sheaf without blemish, golden brown, with luscious kernels. He is the firstfruits of our resurrection. Paul writes about this in 1 Cor 15, telling us that Jesus is our firstfruits and that the wave offering represents resurrection. Christ is the very first man to receive immortality, but he is not the last.

Fifty days later, Pentecost, also called the Festival of Weeks, celebrates the fullness of the barley harvest. Pentecost is usually in late May, the time of year that is the main harvest for winter grains. Just like Passover and Tabernacles, it required a pilgrimage for all Jewish males to appear at the temple in Jerusalem to make a series of sacrifices.

Leviticus 23 specifies that at Pentecost the priest is to make a wave offering of fully baked bread. These loaves of finished bread are to be leavened. However, it is commanded in Lev 2:11 and elsewhere never to burn leaven on the altar of God, so these loaves of leavened bread are only waved above the altar.

Pentecost in ancient Israel was thus an agricultural festival in late spring to celebrate the reaping of the barley harvest, but it doesn't stop there. If the unleavened sheaf at Firstfruits represents the resurrection of Christ, what do you suppose the two loaves with leaven represent?

We, the redeemed, are represented by the loaves of leavened bread. As leaven throughout Scripture represents sin, so, too, we humans are imperfect and include some leaven. Gloriously, we are promised a resurrection just like Christ, by the quickening of the Holy Spirit, to have life eternal. This is the Pentecost message with the waving of the bread. Just as Israel harvested crops, God shall harvest the souls of men.

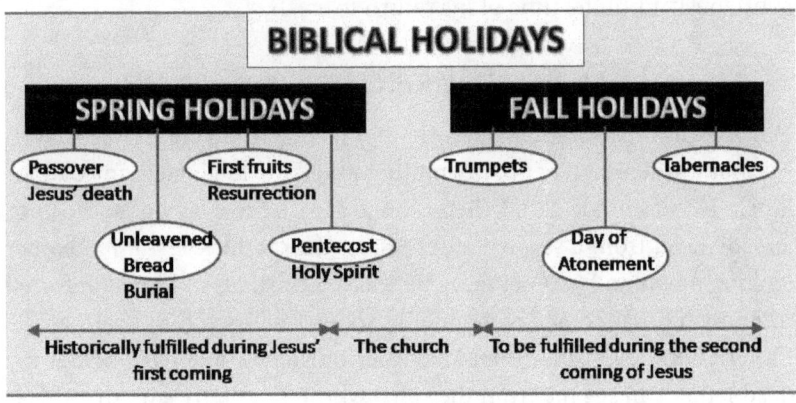

Figure 1 from http://biblicalholidays.com/
Used by permission.

Figure 1 shows the seven festivals and their timing through the course of the year. Christians almost universally recognize that the spring festivals were christologically fulfilled in the first advent of the Lord two thousand years ago.

The spring festivals clearly prophesy about the first coming of the Messiah, so it stands to reason that the fall festivals are also prophetic of his second coming. Between the spring and the fall is the long, hot Israeli summer. In the present age of the Gentile church, we are living in the prophetically long summertime betwixt seasons.

It is curious, and I think indicative of my proposed theory, that the waving of the leavened bread happens with the spring festivals. We will not pursue this tempting line of thought further than to point out that if soul sleep for the redeemed is correct and our resurrection both spiritually and physically is yet in the future at the last trump, then the leavened wave offering should have occurred more aptly in the fall, maybe at Trumpets.

In conclusion, the wave offerings made in the temple are prognostications of the Himalayan event that would occur in the resurrection of the dead. Jesus was the firstfruit. The Pentecostal church with the outpouring of the Holy Spirit is then made spiritually alive to overcome Dead Soul Syndrome. This was symbolized in the leavened loaves brandished by the priest over the altar of God during the spring festival. Our spiritual resurrection is now. Although the body will decay in the grave until the last trump when we physically rise to meet our Lord, now we receive the life-giving Spirit and enjoy the presence of Jesus in heaven consciously until the time of his return to earth.

CAN MY DEAD PARENTS SEE ME TODAY?

When I was thirteen years old my father died. It was a cold winter day in Vermont, where I grew up. My mother asked me to go fetch my dad for lunch. He was in the den. When I found him, he was laying on the floor already dead from a sudden and massive heart attack. I still remember looking down on his quiet face. He was a Christian, so I am comforted in knowing that someday, hopefully soon, I will see him again at the Eastern Gate. Ever since then I have periodically wondered whether my dead father can see me from the spirit world. I'm pretty sure that this is a common question for many of us.

With our physically bound minds, we envision dead saints in heaven leaning over the edge of a cloud and viewing our actions and behavior. Catholics pray to Mary and other saints, thinking that they may be able to intercede for us. Many cultures bury food and beverage with the body for symbolic consumption in the netherworld. In our area of Texas, with a high German Catholic density, interring beer with the casket is quite common, and that is the number-one item (besides the clothed body) to be buried inside the casket, according to our local funeral director. The departed's personal Bible is the number-two item.

Currently our minds and bodies are very much stuck in this physical realm. Paul wrote in 1 Cor 13:12 (KJV), "For now we see through a glass, darkly." The word *esoptron* translated "glass" in the KJV actually means "mirror." The mirrors of the ancient world were not made of glass, as today, but of metal. Bronze mirrors have been discovered in Egyptian tombs dating back to 2000 B.C. The Roman period mirror was commonly about six inches in diameter, shiny bronze with a long handle, very similar to ladies' vanity mirrors still available today. Mirrors of antiquity did not give a clear reflection. The image was similar to what you would get from looking into the chrome bumper of your car.

What Paul means is that we perceive spiritual things as through the distorted view of a bad mirror. Humans have an imperfect perception of reality. Our understanding of our own dimension is fairly good. Our dimension is the real, tangible universe. We live in a three-dimensional space with time. This is what we can hope to know. Spiritual things are, to some degree, beyond our comprehension. This is speculative, but I think that the situation is somewhat similar for the spirits of righteous people who abide currently in heaven. Jesus is currently in heaven, at the right hand of God. As I have already expressed, I think that the spirits/souls of dead saints are with Jesus, but they are incomplete. I think that they are conscious and aware of great spiritual mysteries that we can only dream of knowing. I think that they understand spiritual things, reciprocally as well, as we understand physical things. Likewise, I suspect that they yearn for a fuller understanding of physical life, in an exactly opposite way to how we yearn to understand spiritual life. But until the resurrection, I think they have the same problem that we have: they only understand their own dimension. I suppose they may have some memory and knowledge of the living, but suspect that this memory of the physical world is extremely dim; I suspect further that their understanding of our universe of time and space is totally inadequate.

In conclusion, I do not think that dead people in heaven have the ability to observe our actions or hear our prayers in the land of the living.

ENDNOTES

1. Gill, "How They Met," 20.
2. Thayer, *Thayer's Greek-English Lexicon*, 484.
3. For the classic reference, consult Alfred Edersheim, *The Temple* (Peabody, MA: Hendrickson Publishers, 1994). For a more modern and easier-to-read book, try Robin Sampson, *Family Guide to the Biblical Holidays* (Shelbyville, TN: Heart of Wisdom, 2001).

9

Heaven Not Our Home

I HOPE THAT WE have thus far established that deceased Christians proceed speedily, without hesitation, to heaven. Far too many theologians stop here and exit the train prematurely. The greater glory is yet to be had. The next train stop is the depot, the end of the line—the final state in the saved person's destiny for one's eternal home. You might be surprised to find out that this terminal place is not in heaven. If you thought going to heaven was impressive, just wait until the full manifestation is revealed of what God has in store for us.

THE RESURRECTION

The day is coming soon—many indicators show that it may in fact be very soon—when Christ shall return to Earth and his dead followers will literally rise from their graves. Paul explains the hope of the resurrection in 1 Cor 15.

First Corinthians was written by Paul to the young church in Corinth, Greece. He was in Ephesus at the time, the mid-50s. Corinth is forty-eight miles west of Athens on a narrow stretch of land, the isthmus that joins the Peloponnesus to the mainland of Greece. It is a very strategic city and a major trade hub, so it was quite wealthy. Corinth was home to a major temple to the Greco-Roman goddess Aphrodite. Her temple employed more then one thousand cultic prostitutes. Having sex with the temple prostitute and paying a fee was considered a very pious religious experience. The Corinthian church was surrounded by this and many other pagan beliefs and steeped in Greek philosophy. Greeks believed in the preeminence of the soul. They did not believe in the physical resurrection of the body. According to Greek philosophers, the soul is the real person, the intrinsic you, the ego. The body is a prison that holds down the soul. The soul, they believed, is immortal and lives forever, the spark of the gods that dwells within each human. Greeks, however, did not believe in the immortality of the physical body. For them, the proposition of a bodily physical resurrection would be silly to even suggest. The body just doesn't matter, because it is only temporary.

Ironically, two divergent schools of gnostic thought developed from Greek thought. Both of these gnostic strains appeared in the early church: asceticism and hedonism. Ascetics thought that pleasurable physical activity would hinder spiritual growth, so they lived austere lifestyles in an attempt to put down the body, which they viewed as base, vile, and evil. Hedonists thought that the body totally did not matter. Only spiritual sin was of effect. They lived pleasure-seeking lives in the flesh, rationalizing that the flesh is transient and unimportant. They thought that fleshly actions are of no consequence.

Both heresies felt that only the soul was important; the body was frivolous and trivial. The people who lived in Corinth, even though they were Christians, were heavily influenced by this Greek culture; Paul wrote this part of his letter to clear up some confusion.

First Corinthians 15:12–20: "But if it is preached that Christ has been raised from the dead, how can some of you say that there is no resurrection of the dead? If there is no resurrection of the dead, then not even Christ has been raised. And if Christ has not been raised, our preaching is useless and so is your faith. More than that, we are then found to be false witnesses about God, for we have testified about God that he raised Christ from the dead. But he did not raise him if in fact the dead are not raised. For if the dead are not raised, then Christ has not been raised either. And if Christ has not been raised, your faith is futile; you are still in your sins. Then those also who have fallen asleep in Christ are lost. If only for this life we have hope in Christ, we are to be pitied more than all men. But Christ has indeed been raised from the dead, the firstfruits of those who have fallen asleep."

Things haven't changed very much. The denial or ignoring of a bodily resurrection is still heard today among professing Christians.

The Talpoit tomb, a few miles from the old city of Jerusalem, has received extensive media coverage. *Time*, CNN, and the National Geographic channel have all had specials highlighting the possibility that Jesus is still buried there. Simcha Jacobovici, an Israeli-born Canadian journalist, directed a very controversial documentary about the alleged tomb of Jesus. Supposedly, Jesus, along with his wife, Mary Magdalene, and their family are buried here. There is an ossuary with the inscription "Jesus son of Joseph."[1] Some Christians, such as total preterists, actually claim that this is okay. Spiritual resurrection only is what awaits us, and that's what counts anyway, or so they claim. They think that Jesus spiritually rose from the dead and that he is spiritually now at the right hand of God. I am hopeful that all Evangelical Christians would not agree with the Talpiot claims. By the way, most archaeologists and scholars don't agree either, for purely secular archaeological reasons. Talpiot is not the tomb of Jesus.

Another group of Christian claims, which strikes much closer to home, does not actively deny the bodily resurrection, although they minimize its significance. They ignore the resurrection. Many people seem to think that at death, if you're a Christian, your soul goes to heaven. You are with Christ. You become perfect, and you immediately receive your reward. It is a syrupy and sentimental view of heaven. They envision themselves in an angelic spiritual body sitting on a fluffy pink cloud, strumming a harp and polishing their halo for all eternity. They forget about the resurrection.

I think such believers want immediate gratification when they die. If your soul is in heaven with Jesus, what does resurrection matter? Who cares about that old body? I'm a spirit just like God. That is pagan Greek philosophy, believing in the preeminence of the soul. The concept is not found in the Bible, written by Hebrew men of God. Remember, even the New Testament was written by Jews.

Our eternal life is not going to be ethereal and unreal. It will not be a wispy existence in a dreamlike spiritual dimension. Continue reading in 1 Cor 15:

First Corinthians 15:42–44a: "So will it be with the resurrection of the dead. The body that is sown is perishable, it is raised imperishable; it is sown in dishonor, it is raised in glory; it is sown in weakness, it is raised in power; it is sown a natural body, it is raised a spiritual body."

First Corinthians 15:50–54: "I declare to you, brothers, that flesh and blood cannot inherit the kingdom of God, nor does the perishable inherit the imperishable. Listen, I tell you a mystery: We will not all sleep, but we will all be changed—in a flash, in the twinkling of an eye, at the last trumpet. For the trumpet will sound, the dead will be raised imperishable, and we will be changed. For the perishable must clothe itself with the imperishable, and the mortal with immortality. When the perishable has been clothed with the imperishable, and the mortal with immortality, then the saying that is written will come true: 'Death has been swallowed up in victory.'"

Most of our beliefs about heaven are correct, albeit misplaced. The glory, the perfection, the immortality, the imperishableness are all true, but they take place on Earth after the resurrection and the second coming, not in heaven after death.

ABRAHAM'S PROMISE

Way back in Genesis, in the very beginning, a promise had been made to Abraham—a promise of land. Abraham and his descendants would possess land. He was told to look north, south, east, and west. The land that he saw would belong to Abraham and his heirs. According to Gen 13:15 (KJV), "For all the land which thou seest, to thee will I give it, and to thy seed for ever." We even call it the Promised Land; this is the land of Israel. The same promise was given to his son, Isaac (Gen 26:3), and again it was reiterated to Jacob (Gen 35:12). The very same promise of perpetual land ownership was repeatedly given through Moses and Joshua and the prophets to the children of Israel (e.g., Deut 19:8; 2 Sam 7:16; Ps 105:11; Isa 9:7). More fully, the promise was expanded and came to be for the whole world (Rom 4:13). Abraham's family would rule the entire earth.

While addressing Gentile-born converts in Galatia, the Apostle Paul wrote in Gal 3:16a, 29 (KJV): "Now to Abraham and his seed were the promises made. . . . And if ye be Christ's, then are ye Abraham's seed, and heirs according to the promise." The Christian is an heir of Abraham, and will enjoy the rewards of God's promise along with Abraham. Paul says that if we belong to Christ, then we are grafted into the family of Abraham. We become Abraham's seed, and heirs according to the promise.

What are we heirs to? The promise was for the world; the earth; the physical, temporal planet upon which we now dwell.

Romans 4:13: "It was not through law that Abraham and his offspring received the promise that he would be heir of the world, but through the righteousness that comes by faith."

Abraham was never promised to live in heaven forever. His promise—and the promise to his descendants, both natural and adopted—is to have land on earth in which to dwell.

We can each learn something from everybody. No one group, denomination, or person (including me) has an exclusive contract for correct doctrine. For this section of my study, I have frequently availed myself of the work and sermons of John Ritenbaugh, head pastor of the five-hundred-member Church of the Great God, headquartered in Fort Mill, South Carolina. They are a splinter group coming from the Worldwide Church of God, and still hold to the original doctrines of Herbert Armstrong. Although I may disagree with some of their teachings, I also find great wisdom in Pastor Ritenbaugh's sermons.[2]

MEN ARE TO BE ON EARTH

Psalm 2:6: "I have installed my King on Zion, my holy hill."

Psalm 2:8: "Ask of me, and I will make the nations your inheritance, the ends of the earth your possession."

Psalm 37:9 (KJV): "For evildoers shall be cut off: but those that wait upon the LORD, they shall inherit the earth."

Psalm 37:29: "The righteous shall inherit the land, and dwell therein for ever."

Psalm 115:16 (KJV): "The heaven, even the heavens, are the LORD's: but the earth hath he given to the children of men."

Isaiah 45:12a (KJV): "I have made the earth, and created man upon it."

Jeremiah 23:5: "'The days are coming,' declares the LORD, 'when I will raise up to David a righteous Branch, a King who will reign wisely and do what is just and right in the land.'" Please notice that this passage says that David's branch will reign and do justice in the *land*, not sky.

Revelation 5:9b–10: "And with your blood you purchased men for God from every tribe and language and people and nation. You have made them to be a kingdom and priests to serve our God, and they will reign on the earth."

There are a number of other verses, too. They all say the same thing, which bothers some people; apparently Greek philosophy is still strong in our culture. However, is there anything wrong with having the earth as our eternal inheritance? Would you "settle" for the whole world? Although the redeemed spirits of holy people are today in heaven, we look forward to the resurrection to live on earth. Earth is the future of humankind, and it will be center stage.

DAVID'S ENDURING KINGDOM

David was a humble man after God's own heart. In the phenomenal seventh chapter of 2 Samuel, David desires to build a permanent house for God. David's kingdom is secure, and he is at rest from all of his enemies. Instead of feeling conceited and full of himself, as future generations would during times of plenty, David contemplates the dwelling place of the ark of the Lord. He is comfortable in a palatial house of cedar, yet God is dwelling in a tent, a house of curtains.

David determines that he wants to build a temple for Yahweh. God, however, puts a halt to this idea. Instead, God promises to make David a house (royal line) that will never be obliterated, but will continue forever. We serve a generous and gracious God. David wants to do something for God, and God determines to do much more for David.

This promise is made as an unconditional declaration by God. God promises to deal with David's offspring as a father with his own son and that he would never take away his love and mercy.

Second Samuel 7:16: "Your house and your kingdom will endure forever before me; your throne will be established forever." See also 1 Chr 17:14 for an almost identical verse.

Elsewhere in Scripture, other verses promise an enduring throne for David.

Psalm 89:3–4: "You said, 'I have made a covenant with my chosen one, I have sworn to David my servant, I will establish your line forever and make your throne firm through all generations.' Selah."

Psalm 89:35–37: "Once for all, I have sworn by my holiness and I will not lie to David—that his line will continue forever and his throne endure before me like the sun; it will be established forever like the moon, the faithful witness in the sky. Selah."

David's own last words upon his death bed in 2 Sam 23:5a were, "Is not my house right with God? Has he not made with me an everlasting covenant?"

The well-known promise of God is called a "covenant of salt" by King Abijah, the great-grandson of David, in 2 Chr 13:5: "Don't you know that the Lord, the God of Israel, has given the kingship of Israel to David and his descendants forever by a covenant of salt?"

Salt is a time-proven and consistent preservative that prevents decay and corruption with enduring quality. The forefathers of Israel preserved their food with salt in place of the modern refrigerator. In

Lev 2:13, it is commanded to always salt the offerings that are burned on the altar of the Lord. Salt typifies abidingness, eternity, steadfastness, stability, and permanence. A "covenant of salt," then, suggests an unbreakable covenant.

The Bible clearly promises that David, the chosen of God, will always have a seed, a house, a throne, and a kingdom. But where will this kingdom be? According to 1 Kgs 11:36, "I will give one tribe to his son so that David my servant may always have a lamp before me in Jerusalem, the city where I chose to put my Name."

David's lineage will not reign in heaven. David's throne will not be next to the great white throne. David's kingdom will not exist in an angelic spiritual realm. It will be on earth, specifically in Jerusalem, Israel.

JESUS' STATEMENTS ON THE EARTH

Matthew 5 is known as the Sermon on the Mount. Jesus is in Galilee. The time is about A.D. 30. There is a big crowd following him and the disciples. He walks up a hill. There aren't really any mountains in Galilee, but several big hills overlook the lake with a beautiful view. Matthew says that he sat down while he taught, probably on a rock or a tree stump. I can imagine the disciples sitting Indian style with their legs crossed or laying prone on the slope of the hill. There is a big crowd, too, shoving in, trying to get close enough to hear. In the Sermon on the Mount, Christ says (Matt 5:3 KJV), "Blessed are the poor in spirit, for theirs is the kingdom of heaven."

First of all, what does "poor in spirit" mean? It is those who recognize their own spiritual poverty, those who are not self-righteous and arrogant. Then in verse 5, Christ says, "Blessed are the meek, for they will inherit the earth."

Allow me to ask a question: Are the meek Christians going to have a different reward from the poor-in-spirit Christians? Is this a contradiction? Of course not! The "meek" and the "poor in spirit" are the same thing. They are both humble Christians. They are going to receive the same thing. They shall inherit *the earth* for an everlasting possession, which means the same thing as entering the kingdom of heaven. Notice, as I pointed out before, it does not say kingdom *in* heaven, but *of* heaven, which means the kingdom is owned and operated by heaven. The kingdom owned by heaven will be set up on earth. Those two verses are parallel; they mean exactly the same thing.

A stanza from the Lord's Prayer found in Matt 6:10 (KJV)—and also a similar version found in Luke 11:2—where the disciples ask Jesus to teach them to pray, says, "Thy will be done, in earth as it is in heaven." God's will—or his volition, his power to make decisions—will ultimately be fully manifested upon this earth, just as powerfully as his determination is today in authority within the bounds of heaven. Earth will become heavenly.

What I am trying to establish is that we will live forever on real ground, terra firma, earth—not spiritually or in a metaphysical place. Also, we will have literal, real, touchable glorified bodies. People are earthly beings. Adam came from the ground. We will reign eternally in a perfected body on a perfected earth.

PERMANENCE OF JERUSALEM

I build here upon the assumption that the reader does in fact believe in the eternal life of the redeemed. Jesus used the words "eternal life" on ten occasions. A typical example is John 10:28a (KJV): "And I give unto them eternal life; and they shall never perish." I think all Christians would agree on and believe in the permanence of our existence.

But Christians don't all agree on the permanence of the earth. Sometimes they will quote 2 Pet 3:12, which says that the elements will melt with fervent heat. We discuss that verse later. But for now let me assure you that it does not mean the cessation of the world. That verse and others are representing the birth pangs of the redeemed new earth. It will afterward still be the same earth, but a metamorphosis from ugly caterpillar to beautiful butterfly will occur.

The earth is the location of Israel, and Israel is the location of Jerusalem, and Jerusalem is the location of the temple. The Bible has quite a bit to say that these will last forever.

According to the Bible, the land of Israel will be inhabited perpetually. Joel 3:20 (KJV) says, "But Judah shall dwell for ever, and Jerusalem from generation to generation." Like shoots of good root, planted by God himself, the restored people of Zion will "possess the land forever" (Isa 60:21). God will ultimately "restore them to the land I gave their forefathers to possess" (Jer 30:3). Amos spoke of "that day" when David's fallen tent would be repaired and Israel would be planted "in their own land, never again to be uprooted" (Amos 9:11–15). According to Mic 4:7, then the Lord himself shall rule from Mount Zion "from that day and forever." The prophets all saw an ultimate restoration and perpetual possession of the entire land of Israel as a central theme. See also Ezek 39:25–29; Jer 24:6; 29:10; Isa 49:6; Zech 10:10, and others.

If the land of Israel is to be inhabited forever, then the earth must exist forever. A few chapters ago, when we were speaking about the "*Aeon, aeon*" verses in Rev 14 and 20, I quoted Edward Fudge, who qualifies the word "forever" by stating that its meaning is limited by the inherent properties of the thing it describes. At this point, that definition may need further clarification. The saved people, the glorious earth, the permanence of Jerusalem, and the perpetuity of the temple do not in and of themselves have an inherent everlasting nature. It is conscribed to them by God, who alone owns this nature.

OUR REWARD IS IN HEAVEN RIGHT NOW

The following verses say that something in heaven is waiting for us. I believe the reward is the promise of a glorified body. This is the resurrection. Dead saints who are with Christ today do not yet have their reward. Heaven is not our final destiny. Glorified bodies will be issued after the rapture/second coming. I do not think that our glorified body is literally waiting for us in heaven, like in a glass dome filled with smoke, as in some science-fiction movie. The promise of a glorified body waits for us in heaven, because he who promised it is waiting for us in heaven, and his word is as good as reality.

Matthew 5:12a (KJV) states, "Rejoice, and be exceeding glad: for great is your reward in heaven."

Matthew 6:20: "But store up for yourselves treasures in heaven, where moth and rust do not destroy, and where thieves do not break in and steal."

First Peter 1:4 (KJV): "To an inheritance incorruptible, and undefiled, and that fadeth not away, reserved in heaven for you."

Second Corinthians 5:2 (KJV): "For in this we groan, earnestly desiring to be clothed upon with our house which is from heaven."

This is our hope, for which we wait patiently (Rom 8:29).

GLORIFIED BODY

At the resurrection, according to Paul, all believers receive a somatic immortality in the form of a glorified body. Paul himself longed to be clothed with his heavenly form, this glorified body. A glorified body is a real, physical body. It is exactly like what Jesus had after his resurrection, while he walked on earth for forty days. The angels, which are spiritual beings and do not have bodies at all, in Luke 24:5b asked the women at the tomb, "Why do you look for the living among the dead?" The actual, physical, three-dimensional, molecular, flesh-and-blood body of Christ had been raised from the natural physical dead.

However, the glorified body is a super-special version of a body. First Corinthians 15 says that it is immortal, and incorruptible. "Immortal" obviously means that it will never die again. The body is impervious to rot, decay, and disease. "Incorruptible" means that it is not inclined to sin. The body is pure and perfect. Glorified bodies also have the extra capabilities that Jesus had. They may appear inside locked doors, and then disappear in a flash. I believe a glorified body is a holistic synthesis of the spiritual and physical. It has most attributes of both worlds. Today, the spiritual world and the physical world are separate universes. They are different dimensions. In our physical world, we know very little of spiritual things (except as the Spirit reveals), and, I suspect, the citizens of that spiritual world (i.e., the dead saints in heaven) groan for physical knowledge.

The promise of a glorified body is found in a number of passages:

Second Corinthians 5:1: "Now we know that if the earthly tent we live in is destroyed, we have a building from God, an eternal house in heaven, not built by human hands."

Philippians 3:20b–21: "The Lord Jesus Christ, who, by the power that enables him to bring everything under his control, will transform our lowly bodies so that they will be like his glorious body."

First John 3:2b: "But we know that when he appears, we shall be like him, for we shall see him as he is."

John 11:25–26a: "Jesus said to her, 'I am the resurrection and the life. He who believes in me will live, even though he dies; and whoever lives and believes in me will never die.'"

Romans 8:29a: "For those God foreknew he also predestined to be conformed to the likeness of his Son."

The Bible does not contradict itself. Wonderfully, each verse tells us a little something about the topic. There will be a bodily resurrection. We will literally have real, perfected bodies. Our assurance of an imperishable body is that Jesus had an imperishable body when he rose from the dead on that Easter day some two thousand years ago.

This promise is absolute. It does not matter how the body had been disposed of at natural death. This miracle of new life will be eternally perfect. Unfortunately, we are told very little about what our glorified body will be like. We know that it is impervious to sin, sickness, aging, and death.

I think that we can glean some traits of glorified bodies by studying the body that Jesus had. Some details are listed in every single one of the four Gospels.

A glorified body can eat fish (John 21:13; Luke 24:42) and bread (Luke 24:30). In Luke 24:41, the newly resurrected Jesus asked the disciples if they had anything available to eat. I don't think Christ was hungry, I think he wanted to assure them that he was real and not a ghost.

Also, earlier in Luke 24, Jesus walked seven miles to Emmaus. That's a good trick for a guy who had been brutally beaten and crucified only three days earlier.

He could hide his identity from mortals. Mary Magdalene thought he was the gardener (John 20:15), while the guys on road to Emmaus didn't know who he was (Luke 24:16). He could flit in and out at will (John 20:19). He could teleport. He came through locked doors (John 21:26). He apparently had control over the time/space continuum and could appear and disappear at volition. At the end of the Fourth Gospel, the risen Jesus breathes on the disciples, and they receive the Holy Ghost. In his glorified body, I guess, he must have lungs. Breath is a symbol of life. Once before, the same Son of God also breathed on the lifeless form of Adam, and he became alive.

Jesus was the same person after his resurrection as he had been before. The tomb was empty; this was the very same body and flesh that been crucified. However, it had been totally changed by the Spirit of God's resurrection, and it was also entirely different. As the same person, Jesus assured his disciples in Luke 24:39, "It is I, myself!" He had the same personality, the same character traits, and the same mannerisms. So, too, will we in our glorified bodies be exactly the same people whom we are today, yet totally different.

Jesus ate fish in his glorified body. Revelation 19 talks about the wedding supper of the Lamb. Ever since my days of living in Israel, I love Middle Eastern food. In our glorified bodies at the wedding, we're going to eat some mutton and have a glass of wine. I suppose there will be pita bread, hummus, and maybe baklava for dessert. Will we poop when we go to the bathroom? Probably an inappropriate question, but I can't suppress from asking.

Mark 16:12 says that Jesus appeared to a couple of unnamed disciples "in another form." This is curious. I assume that "in another form" refers to a spiritual apparition, not a human body. Glorified bodies have this power over the fourth dimension of the invisible spirit world.

Humans could see the glorified Jesus. Paul tells us in 1 Cor 15 that, during an unspecified appearance, he was seen by over five hundred people all at the same time. Paul is chiding the Corinthians, rebuking them for entertaining any thought that Jesus could still be in the tomb. If five hundred people witnessed any such event today, we can rest assured that it would be on the news, blogged on the Internet, posted on YouTube, and recorded as a bona fide historical event.

Most important, and this is my main point, a glorified body can be touched. It's real. It has flesh and bones. Remember doubting Thomas in John 20:24? He touched the palms and the side of the risen Christ. Glorified, resurrected bodies are physical and real, yet fully spiritual, too. We will be so much more than a ghostly spiritual essence.

As an interesting side note, you know that we are not going to have any imperfections or sicknesses in our resurrection, glorified bodies—with one exception. Jesus himself will for all eternity bear those marks in his hands and on his side. It will be a reminder to me and you and Thomas of what he did for us.

ENDNOTES

1. Meyers, "The Jesus Tomb Controversy," 116.
2. **Church of the Great God, 10409 Barberville Road, Fort Mill, South Carolina 29707,** http://cgg.org/.

10

The New Spiritual World

MIRROR IMAGE OF GLORIFIED BODY AND NEW EARTH

Our current mortal body suffers from many imperfections and ailments. Our promised resurrection body will be incorruptible and gloriously powerful. Our present earth is plagued with pestilence, deforestation, famine, open strip mines, landfills, and nuclear waste. Our promised new earth, when Jesus restores all things—as Christ promised in Matt 19:28—will be beautiful, bountiful, and pristine. There is an analogy herein that is important to understand. God loves symbolism and analogies and mirror images. As the glorified body is to the human body, so is the new earth to the old earth.

The entire creation will be redeemed. The stars will be stronger, the moon will be better, the earth will be fixed, and the animal kingdom will be healed. The entire cosmos that was cursed in Gen 3 will be restored to its pre-curse glory and pristine condition.

Romans 8:18–23 states, "I consider that our present sufferings are not worth comparing with the glory that will be revealed in us. The creation waits in eager expectation for the sons of God to be revealed. For the creation was subjected to frustration, not by its own choice, but by the will of the one who subjected it, in hope that the creation itself will be liberated from its bondage to decay and brought into the glorious freedom of the children of God. We know that the whole creation has been groaning as in the pains of childbirth right up to the present time. Not only so, but we ourselves, who have the firstfruits of the Spirit, groan inwardly as we wait eagerly for our adoption as sons, the redemption of our bodies."

Matthew 19:28–29: "Jesus said to them, 'I tell you the truth, at the renewal of all things, when the Son of Man sits on his glorious throne, you who have followed me will also sit on twelve thrones, judging the twelve tribes of Israel. And everyone who has left houses or brothers or sisters or father or mother or children or fields for my sake will receive a hundred times as much and will inherit eternal life.'"

Acts 3:21 (KJV): "Whom the heaven must receive until the times of restitution of all things, which God hath spoken by the mouth of all his holy prophets since the world began."

Gary North, a Presbyterian, points out, "The word 'save' is related to 'salvation,' which in turn is related to 'salve.' A salve is a healing ointment. This is a very good description of Christ's work at Calvary. Christ healed the whole universe by His death. Because of this, God did not destroy the world on the day Adam rebelled. This salve heals some men's souls and all men's environment. This is why Christ's salvation is comprehensive. It affects everything, for it was designed to heal everything progressively and finally on the Day of Judgment."[1]

A DARK WORLD MADE LIGHT

Right now, for us, the spiritual dimension is unseen. It is a dark world, not illuminated for us, and we do not comprehend spiritual things fully. Paul said in 1 Cor 13:12a (KJV), "For now we see through a glass, darkly." As we discussed in a previous chapter, the "glass" here is a mirror—not made of glass at all, but a sheet of tin or bronze, offering a much-distorted reflection. Paul says that this is how we perceive spiritual things right now.

Paul writes in 1 Cor 2:14, "The man without the Spirit does not accept the things that come from the Spirit of God, for they are foolishness to him, and he cannot understand them, because they are spiritually discerned."

The only way for us in our current human bodies to understand spiritual things is for the Spirit of God to lead us and show us.

The spiritual world is very real. Angels, demons, our born-again soul, heaven, and God all exist. It is all very real, but these items are in another dimension. We have great difficulty understanding spiritual things. We are three-dimensional beings; the spiritual world is a fourth dimension, probably all around us, but it might as well be a separate universe. Because of our limitations, we don't recognize the spiritual world.

First Corinthians 13:8–12 (KJV): "Charity never faileth: but whether there be prophecies, they shall fail; whether there be tongues, they shall cease; whether there be knowledge, it shall vanish away. For we know in part, and we prophesy in part. But when that which is perfect is come, then that which is in part shall be done away. When I was a child, I spake as a child, I understood as a child, I thought as a child: but when I became a man, I put away childish things. For now we see through a glass, darkly; but then face to face: now I know in part; but then shall I know even as also I am known."

Paul reveals to us that when perfection comes, I will know as I am known, and we will see him face to face. For this reason, I cannot accept, as some non-Charismatics have proposed, that the perfect and complete thing refers to the complete canon of Scripture. Even with the whole Bible, we do not, and cannot hope to, "know as we are known." The completed, whole, perfected thing, I believe, must refer to us. This is our glorification in the resurrection. This is our completion as God's people. This is the perfection and climactic finishing of the Creator's work with the resurrection for our glorified body.

The problem of a dark world and poorly understood spiritual dimension will be rectified at the resurrection. I believe the glorified body is a holistic synthesis of the spiritual and physical. It has all the attributes of both worlds. It is physical: you can touch it, and you will eat. Glorified bodies also are fully spiritual, like an angel's. The spiritual element of our nature is called the spirit or soul. However, currently the soul is quite opaque. At the resurrection there will be a meshing, a synthesis, an intertwining of the physical and spiritual bodies. My ethereal soul and my material body will become one. We will become able to literally see spiritual bodies.

Likewise, in due time, heaven and earth will merge. Just as our new glorified body is both physical and spiritual, the new earth will also be physical and spiritual. John MacArthur points out, "The New Heaven and New Earth are seen blending together in a great kingdom that incorporates both realms. The paradise of eternity is thus revealed as a magnificent kingdom where both heaven and earth unite in a glory that surpasses the limits of the human imagination and the boundaries of earthly dimensions."[2]

I look forward to a synthetic world, where the spiritual and physical are fully laced together, inseparably intertwined, and meshed together. It is a synthetic merger of physical, real, touching matter and spiritual glory. This is a holistic view. I cannot accept a materialistic view, with the physical dominating, nor can I approve of a spiritual view, which is heavenly only. They must be tandem and balanced with each other. In this world, the resurrection body of Christ gives an example of the completeness of both the physical and the spiritual within ourselves and the cosmos. In that day, spiritual and physical shall become one.

Today the spiritual and physical are antithetical, but I eagerly anticipate the resurrection at the coming of Christ, and finally at the end when all things shall be restored. I will know as I am known, and we will reign with Jesus forever on a glorious new earth. This is the ultimate promise of Easter.

Marriage of Heaven and Earth

The marriage covenant has been divinely instituted as being exclusively between a man and a woman. Liberal progressives today attempt to forward the agenda of homosexual marriage. A quick search in any concordance reveals more than five hundred biblical references to the words "marriage," "married," "husband," and "wife." Marriage is very scriptural. Our understanding of traditional marriage has implications for our understanding of the relationship between God and man and for the prophetic union of heaven and earth. This is why it is important to keep the original meaning and context clear. Traditional human marriage was ordained by God in the garden of Eden for Adam and Eve. It is still applicable in its original form to us today.

Genesis 2:23–24 (KJV): "And Adam said, This is now bone of my bones, and flesh of my flesh: she shall be called Woman, because she was taken out of Man. Therefore shall a man leave his father and his mother, and shall cleave unto his wife: and they shall be one flesh."

Jesus referred to this oneness in Matt 19:6 (KJV): "Wherefore they are no more twain, but one flesh. What therefore God hath joined together, let not man put asunder."

The union of Adam and Eve, and all marriages ever since, have been pointing toward something bigger.

Ephesians 5:23, 30–32 (KJV): "For the husband is the head of the wife, even as Christ is the head of the church: and he is the savior of the body. . . . For we are members of his body, of his flesh, and of his bones. For this cause shall a man leave his father and mother, and shall be joined unto his wife, and they two shall be one flesh. This is a great mystery: but I speak concerning Christ and the church."

The marriage contract executed millions of times every year by couples around the planet points toward Jesus Christ as husband and redeemer of humanity. Marriage represents the union and the oneness to be had between Christ and believers. Jesus, the Living Stone (1 Pet 2:4) will be mortared together, inseparable from his wife, the bricks of the church. We come from his side and ribs, just as Eve was part of Adam. Man was given woman as a helper and aide. They are to be equal but different. God's purpose in designing the marital institution was for companionship and intimacy.

Another union that will occur in the cosmos also points toward Christ. This union too will become intimate, though previously they were apart. The fleshly earth and the spiritual heaven will be joined together in perpetual bliss and mutual satisfaction. The interlocking of heaven and earth is another manifestation of the prophetic nature of the marriage covenant. The marriage of heaven and earth is the enosis of the two. They merge into one being. They become inseparable—just like man and woman, just like Christ and believer.

When heaven and earth join, which one do you think is represented by males and which by females? We are told that in the ultimate fulfillment of marriage typology that Christ is the husband and the church is the bride. Some people may preliminarily draw the conclusion that spiritual heaven is the groom and the fleshly earth is metaphorically the wife. But I would not think or conclude that too quickly. They are equal, but different. They will complement each other and fulfill each other.

All mirrors and types in the Bible always point toward Jesus. The Apostle Paul urges his readers to focus on Christ. Paul warns them that time is short, and soon this world, as we know it, will pass away; see 1 Cor 7:31b (KJV): "For the fashion of this world passeth away." The "fashion" of this world is, I think, the three dimensions in which we live. The new world order will include four.

FOURTH DIMENSION

Although the disciples looked up as they watched Jesus ascend into heaven in Acts 1:9, I seriously doubt that the location of heaven is "up," just behind Jupiter. Nor is heaven located in all of the intergalactic space of the universe. Most likely the immaterial realm of heaven exists concomitantly with the physical cosmos. It is superimposed, as it were, across our world. If heaven is the fourth dimension, then it is all around us. Unfortunately, biblical texts are unconcerned about querying such thoughts, and they leave us with a plethora of unanswered questions. This section is purely speculative, as I have very little biblical citation for anchoring.

In geometry we learn that a line is a one-dimensional object. It extends forever in either direction, but does not exist above or below, or to the left or right. Likewise, a plane is a two-dimensional object. It extends within its paper space forever in both directions, but it has no up and down. If I poke a pencil from above through a piece of paper, the pencil and the paper come together at the intersection of the two-dimensional space, but not above it and not below it, because above and below are not within the two-dimensional plane of the piece of paper. Now, if there were two-dimensional beings to see the intrusion of the pencil into their two-dimensional world, then they would only see the pencil at the intersection of their worlds. This is similar to how an MRI (magnetic resonance imaging) device takes photographic cross-sections of a patient's body. If the pencil just barely penetrated the plane of paper, then the exceedingly short two-dimensional beings would see the lead. If the pencil was pushed nearly through, then they would see the eraser. If the pencil went somewhere in between its own length, they might read one of the letters of "Ticonderoga." They would never be capable of seeing the entire manifestation of the whole pencil. They would most likely have a much distorted idea of what a pencil looks like.

So it is with our understanding of the fourth dimension. This is a silly analogy, of course. It is based on the classic science-fiction book written over one hundred years ago by the English mathematician Edwin Abbott Abbott, *Flatland: A Romance of Many Dimensions*. It is the story of the adventures of an enlightened square geometric figure who lives in a two-dimensional world called Flatland. This world is inhabited by many similar living geometric beings. Trapped in their planar world, not capable of seeing above and below, they believe that their plane is the total existence of the cosmos. But our hero, the square, discovers the existence of a third dimension. At times the story is comic. The book is meant to stimulate us into realizing higher dimensions and is highly recommended.[3]

The spiritual world is the fourth dimension in my estimation. For this discussion, I am discounting Einstein's theory of time as the fourth dimension, although I do not doubt that assertion. I am concerned with higher dimensions of Euclidean space. The spiritual world envelops our three-dimensional world. It permeates us and is all around us, but unless it chooses to intersect at our meeting point (within 3D space), it is totally invisible and undetectable to us.

Christ's glorified body, demons, and angels all have the ability to transcend space-time limitations. I believe that spiritual beings are all around us. They have the power to superimpose themselves into our framework to be seen, as they wish to be seen, at any moment. They could appear in human form, animal form, demonic form, or any form or likeness that they choose, simply by revealing a different piece of their "anatomy" into our plane of existence. Angelic beings could be in Texas one moment, and then very quickly take a shortcut through the fourth dimension to appear in China the next moment. I think that this is the method that demons use to appear to tell the future to their clairvoyant mediums. Demons and angels do not know the future. Only God is omniscient. But demons do have the ability to travel through the astral plane and then reappear with fresh information that no human could ever possibly know. They may communicate this knowledge to satanic mediums, which may then make remarkably accurate predictions.

Scripture specifically precludes us from attempting to communicate with spirit beings (Deut 18:10 and many others). We are commanded to pray only to God. In today's messed-up world, neo-Platonic and esoteric philosophies, like New Age mystery religions, have strived for out-of-body experiences, astral projection, and other metaphysical adventures. There was even a popular U.S. television show called *Crossing Over* where psychic John Edward consulted the dead relatives of audience members.

These people do not comprehend the forces with which they are dabbling. I suppose astral projection may be theoretically possible (but only for the saved, as we shall see). The Apostle Paul, John of Patmos, Isaiah, and Ezekiel are some who had visions and experiences within the heavenly realm. Paul himself admits that he does not know whether his heavenly revelation was a vision in his body or actually traveling in another plane of existence (2 Cor 12:2). The biblically correct use of the fourth dimension is in our prayer life. We should build up and strengthen the spiritual life that we possess in that realm, not for entertainment and adventure, but for the glory of Christ.

In this age, after the ascension of Christ (forty days from his resurrection) or possibly after Pentecost (fifty days from his resurrection), Dead Soul Syndrome has been conquered. Today, upon the new birth, a spiritual entity (the soul/spirit—that third magnitude of man's aspect) is regenerated. It is real. It is a literal force of our being and resides in this fourth dimension, the heavenly spiritual dimension. When Scripture speaks of a new creature (2 Cor 5:17), of being born again (John 3:7), or of being seated in the heavenly realm with Christ (Eph 2:6), it speaks of a reality of existence, not just a favorable status with God, but an actual existence within the fourth-dimensional spiritual realm.

See Eph 2:4b–6: "God, who is rich in mercy, made us alive with Christ even when we were dead in transgressions—it is by grace you have been saved. And God raised us up with Christ and seated us with him in the heavenly realms in Christ Jesus."

Please note—and I am emphatic about this—that unregenerate sinners do not have a sentient force within the fourth dimension. This is the world to which they are dead. This is the world in which they have no understanding. This is the immaterial realm that is exclusive to the believer's incorruptible nature. The unsaved have no share in this vibrant, powerful kingdom. They don't even exist.

Dead Soul Syndrome caused a rip in the fabric of the cosmos. It is the cause of the death of man's spiritual nature, but also it appears to be responsible for the cleaving of the fourth dimension away from the other three. Maybe this is part of the curse on Adam. Today, even with the quickening of the Spirit and our new life in Christ, we still do not have 4-D vision. We live in that world, but it is disjointed. We must wait for the redemption of the cosmos in order to be whole again.

I mentioned earlier that astral projection may be theoretically possible, but only for the saved. This is because the unsaved have no existence in the fourth dimension due to Dead Soul Syndrome. Satanic mediums, New Age clairvoyants, and others who profess to have had these experiences are either lying or deluded. Certainly dreams or mental visions may be satanically inspired, but truly traveling into the fourth astral/spiritual dimension is simply not possible for them. Legitimate saved believers do have a real presence in this astral world, so for them it would be theoretically possible. However, it would be infinitesimally probable, since legitimate saved believers should not be flirting with the world of spirits. The Lord's method of communicating with people is for him to come to us, not for us to go to him. In order for the communion to be successful, God must take the initiative. Christ must be the leader and the instigator.

DESTRUCTION OF THE "UNSEEN" AND "KEYS" TO HEAVEN

In chapter 1, we studied the meaning of the Hebrew word *sheol* and the Greek word *hades*. Although I concluded that they figuratively refer to the grave, literally they mean the unseen world. At the close of Revelation, near the great white throne, John witnesses a preview of the end of this current cosmos and the birth of the new order: Rev 20:14a states, "Then death and Hades were thrown into the lake of fire." The unseen is destroyed in the lake of fire, which is indicative of my point that nothing will remain unseen. All spiritual mysteries will become plainly visible upon that day.

Also, in chapter 7 we reviewed the meaning of the phrase "kingdom of heaven." As Matt 16:19 (KJV) states, "And I will give unto thee the keys of the kingdom of heaven: and whatsoever thou shalt bind on earth shall be bound in heaven: and whatsoever thou shalt loose on earth shall be loosed in heaven."

Keys open doors. Keys provide access from room to room, from area to area. Jesus in this verse is promising to give to Peter and all Christians access to the fourth dimension. They will overcome Dead Soul Syndrome.

THE POWER OF GOD IS IN THE FOURTH DIMENSION

Jesus of Nazareth was born of a virgin and never sinned. He alone of all men did not suffer from Dead Soul Syndrome during his life, except for the last few minutes upon the cross when God turned his back on his only begotten son. Jesus lived for thirty-something years. According to my theory, Jesus had a living soul fully vested in the fourth dimension during his bodily life, which means that he was the first person since Adam's pre-fall days to actually have control and power within the heavenly realm of the fourth dimension. I think Jesus may have been able to see spiritual things; Heaven, God's throne, demons, angels, and the heavenly ark all might have been plainly visible to Christ even before his resurrection. In a couple of verses, Jesus claims that he can see the Father:

John 5:19–20: "Jesus gave them this answer: 'I tell you the truth, the Son can do nothing by himself; he can do only what he sees his Father doing, because whatever the Father does the Son also does. For the Father loves the Son and shows him all he does.'"

John 8:38a (KJV): "I speak that which I have seen with my Father."

During the transfiguration, Jesus holistically merged his physical body with his spiritual body for a temporary period. He allowed his true fourth-dimensional, glorious nature to be manifest to his disciples before the resurrection.

I believe that the fourth dimension is the place from which Jesus received his power. Remember that the success of Jesus over temptation was performed as a man. Certainly, he was God incarnate, but Jesus did what Adam could have done. None of us today are capable of living a totally sinless life (although we can have great victory in the Spirit), because we are born with the consequences of Dead Soul Syndrome as sinners. Jesus Christ, however, was born of a virgin without the corrupted Y-chromosome. He was the second Adam. He triumphantly accomplished where the first Adam had failed. The power for the miracles that Christ performed is readily available in this fourth heavenly realm. As Christians today we have access to this great power. The same power that Jesus used to raise the dead and cast out demons is available to us. However, it is sadly almost entirely untapped, and most of us, myself especially, have barely scratched the surface of the vast spiritual power and victory that could be ours. Someday, I hope very soon, the fourth-dimensional heavenly power will be made manifest for all to dwell within.

In the day of God's choosing, at the end of time, Jesus Christ, who has been authorized and commissioned by his Father, will create a new heaven and a new earth. Premillennial eschatology tells us that this day is after the millennium, with which I tentatively concur. Amillennial eschatology tells us that this day is at the second coming. I have great respect for amillennial thinking; however, on this and kindred subjects, time forbids me to dwell. On this remarkable day, whenever it occurs, heaven and earth will merge together. The fourth dimension and all its magnificent power will become part of our perceived reality.

ENDNOTES

1. North, *75 Bible Questions Your Instructors Pray You Won't Ask*, 193.
2. MacArthur, *Glory of Heaven*, 60.
3. Abbott, Edwin Abbott, *Flatland: A Romance of Many Dimensions* (Mineola, NY: Dover Publications, 1992).

11

The New Physical World

I HAVE MORE TO say about the redemption of the material universe than I had about the redemption and unity with the spiritual universe. The reason is that I am stricken, just like every other human, with three-dimensional understanding. Because of Dead Soul Syndrome, our sight is myopic.

OLD EARTH TO PASS AWAY

Several biblical passages claim that the existing earth will pass away, perish, and be dissolved. They clearly use an element of apocalyptic metaphor, so frequently favored by the Jewish writers. The literary conventions of that day meant that apocalyptic language was used symbolically to emphasize God's dramatic intervention in world affairs. In that sense, heaven and earth will be changed so drastically that they will be like new. This cataclysmic renewal process of God's new order will totally remove the old, sinful world and begin a reign of peace and unity. When God acts to renew creation, all evil and injustice will be swept away, never to return. All of the current institutions and relationships in the world will be radically realigned, so there is no more pain, suffering, enslavement, or exploitation, but rather harmonious participation in the life of God. Paul talks about the liberation of Creation, and he also talks about Christians working to help build up the kingdom of God, which says to me that God does not plan on annihilating the universe. Rather, our good works will have eternal significance. When God tumbles the mountains, lifts up the valleys, throws down the thrones, crushes the enemy in a grape press, and burns the stubble—hopefully you get the picture. We might say today something quite different—like God pulling the plug on the world, turning off the lights, or setting off the bomb. The biblical writers are fond of metaphor, and their frequent use of it is no excuse to deny the reality behind their words, but we must be careful, for neither is it an excuse to always demand pure literalness.

Verses that foretell the passing away of this world are as follows:

Psalm 97:5: "The mountains melt like wax before the LORD, before the Lord of all the earth."

Psalm 102:25–27 (KJV): "Of old hast thou laid the foundation of the earth: and the heavens are the work of thy hands. They shall perish, but thou shalt endure: yea, all of them shall wax old like a garment; as a vesture shalt thou change them, and they shall be changed: But thou art the same, and thy years shall have no end." This verse is also quoted at Heb 1:10–12.

Isaiah 24:19: "The earth is broken up, the earth is split asunder, the earth is thoroughly shaken."

Isaiah 34:4 (KJV): "And all the host of heaven shall be dissolved, and the heavens shall be rolled together as a scroll: and all their host shall fall down, as the leaf falleth off from the vine, and as a falling fig from the fig tree."

Isaiah 51:6: "Lift up your eyes to the heavens, look at the earth beneath; the heavens will vanish like smoke, the earth will wear out like a garment and its inhabitants die like flies. But my salvation will last forever, my righteousness will never fail."

Isaiah 65:17: "Behold, I will create new heavens and a new earth. The former things will not be remembered, nor will they come to mind."

Nahum 1:5–6: "The mountains quake before him and the hills melt away. The earth trembles at his presence, the world and all who live in it. Who can withstand his indignation? Who can endure his fierce anger? His wrath is poured out like fire; the rocks are shattered before him."

Matthew 5:18 (KJV): "For verily I say unto you, Till heaven and earth pass, one jot or one tittle shall in no wise pass from the law, till all be fulfilled."

Matthew 24:35: "Heaven and earth will pass away, but my words will never pass away." See also Mark 13:31 and Luke 21:33.

First John 2:17: "The world and its desires pass away, but the man who does the will of God lives forever."

Second Peter 3:10–13 (KJV): "But the day of the Lord will come as a thief in the night; in the which the heavens shall pass away with a great noise, and the elements shall melt with fervent heat, the earth also and the works that are therein shall be burned up. Seeing then that all these things shall be dissolved, what manner of persons ought ye to be in all holy conversation and godliness, Looking for and hasting unto the coming of the day of God, wherein the heavens being on fire shall be dissolved, and the elements shall melt with fervent heat? Nevertheless we, according to his promise, look for new heavens and a new earth, wherein dwelleth righteousness."

Rev 20:11a (KJV) describes the great white throne judgment, "And I saw a great white throne, and him that sat on it, from whose face the earth and the heaven fled away." Could this be the same day as described above in 2 Pet 3:10?

MAKING OF THE NEW EARTH

Many of the above verses give a strong impression that the old world will completely vanish when it passes away, yet I have attempted to make the point that we as redeemed men and women will live on earth. I have pointed out Scripture references that show the permanence of Jerusalem, the never-ending reign of David's line, the earthly promise to Abraham, and the eternal nature of the glorified body upon the redeemed earth.

Are these verses contradictory? Is the earth to vanish and pass away, or will God remodel it and give it a freshening up? Simply because we admit to the metaphorical language, does that mean that this total destruction is not going to happen? Do the above verses about the passing of earth and the destruction of the heavens mean that God will start from scratch when he creates the new earth?

I pondered this question until a theologian friend from Walsall, England, offered the following:

> I think the answer to this dilemma needs also to take into account the seed from which the whole renewal of creation grows: namely, the resurrection of Jesus. In 1 Corinthians 15, Paul speaks at length of resurrection, applying the fact of Jesus' resurrection to the certainty of its fulfillment in the final resurrection at the end of the age—the time when the last enemy, death, is finally defeated. Paul draws parallels between the resurrection of Jesus (v. 20 ". . . Messiah is risen from the dead, and has become the firstfruits of those who have fallen asleep") and ours.
>
> We need to be aware of at least two features of this: first, Paul addresses a hypothetical objector who asks (v. 35) "How are the dead raised up? And with what body do they come?" Paul's

answer is that it is a foolish question because that which is sown bears no apparent resemblance to that which subsequently grows. The grain that is sown doesn't really tell us what the plant will be like—and yet it is the same entity! The grain has to be buried and to "die" in order for the wheat to grow—and yet it is the same creature! So (I extrapolate) it is with the whole creation. It is the same, but new. It is the same, but unrecognizably different.

Second, Paul implies a narrative taking us back to the law of Jubilee. In vv. 51–53 he says, "Behold, I tell you a mystery: We shall not all sleep, but we shall all be changed—in a moment, in the twinkling of an eye, at the last trumpet. For the trumpet will sound, and the dead will be raised incorruptible, and we shall be changed. For this corruptible must put on incorruption, and this mortal must put on immortality." Whilst Handel's setting of this passage is extremely beautiful and stirring, it might give us the wrong idea of the trumpet. The trumpet in Paul's mind will have been the ram's horn trumpet. And this ram's horn, which is to usher in the day of resurrection, is taken from the ram's horn/trumpet that was to usher in the day of jubilee. On that day the slaves were freed, the properties restored equity and justice re-established, and Israel set to rights. The year of jubilee was the acceptable year of the Lord (Luke 4:17–21, citing Isaiah 61:1–2 [read the rest of the chapter]). That great renewal is seen by Paul (confirmed by his reference to the trumpet) as the ultimate application of Jubilee to the whole creation.

The creation that will emerge from that glorious, cataclysmic event will be the new heavens and the new earth spoken of by Peter. As with Jesus, so with the resurrection, so with the renewal of all things: it is the same but changed. It was the seed; now it is the full-grown plant. The same, but different, transformed, re-made, but grown from what was formerly there. I hope you will agree that this is rather more than "freshening up." There's plenty more that could be said about this, but I hope this little bit helps.[1]

NO MORE SUN, MOON, AND SEA?

Let's review what we know for sure. Our eternal life for the redeemed shall never end. By the power of the Spirit, our human frailty will be regenerated into incorruptible and everlasting glory. The resurrection is "a lively hope" (1 Pet 1:3 KJV) for the dead in Christ. We are promised by the Easter testimony that we, too, will receive a glorified body similar in character to Jesus' new body. Earth shall be our everlasting possession. Alongside Christ, who will reign from Jerusalem, we will live forever on this planet. It is not in heaven, not somewhere else, but right here on earth that we are destined to live. The earth will be reborn into what the apostles and prophets call the new earth. By the power of resurrection, all things will be renewed. This is the very same Spirit of resurrection that had brought Christ out of the grave. The new earth will be glorious, fresh, and immaculate; similarly our glorified bodies will be eternal, incorruptible, and immune from disease. At the redemption of the cosmos, Dead Soul Syndrome will be vanquished. An enosis, or complete merging, between the spiritual world and the physical world will restore our knowledge into perfection. The heavenly realm, spiritual beings, and God's very nature will become plainly visible, just like your own hands in front of your face.

That is the part that we have studied so far. Most of it is biblically grounded. Some of the latter things yet to be are clearly conjectured. Some verses in Scripture are even less readily understandable. These require silence on the part of a wise commentator. Those foolhardy enough, like myself, to attempt to tackle them must acknowledge, as I do now, that my understanding is feeble and my hypothesis may well be overturned shortly. But that is okay. Paul speaks of hidden wisdom in 1 Cor 2:7 (KJV): "But we speak the wisdom of God in a mystery, even the hidden wisdom, which God ordained before the world unto our glory." Paul is, in context, referring to the gospel. God's free offer of salvation was a hidden mystery that was unknown to all of humanity. I will take the liberty of expanding the meaning to include that all hidden wisdom of Scripture has been preordained to bring blessing and glory to Christians. I think the eighth chapter of Proverbs, about Lady Wisdom, would agree. In that vein, we will humbly attempt an insight into some of the most perplexing issues surrounding the new earth. These difficult passages mention that in the new earth there will possibly no longer be a sun, moon, or sea.

Sea

Revelation 21:1: "Then I saw a new heaven and a new earth, for the first heaven and the first earth had passed away, and there was no longer any sea."

Does this literally mean, as it appears at first to say, that there will not be oceans in the new world? That is probably the view of many literal dispensationalists. I hope that they are wrong. Personally, I love to scuba dive, deep-sea fish, and go on cruises. If the new earth literally has no oceans, then I suppose that there would be no coral reefs, no whales, and no surfing at high tide. Currently oceans cover almost three-quarters of the surface area of the planet. I think John is more likely being figurative and symbolic with his vision of no sea in the new earth.

There are two potentially symbolic understandings and one semi-literal understanding that I would like to present with regard to the Revelation statement. However, first we must understand that God's ultimate plan has never been to eliminate this planet and start from scratch in the new world. According to Jesus in Matt 19, all things will be "renewed." According to Paul in Rom 8, the whole creation waits in eager expectation to be liberated from the frustration that it was subjected to by sin. God's plan has always been to restore creation to its pre-fall status. Adam's fall into sin is the "subjection to frustration" that Paul mentions. The earth along with the redeemed will be taken out of the iron furnace of Egypt (Deut 4:20). We are freed from the bondage of sin. Nowhere does the Bible claim that God will eliminate the earth and start over.

The first symbolic theory that I find plausible is that the sea represents chaos, danger, death, and fear. Throughout the Old Testament, the sea is viewed as a fearful place. It is massively vast, so as to lose a man forever in its fathomless depths. It is violent and tumultuous, so as to drown a man in its cresting swells. It is unrelenting in its power, so as to erode and destroy whatever men can build by its billowing waves. The Israelites were not a seafaring people, unlike their neighbors the Phoenicians and Philistines. Israelites descended from Abraham. He was a desert nomad who lived in tents and bred camels. The Mediterranean coast of Israel is very smooth, with no harbors or good anchorage for a navy. I'm sure that had an effect in their lack of sailing experience. Many verses in the Hebrew Bible express this fear of the ocean:

Psalm 65:7: It is God "who stilled the roaring of the seas, the roaring of their waves, and the turmoil of the nations."

Psalm 89:9 (KJV): "Thou rulest the raging of the sea: when the waves thereof arise, thou stillest them."

Isaiah 17:12: "Oh, the raging of many nations—they rage like the raging sea! Oh, the uproar of the peoples—they roar like the roaring of great waters!"

Isaiah 57:20 (KJV): "But the wicked are like the troubled sea, when it cannot rest, whose waters cast up mire and dirt."

Jeremiah 6:23a (KJV): "They shall lay hold on bow and spear; they are cruel, and have no mercy; their voice roareth like the sea." See also Jer 49:23; 51:42; Ezek 28:8.

Jude 1:13a: "They are wild waves of the sea, foaming up their shame." Jude is, of course, in the New Testament. However, he was a Jew (half-brother of Jesus) who probably had the same cultural anxiety about the ocean.

It is possible that what John meant was that there will no longer be any turmoil, chaos, and strife in the new world. He is not really talking about waves and water, but about the emotions that those waves and water bring on. According to this theory, there will still be oceans in the new world. However, there will never again be any death, marooning, shipwrecks, drowning, shark attacks, or other catastrophes to life and limb that these seas cause so mercilessly.

The second symbolic theory has less scriptural and cultural backup, but it ties directly into my theory of Dead Soul Syndrome; so as you can imagine, I like it. The sea represents enormous distances of thousands of miles, causing the separation of people of like faith. By John's time, about A.D. 95, the Diaspora of the Jewish nation encircled the Mediterranean. Jews lived in Spain, Italy, Greece, North Africa, and every point in between. The sea separated them from communication, trade, and fellowship. Likewise, a great spiritual gulf has separated people from God. This is the ripping away of the fourth dimension from perceived reality, so spiritual things are foreign to us.

Ezekiel and John both had visions of heaven. In each of their visions they saw something like a sea underneath the throne of the Almighty. They both likened this expanse to crystal:

Ezekiel 1:22, 26 (KJV): "And the likeness of the firmament upon the heads of the living creature was as the color of the terrible crystal, stretched forth over their heads above.... And above the firmament that was over their heads was the likeness of a throne, as the appearance of a sapphire stone: and upon the likeness of the throne was the likeness as the appearance of a man above upon it." See also Ezek 10:1.

Revelation 4:6: "Also before the throne there was what looked like a sea of glass, clear as crystal."

It appears that Ezekiel of Chebar around 584 B.C. and John of Patmos around A.D. 95 are describing the same thing. With almost seven hundred years between them, the throne of God is still separated from earth by a sea, a firmament, an expanse of what looked like crystal. This theory proposes that the sea of crystal is what Rev 21:1 announces will no longer exist. The sea of crystal is the separation of God and people because of sin. It is the tearing asunder from our grasp the fourth dimension, and the cause is Dead Soul Syndrome. "There was no longer any sea" is figurative of the unity and enosis between heaven and earth that will come about in the restoration by fire. The cosmos will once again remerge, as it had been in Eden, so that God is with us in the flesh, everywhere, all the time, and forever.

I like both of these ideas. I think it is possible that both meanings are conveyed and both will come to fruition with the elimination of the sea. I do not find any scriptural substance to support the wholesale removal of large bodies of saltwater from the new earth. Oceans in and of themselves are not evil. As a matter of fact, God had originally said that they were good (Gen 1:10). I do believe that God frequently implies multiple meanings with his prophetic word. It is entirely possible that the seas will be rebuilt and redesigned to incorporate literally the symbolic truth of the message. This next interpretation is semiliteral, as it really does change the physical nature of the oceans, but does not eliminate them.

Let us start at creation. On the third day of the week (however long that day lasted), God made the oceans. According to Gen 1:9–10, "And God said, 'Let the water under the sky be gathered to one place, and let dry ground appear.' And it was so. God called the dry ground 'land,' and the gathered waters he called 'seas.' And God saw that it was good."

Then on the fifth day God made the sea creatures; Gen 1:20–23 (KJV) states, "And God said, Let the waters bring forth abundantly the moving creature that hath life. . . . And God created great whales, and every living creature that moveth, which the waters brought forth abundantly, after their kind . . . and God saw that it was good. . . . And the evening and the morning were the fifth day."

He declared his creation "good." This was before the fall of mankind. If oceans existed in the perfect world of Eden, then I think they will continue to exist in the restored perfect world of eternity. Instead of literally eliminating the sea, I think the sea will more likely be restored and purified to be gloriously bountiful with all peace and serenity. The seas will no longer be a threat to people for harm, and they will no longer cause separation of friends and loved ones by vast distances.

Geologists and paleogeographers tell us that hundreds of millions of years ago, all of the land mass of the earth was bundled together near the equator into a supercontinent called Pangaea. Scientific evidence for a Pangaea theory is found in the rock sediments of adjacent continents. The eastern coast of South America and the western coast of Africa have strikingly similar matching geological trends. Additional evidence for Pangaea is found in the fossil record. Paleontologists have found identical species in the fossil records of continents that are now great distances apart.

Figure 2 modified from http://commons.wikimedia.org/wiki
/File:Pangaea_continents.svg. Used by permission.

Figure 2 shows the scientific community's idea of how the supercontinent was arranged. It was shaped into a giant letter C. The body of water that was enclosed within the resulting crescent has been named the Tethys Sea. Israel, Iraq, and the entire Middle East area would have been on the south shore of this humongous bay. Part of that area may have been under the sea, as many sea fossils have been found very far inland.

My speculative suggestion is that possibly during the time of the garden of Eden (before the fall), all dry earth was together in a Pangaea-like mass. After the fall—maybe during the flood, or some say possibly in the days of Peleg when "the earth was divided" (Gen 10:25)—massive tectonic movements separated the continents into our current configuration. At the restoration in the end time, at the birth of the new world, the earth will return to a Pangaea-like grouping of all landmasses. Oceans will still exist. Whales, sharks, coral reefs, kelp forests, and oyster beds will be plentiful. However, the sea will no longer be a barrier to separate people from each other. The sea will no longer be an impassable blockage between heaven and earth. The single super-ocean will be calm and gentle, like the tropical South Pacific. Never again will it roar up with ferocity. I look forward to scuba-diving opportunities in this pristine giant aquarium. I am quite sure all of the sea life will be vibrant and lively, yet friendly and nondangerous. I am inclined to believe that the sea will be reconfigured but not superseded.

In conclusion, see Ps 72:8 (KJV): "He shall have dominion also from sea to sea, and from the river unto the ends of the earth." Many of the psalms are messianic. They promise an enduring righteous kingdom in which God will reign forever. This psalm confidently assures us that large bodies of water will still exist in the messianic kingdom of the millennium and eternity.

John's vision is clearly symbolic and maybe also semiliteral. In the new earth, the words of Habakkuk 2:14 (KJV) will come true: "For the earth shall be filled with the knowledge of the glory of the LORD, as the waters cover the sea."

Sun and Moon

Several verses appear to speak of strange celestial behavior during the tribulation, immediately preceding the Parousia. For example, Joel 2:31 (KJV) states, "The sun shall be turned into darkness, and the moon into blood, before the great and terrible day of the LORD come."

Similar Day of Judgment solar/lunar signs and problems are also seen in Isa 13:12; 24:23; Joel 2:10; Ezek 32:7; Hab 2:11; Matt 24:29; Mark 13:24; Luke 21:25; Acts 2:20; Rev 6:12; 8:12. The darkening of the sun and the sanguination of the moon I accept as real and literal miracles preceding the second coming of Jesus. However, these verses are not relevant to our current interest in the possible cessation of these heavenly bodies in the new creation.

Revelation 21:23 (KJV): "And the city had no need of the sun, neither of the moon, to shine in it: for the glory of God did lighten it, and the Lamb is the light thereof."

The penultimate chapter of the New Testament is John's vision of the new Jerusalem. Near the end of the vision, we find this verse. It is very frequently, I believe involuntarily, forced by literalists to mean that the sun and moon will be extinct during the glorious eternity of the new earth. Isn't it ironic that these hyperliteralists envision the expungement of the inanimate sun, moon, and sea, yet they interpret the desperately wicked to remain in God's view for all eternity?

John's statement is clearly in reference to the vision of the new Jerusalem, not in reference to the new earth. These two must not be confused with each other. The new earth is very real—just as real and physical and touchable as the risen, resurrected body of Jesus had been. The new Jerusalem, however, we deal with in an upcoming chapter.

John's language of the ineffective nature of the sun and moon comes from the prophet Isaiah, from whom he borrows without abash. Isa 60:19–20 (KJV): "The sun shall be no more thy light by day; neither for brightness shall the moon give light unto thee: but the LORD shall be unto thee an everlasting light, and thy God thy glory. Thy sun shall no more go down; neither shall thy moon withdraw itself: for the LORD shall be thine everlasting light, and the days of thy mourning shall be ended."

Chapter 60 of Isaiah[2] deals with the millennium, although much of it probably spills over into the new earth. In an upcoming chapter of this book, we learn about the millennial temple as prophesied by Ezekiel. It will be built by the Messiah himself after the second coming. It will become the focal point of global society for one thousand years during a literal reign of Christ on earth. The light of the *shekinah* power of God will be poured into that temple and will be the visible splendor of his glory. As I accept the Messiah's temple as literal and future, I also accept the Messiah's radiance and illumination as literal and future. The entire city of Jerusalem will be flooded with that supernatural light. The photons do not emanate from a mechanical, electrical, or nuclear source—only the glory of God himself, who will then dwell in Israel.

The holy of holies at the temple in Jerusalem is the epicenter of this light. It is exceedingly bright, infinitely brighter than the shining of the sun. The light will be of a certain wavelength that will not cause blindness or squinting when looking directly into its core. Priests, tourists, and businesspeople in the area of Jerusalem will not need sunglasses, as it causes no pain, skin cancer, or retinal damage. John Gill, the eighteenth-century English Baptist, said in *Exposition of the Entire Bible*, which was his magnum opus, "Because of the exceeding brightness, splendour, and lustre of the divine majesty of Christ, who will appear personally among his people, neither sun nor moon will be able to give any light: as the light of a candle is made useless and unnecessary by the light of the sun, so the light of the sun and moon will be made useless and unnecessary by the vastly superior light and glory of Christ."[3] This light is continual, twenty-four-hour, all day and all night. The temple and its surroundings are bathed in light in perpetuity.

This passage may be entirely figurative and symbolic; however, I leave room open for this to be a literal light. Even if literal, I do not interpret this as a global phenomenon. It will be centered on Jerusalem. I'm sure it will be seen for many miles from the city, as Jerusalem is prophesied in Zech 14:10–11; Mic 4:1–2; and Isa 40:4 to be lifted up around the surrounding countryside. In Isa 30:17, Jerusalem is to be a beacon for the nations. These prophecies may be literally fulfilled during the millennium, or at least in the new earth. I can picture Jerusalem lifted up on a pedestal with a bright light pouring from the holy of holies like a lighthouse on the foggy coast of Maine. Even if these prophecies are literal, the light of temple glory would not be visible for more than forty or fifty miles due to the curvature of the earth's surface. Elsewhere on the planet, day and night cycles will continue. During the millennium, I expect night owls to catch mice, flying bats to eat nocturnal moths, and lions to prowl in the dark.

Even when literally understood (which is always my first preference for Scripture interpretation), Rev 21:23 and similar verses do not say that the sun and moon will no longer exist. It only claims that their light is not needed. I think that the sun and moon will continue to bless us with their presence. The planetary orbits of the galactic bodies will remain as they are today. The earth will spin on its axis and move in its orbit.

Here is additional evidence that the sun and moon will not disappear and fade during future eternity:

Psalm 72:5 (KJV): "They shall fear thee as long as the sun and moon endure, throughout all generations."

Psalm 72:7 (KJV): "In his days shall the righteous flourish; and abundance of peace so long as the moon endureth."

Psalm 89:35–37 (KJV): "Once have I sworn by my holiness that I will not lie unto David. His seed shall endure for ever, and his throne as the sun before me. It shall be established for ever as the moon, and as a faithful witness in heaven. Selah."

Jeremiah 31:35–36: "This is what the LORD says, he who appoints the sun to shine by day, who decrees the moon and stars to shine by night, who stirs up the sea so that its waves roar—the LORD Almighty is his name: 'Only if these decrees vanish from my sight,' declares the LORD, 'will the descendants of Israel ever cease to be a nation before me.'"

These verses state that the endurance of the sun and the moon is a type of the endurance of his people. We know that his people will never die out, so I conclude that the sun and moon will never die out either.

ENDNOTES

1. Shakespeare, "What N. T. Wright Really Said."
2. By the way, Isa 60:5 claims that "the wealth on the seas will be brought to you" (Jerusalem), so apparently at this point the oceans still exist.
3. Gill, "Isaiah 60," in *Exposition of the Entire Bible*.

12

Redemptive and Judgmental Fire

In Part 1 of this book, I had a chapter seemingly juxtaposed out of sequence. In chapter 3, we discussed the organically living soul of the believer, even though part 1 was more focused on the fate of the damned. Now, again, I repeat the habit. This second section of the book is interested in the nature of heaven for the redeemed; however, this chapter reverts back in part to the nature of Gehenna. Jesus used the term "Gehenna" in the Gospels as a metaphor for the lake of fire, the place of destruction for the wicked. I use the terms interchangeably. I saved this chapter for now, because it is necessary to understand several things about the spiritual world before delving into the more detailed characteristics of Gehenna. The fourth dimension (I believe) is concomitant and superimposed across our current plane of existence, yet fully invisible. In the resurrection, the spiritual world will merge with the physical world, becoming holistic and full. It will be a hybrid universe of physical and spiritual. In that day, spiritual things will become touchable and tangible, and they will occupy real Euclidean space. Likewise, physical things will become fully ethereal, with mystical powers beyond comprehension. Homogenization with equal measures of body and spirit is the recipe for the new world.

At the birth of the new earth, we are told, it will be purified as gold, silver, and gems are refined. This is the "renewal of all things" that Jesus speaks of in Matt 19:28 and the liberation of "the creation itself" that Paul speaks of in Rom 8:21. It is that to which I eagerly look forward. The earth is made out of rock and dirt, and nothing is intrinsically wrong or bad with dirt. Just like everything else God created, God said that it was good. The soil and stones will by fire be regenerated, along with every good material object made out of them. The creation itself will be redeemed and returned to a pre-fall status. The restored temple will be built during the millennium (an upcoming chapter deals more fully with that), but the temple will endure forever. Likewise, the physical bodies of Christians will last forever in the resurrection. Remember, this is based on the fact, which is our promise, that the glorified body of Christ is the same, but vastly improved, as the physical body that Jesus had had in life. The physical is the seed that is planted; the glorified is the mature tree that springs forth. The tree has the same DNA as the original seed. It is still the same organism, yet incomparably metamorphosed. My point is that there is a continuation of all things. Our world is holistic, not to be discarded and started over. N. T. Wright points out that Jesus promises in Rev 21:5 to "make all things new, not to make all new things."[1]

First Corinthians 3:12–15 (KJV): "Now if any man build upon this foundation gold, silver, precious stones, wood, hay, stubble; Every man's work shall be made manifest: for the day shall declare it, because it shall be revealed by fire; and the fire shall try every man's work of what sort it is. If any man's work abide which he hath built thereupon, he shall receive a reward. If any man's work shall be burned, he shall suffer loss: but he himself shall be saved; yet so as by fire." Others have noted with wisdom that "God's fire will not destroy the whole Earth; it will destroy all that displeases Him."[2]

The day mentioned in verse 13 is the final Day of Judgment. This likely coincides with the Last Judgment spoken of many times in Holy Writ. The analogy in this verse is to a house fire where the occupants are saved, but all of their possessions are lost. The homeowner barely escapes with his life, still smelling of smoke. Jude 1:23 (KJV) says that he may be "pulled out of the fire," and Zech 3:2 (KJV) likens one removed from God's judgment as "a brand plucked out of the fire."

Our actions upon this current earth are not inconsequential. Everything that we build and do now will be tested and purified as it enters into the regeneration. The millennial light of the temple will continue and spill over into the eternal temple of the new earth. All good deeds and processes will not be discarded in the regeneration; they will be heightened and intensified. Good things, actual material objects and products, will survive and be refined like gold by the judgment of God. Our godly actions of helping the poor, sharing the gospel, and even friendly smiles will follow us into eternity. The applicational truth found herein is that our current good deeds, holy thoughts, and productive actions today will follow us into eternity. Instead of destroying and cutting down, we need to build up and strengthen.

Beautiful things like waterfalls in Hawaii and the natural beauty of the Rocky Mountains will be improved, not destroyed. Randy Alcorn and Albert Wolters have suggested that cultural, sociological, artistic, literary, athletic, scientific, and intellectual achievements of humanity such as "the music of Bach and Mozart, the painting of Rembrandt, the writing of Shakespeare, the discoveries of science"[3] will not be lost to fire or destroyed by judgment; instead, they will be given to the regenerated saints, who will rule the new earth as "the stewards, the managers of the world's wealth and accomplishments."[4] Alcorn observes that we will not have to literally reinvent the wheel.[5] The technological advances of mankind will be remembered, and the earth will pick up where she left off. All of the healthy knowledge that humans have accrued over the centuries will be retained in the new world after the purging fire. Just as individuals will not forget their memories nor have their identities erased, so, too, the planet will not forget its history and social achievements. This is feet-on-the-ground theology, viewing the resurrection as more far-reaching then typically understood. Even the inanimate planet Earth is physically resurrected. I find this reasonable and will tentatively concur with the concept, although the details may stretch beyond the direct purview of biblical revelation. N. T. Wright, the scholarly bishop of Durham, for the most part agrees with and recommends Alcorn's book,[6] as do I. My only caveat with Alcorn is that we must be careful not to present a predominantly physical view of the new earth. Our existence will be equally spiritual, with an intimate relationship with God, who is a spirit.

There is a flip side to all of this. God is logically consistent, and our theologies should not self-contradict. Paul clearly states that the wood, hay, and stubble will burn. The bad deeds, products, and evil cultural things will burn up. Selfish behavior, hatred, and similar emotions will be burned like chaff. Bad things—actual physical objects like porn magazines, guillotines, and weapons of mass destruction—will be totally charred by flame and leave no trace. Evil, worthless cultural/sociological achievements like Canaanite altars, Buddhist shrines, and pagan Wicca votive rites will be consumed like hay in this fire. None of these evil objects will exist in the restored new world.

The fire may very well be the same fire as described in 2 Pet 3:10 (KJV), wherein "the elements melt with fervent heat." These worthless objects and practices, Paul says, will be destroyed with fire. In context, the passage of 1 Cor 3:12–15 is speaking of a Christian's actions, but it is indicative of the judgment. Other verses speak of this purification process by fiery judgment:

Deuteronomy 32:22: "For a fire has been kindled by my wrath, one that burns to the realm of death below. It will devour the earth and its harvests and set afire the foundations of the mountains."

Jeremiah 23:28b–29 (KJV): "What is the chaff to the wheat? saith the LORD. Is not my word like as a fire? saith the LORD; and like a hammer that breaketh the rock in pieces?"

Zechariah 13:9: "This third I will bring into the fire; I will refine them like silver and test them like gold. They will call on my name and I will answer them; I will say, 'They are my people,' and they will say, 'The LORD is our God.'"

Malachi 3:2–3 (KJV): "But who may abide the day of his coming? and who shall stand when he appeareth? for he is like a refiner's fire, and like fullers' soap: And he shall sit as a refiner and purifier of silver: and he shall purify the sons of Levi, and purge them as gold and silver, that they may offer unto the LORD an offering in righteousness."

Matthew 3:12 (KJV): "Whose fan is in his hand, and he will thoroughly purge his floor, and gather his wheat into the garner; but he will burn up the chaff with unquenchable fire."

Do you suppose that the porn magazines and other above-mentioned worthless things are utterly *destroyed* in this fire? Are they abolished? Do they become extinct? Are they annihilated and expunged from reality? Or do you suppose that the fire eternally relocates sinful objects, real physical objects, to an unspecified corner of the new cosmos, to burn in this judgmental fire for all eternity?

By now, you probably see where I'm headed. I perceive an inconsistency between the renewal and destructive fire of the judgment with the eternal conscious torment of lost sinners. If the wicked lost anguish forever in Gehenna's flame, then the porn magazines and Buddhist shrines will not be burned up as straw; they will burn, yet never perish.

Alcorn coins the term "Christo-Platonism" for a philosophy that has blended elements of Platonism with Christianity, and "in so doing has poisoned Christianity and blunted its differences from Eastern religions."[7] Christo-Platonists believe that physical things, including our bodies, are an intrinsic liability. Therefore, eternal life will be an exclusively spiritual existence, and all physical matter will be eternally destroyed. Many Evangelical theologians acknowledge a Greek, nonbiblical origin of Christo-Platonism, yet most deny any influence in their own theology. Ironically, many Christians have some deep-rooted elements of it within their own worldview. Christo-Platonism has a strong hold on most Western Evangelical Christians.

THE REALITY OF LAKE OF FIRE

Revelation 20:14–15 states, "Then death and Hades were thrown into the lake of fire. The lake of fire is the second death. If anyone's name was not found written in the book of life, he was thrown into the lake of fire."

We are expressly told that the residents of the lake of fire will suffer a second death. This text is, however, very careful not to flippantly use the words "resurrection," "alive," "life," or other words expressing renewal of vitality. There is a parenthetical comment at Rev 20:5: "The rest of the dead did not come to life until the thousand years were ended." The wicked dead are resurrected and do come to life, but it is of a different nature than the first resurrection and second life awarded to overcomers. The second resurrection is not permanent. The resurrection of judgment is literal and physical, but not eternal or God-breathed.

It says that they "come to life." In a Hebraic perspective, this can only mean bodily resurrection. Resurrection means reanimation. It revolves around the continuity of the same body that had been buried, cremated, or eaten by fish in the sea. Disposal procedures make no difference to an Almighty God. The very same molecular patterns from the first life are reconstructed into the new, resurrected body of the second life. The unsaved dead standing before the great white throne in Rev 20 have physical, real, flesh-and-bone bodies. Their resurrection is similar to ours in that it is real, tangible, and literal. However, it is fundamentally different from ours in that they do not receive incorruptible, imperishable, powerful, glorified bodies. They most likely have a pretty much regular body as it had been at the point of death. I don't need to speculate on all the details here, but it is most definitely *not* a glorified body.

My repeated message has been that the redeemed new world will be holistic: fully spiritual and fully material. These worlds are currently separated by the curse of Dead Soul Syndrome. In the restoration they will be folded back into each other. It is usually the Christo-Platonists who banish the unsaved lost into some metaphysical torment realm of Dante's hell. Realists, like me, understand God to redeem his actual physical creation. He will perfect it and expunge all the flaws. If the new earth is a real, material, physical place (yet fully powerful in the spirit), then so too is the lake of fire, also known as Gehenna, a real, tangible, physical place. The lake of fire must also have a complete spiritual side since Satan is a spirit. Gehenna has actual hot flames and physically resurrected sinners. The flames so clearly described throughout Scripture, I believe, are actual pyrotechnics of fire. As well as being fully physical, they are also fully spiritual flames, because we are told that these can and will destroy bad attitudes, sin, and evil deeds. The second resurrection—out of the sea and graves, to stand before the great white throne—is a resurrection of real bodies with a spiritual nature. If heaven is tangible, then Gehenna is tangible. To spiritualize Gehenna into emotional anguish in a spiritual realm is Christo-Platonism and is self-contradictory with a resurrection theology of the new earth.

In a tangible, real, physical universe, it has been suggested that we may be capable of traveling to other planets. Why not? If now, under the curse, mankind is capable of traveling to the moon, how much farther may we be able to travel when that curse is lifted? This is speculative, but cool. I like it. The entire cosmos, including faraway galaxies and planets, have been created to glorify God and will be ruled by the sons of God. In this new earth/new cosmos, behind which planet would a literal, tangible Gehenna still exist? Would this evil kingdom be off-limits to the saintly kings of the new earth? It requires Christo-Platonism to spiritualize the existence of sinners in some other ethereal realm to suffer eternally.

My conclusion is that if a Bible student takes the resurrection literally and believes in a bodily, physical life (complete with spiritual powers, of course), then believing in a tangible new earth will follow. If a Bible student acknowledges the earthly, eternal life of the redeemed within a real, tangible universe, then the concurrent existence of sinners in Gehenna, who are equally real and tangible, becomes extremely unlikely. Hence, resurrection theology invariably leads to conditional immortality.

WHERE IS GEHENNA LOCATED?

According to my theory, heaven is located right here all around us on earth. There could be an angel standing next to you right now. That angel is in heaven. Heaven is so very close, yet so far away. In the redemption, the three dimensions of reality will reunite in perfect unity be born out of the molten formless void. I definitely want to witness this one.

An interesting couple of verses fit well into this model of Earth being the location for the lake of fire. See 2 Pet 3:7: "By the same word the present heavens and earth are reserved for fire, being kept for the day of judgment and destruction of ungodly men." Read this verse carefully. It plainly says that the destruction of the ungodly is to occur on the present earth.

Malachi 4:1, 3: "'Surely the day is coming; it will burn like a furnace. All the arrogant and every evildoer will be stubble, and that day that is coming will set them on fire,' says the Lord Almighty. 'Not a root or a branch will be left to them. . . . Then you will trample down the wicked; they will be ashes under the soles of your feet on the day when I do these things,' says the Lord Almighty."

The redeemed will literally walk on the ashes of the wicked. The same planet Earth that had been their hell will be transformed into our heaven. The glorious new earth will then become our eternal home with Jesus as King and husband.

ENDNOTES

1. Wright, *Surprised by Hope*, 96.
2. Alcorn, *Heaven*, 128.
3. Wolters, *Creation Regained*, 37. Quoted in Alcorn, *Heaven*, 235.
4. Alcorn, *Heaven*, 223.
5. Ibid., 234.
6. Wright, *Surprised by Hope*, 298.
7. Alcorn, *Heaven*, 459.

13

Removal of the Curse

MAYBE IT IS BY design that chapter 13 is about the curse on humanity due to Adam's sin. Sin has been our unlucky companion since the beginning of civilization. We are promised that this curse will be removed.

Our eternal life will be earthly and terrestrial. Our beautiful planet will be remade by the Creator into perfection. Death and disease will cease. Some people think that "perfection" means no decay, rotting, decomposition, or fermentation. They frequently quote Rom 8:21: "That the creation itself will be liberated from its bondage to decay and brought into the glorious freedom of the children of God." The Greek word *phthora* translated here as "decay" also has the meaning of corruption, destruction, and perishing.

The second law of thermodynamics states that in a closed system entropy always rises. In other words, you could say that decay always increases. Over time, without the work of new energy, an organized system loses its organization. This is the law of the natural universe with which we live. Since the current earth recycles its own deleterious matter, life as we know it would not be possible without the law of decay. Decay allows our intestines to digest our food. Decay allows gardens to absorb nutrients from organic fertilizers. Decay allows mountains to erode into sand. Decay allows the circle of life to pass from one generation to the next, constantly renewing the earth with youth and vigor. Are these cycles to stop in the new earth? Will chemical decay no longer exist? Will deciduous trees no longer drop their leaves? Will death on a bacterial level and even on an animal level cease to operate? Scripture does not claim that the natural cycles of chemical decomposition or death of animals will cease in eternity. This would require a static cosmos, which

I find unlikely. The Creator and Designer of our world appears to prefer extremely complicated and dynamic systems.

In Gen 2:15, God placed Adam in the garden of Eden and told him to work it and take care of it. The implication here is that without Adam's effort, the garden's pristine beauty would deteriorate. I see nothing innately cursed, evil, or wrong with a death cycle and decomposition among minerals, vegetables, and lower animals, which have no sentient life force and cannot die in the biblical sense. Those things are simply resources. Plants and lower animals are renewable resources. They are not said to have the breath of life (Heb. = *nephesh*) or blood in the same sense as vertebrates. By "lower animals," I mean to include bacteria, protozoa, and all invertebrates (such as worms, shrimp, and insects). Death of higher animals, I think, is a direct result of Adam's curse. By "higher animals," I include upper vertebrates such as mammals, birds, and humans, for sure. I am unsure of where fish and reptiles fit.

The last chapter of the Bible—specifically, Rev 22:3a (KJV)—states, "And there shall be no more curse."

Commentators seem to agree what this means. The curse in Gen 3 that was placed upon Adam and Eve and upon the whole earth because of Adam's sin will be removed in the new earth. This curse included sweaty toil by farming to produce food, an abundance of weeds and thistles instead of edible fruit, pain in childbirth, domination of women by men, fear and hatred of snakes, antagonism with Satan, and of course, the mother of all curses: death. The death curse included immediate death of the spiritual nature and eventual physical death of the body. Additionally, it rent the spiritual fourth dimension away from the temporal three-dimensional world.

Although some dispensationalist commentators think that this curse will be removed during the millennium, I disagree (even though I do accept a dispensationalist millennium). I think it will be removed only at the creation of the new earth. A major part of the curse is death. Death will cease to exist only after the final great white throne judgment, which follows the millennium, per Rev 20:14.

Man dwelt in the garden of Eden right after creation. It was a paradise without sin. This paradise was lost by the rebellious and foolish actions of Adam and Eve. In the new world after sin is expunged, it will be paradise regained. I think the new world will be very similar to how Eden had been before the fall, except better. Instead of merely being innocent, it will be redeemed by Divine blood.

Isaiah 51:3: "The Lord will surely comfort Zion and will look with compassion on all her ruins; he will make her deserts like Eden, her wastelands like the garden of the LORD. Joy and gladness will be found in her, thanksgiving and the sound of singing."

My theory is that, before the fall, before Dead Soul Syndrome struck the earth, the world was a four-dimensional place. When Adam walked with God in Eden, it was in full communion and fellowship. Adam transcended all dimensions into the astral plane as a triune being living in a four-dimensional universe. In those early days after creation, Adam could literally see God. Upon the fall, his soul died, and the fourth dimension was separated. With the death of his metaphysical man, the higher planes of existence became invisible and disjunct. They were still there, but Adam was blinded to their existence. This is the full punishment of Dead Soul Syndrome. As a blind man, who just had his eyes put out, he must have been very scared. No wonder he hid himself in fear. Surely, he was trembling with confusion and panic as he tried to sew together fig leaves. Upon that still-future day of God's mighty work, when heaven and earth shall merge, the curse will be purged and removed. In that day, all sin and rebellion will be extinct, and God will be all in all.

NO MORE FARMING OR PREDATION

An interesting part of the curse is that Adam would have to sweat and toil to find his food. After working hard to prepare his fields and gardens, Murphy's Law would bring forth weeds and pests. Farming is going to be hard work.

Genesis 3:17b–19 (KJV): "Cursed is the ground for thy sake; in sorrow shalt thou eat of it all the days of thy life; Thorns also and thistles shall it bring forth to thee; and thou shalt eat the herb of the field; In the sweat of thy face shalt thou eat bread, till thou return unto the ground; for out of it wast thou taken: for dust thou art, and unto dust shalt thou return."

The early chapters of Genesis state that God gave all plants, fruits, and vegetables for food to Adam and all animals. They did not become carnivorous until after the fall.

Genesis 1:29–30: "Then God said, 'I give you every seed-bearing plant on the face of the whole earth and every tree that has fruit with seed in it. They will be yours for food. And to all the beasts of the earth and all the birds of the air and all the creatures that move on the ground—everything that has the breath of life in it—I give every green plant for food.' And it was so."

Genesis 2:9a (KJV): "And out of the ground made the LORD God to grow every tree that is pleasant to the sight, and good for food."

Mankind was not specifically granted meat for food until after the flood in Noah's day.

Genesis 9:3 (KJV): "Every moving thing that liveth shall be meat for you; even as the green herb have I given you all things."

Apparently, before the fall, food was abundant. Adam did not have to plow and cultivate to produce it. Surely there was some management or light-duty work, but not hard, sweaty work. Green plants are almost everywhere. In cities, flowering bushes and trees line the sidewalk. In deserts, sage grass and cactus abound. My own backyard is aflood with plant growth. Hedges surround the house. Trees line the driveway. Carpet grass is under foot. However, even with all of this plant life, precious little of it is edible.

The basic structure of plants is cellulose—the major component of all plants and estimated to be the most common organic compound on earth. Cotton is 91 percent cellulose. Wood is about 42 percent cellulose. On average, about one-third of all plant matter is cellulose. Sticks, leaves, grasses, flowers, roots, and logs are all made in large part of the plant fiber cellulose, which is a long chain of glucose sugar molecules. Glucose is the basic sugar that all animal life relies on for nutrition. The glucose molecules in a cellulose chain, however, are chemically bound together in such a way that humans and all animals do not have the ability to digest it.

From a nutritional standpoint, we call cellulose dietary fiber. It is good for roughage, but is totally indigestible. It simply passes through the gut without any breakdown. Ruminants (cows, sheep, etc.) have a certain symbiotic anaerobic bacterial flora that lives inside their intestines. These bacteria are capable of breaking down cellulose. They (along with fungi and a few protozoa) possess a certain gene that metabolizes an enzyme. The enzyme breaks down the cellulose fiber into glucose. The resultant glucose is then readily digested by the host mammal. Cellulolysis is the name of the process in which cellulose is broken down. Termites have a similar cooperative arrangement with a gut protozoan.

If it were not for these micro-organisms, no animal or insect on earth could digest cellulose. It is biochemically locked, and yet it is the most abundant resource on the planet.

Chris Ashcraft, a biology professor with the Northwest Creation Network, has proposed a theory that man and animals were originally created with the genetic ability to metabolize cellulose.[1] All creatures were originally vegetarians, as Scripture claims. Farming was not needed because every leaf, twig, and blade of grass was potentially lunch. After the fall, part of the curse was the removal of this valuable gene from our DNA. Now only the lowest microbes and fungus can break down plant fiber. Instead, we are cursed to eat starches and simple sugars, which have a different type of chemical bond and are easier to break down into blood glucose molecules. Starches are found in concentrated amounts in cereals, tubers, and some greens. Fruits have lots of simple sugar.

Adam was forced to cultivate wheat, only the kernels of which contain a significant amount of starch. The rest of the wheat grass is inedible cellulose. It is waste, only to be turned under by the plowman for decomposition by microbes. Adam may have planted an orchard with peach trees. Less than 0.1 percent of the biomass of the tree is edible, and those fruit only appear in seasonal spurts. Wildlife, too, lost the gene, and instead of eating green grasses, God altered their diets and dental work to eat each other. Many species turned to predation and developed carnivorous appetites.

In the new earth, part of the removal of the curse as promised by Rev 22:3, I think, will be the restoration of the cellulolysis-inducing gene. Addition of this bacterial gene to our chromosomes will eradicate hunger and starvation. No animal or person will ever again be without food. The most abundant energy source in the world will be unlocked for consumption. All higher animals will once again return to their Edenic vegetarian state. Scripture specifically promises this.

Isaiah 65:25 (KJV): "The wolf and the lamb shall feed together, and the lion shall eat straw like the bullock: and dust shall be the serpent's meat. They shall not hurt nor destroy in all my holy mountain, saith the LORD."

Isaiah 11:7 (KJV): "And the cow and the bear shall feed; their young ones shall lie down together: and the lion shall eat straw like the ox."

Have you ever heard the expression, "The lion shall lay down with the lamb"? It brings to mind the vision of a helpless newborn lamb sweetly nestled into the side of a powerful lion's big shaggy mane. It has become a popular image that has filtered into pop culture and that resonates in our mind. Unfortunately, it is not in the Bible. Let's read Isa 11:6 (KJV): "The wolf also shall dwell with the lamb, and the leopard shall lie down with the kid; and the calf and the young lion and the fatling together; and a little child shall lead them."

Even though the imagery is incorrectly juxtaposed, it causes no damage to the meaning of the prophecy.

Some Bible teachers have suggested that the lion eating straw (which represents a return to vegetarianism) and the dwelling together of the wolf and the lamb (which represents the cessation of predation) all occur during the millennium, but I find some particular Bible verses that stand as a refutation to such an idea. Remember, these concepts go hand in hand with Adam's curse to farm, toil, and sweat.

Amos 9:13a (KJV): "Behold, the days come, saith the LORD, that the plowman shall overtake the reaper, and the treader of grapes him that soweth seed." This verse means that the bounty of the agricultural harvest will be so ridiculously abundant during a future promised period (the millennium) that the reaper of grain and the people treading grapes to make wine won't be able to harvest the entire crop before springtime when it is season again to plow and sow. Imagine a field with so much wheat that farmers don't have enough time to get it all into the barns before spring, when it is time to start all over again. This is a millennial promise of bounty and productivity. However, it still requires hard work of sowing, reaping, threshing, and milling. This is not yet the Edenic state wherein farming is obsolete.

Isaiah 2:4a: "He will judge between the nations and will settle disputes for many peoples. They will beat their swords into plowshares and their spears into pruning hooks." This verse promises peace and prosperity during Israel's Golden Age. It also clearly says that, during the millennium, plowing and pruning—in other words, farming and sweating—will still be needed in order to put food on the table during the glorious reign of the Messiah.

In the new world to be created, the sweat and savagery of this natural world will not be present. This cessation of carnivorous behavior has further implications for temple worship in the new earth, which we shall address soon.

CURSE OF BABEL

Another curse was pronounced upon humanity in Gen 11. The proud men of early Babylon tried to build a city and tower to reach heaven. The tower of Babel was probably an early ziggurat with an impressive spire. The real problem was the haughty and conceited spirit of the architects and builders. They wanted to make a name for themselves with a famous landmark. The sin of pride is indicative of the Babylonian system. Still today, pride is the stereotypical feature of the world's Babylonish system. The curse with which God affected all people is the diversity and confounding of languages. The result was chaos and a cacophony of noise without comprehension. The inability to communicate stifled the work progress and cooperation. It turned into a requiem of misunderstanding. From there the nations were dispersed. It is very probable that this curse will also be reversed in the creation of the new world order.

Zephaniah 3:9 (KJV): "For then will I turn to the people a pure language, that they may all call upon the name of the LORD, to serve him with one consent."

Some Bible teachers say that the miracle at Pentecost in Acts 2 was the fulfillment of Zephaniah's prophecy. During that momentous festival, Jews from many foreign nations were able to understand Peter's speech in their own language. I think Pentecost may be the firstfruits of fulfillment, but it was not the final and total removal of the communication barrier.

Some have speculated that before Babel the original language of men was Hebrew, and that after the curse removal, the universal language will once again be Hebrew. הַלְלוּיָהּ (Hallelujah.)

In the new earth, I expect to be able to communicate freely with brother and sister saints from all regions, all nations, and all centuries of time. I hope that there will still be cultural variety. I greatly enjoy ethnic foods and music. Differing cultural traditions make for an interesting and multifaceted world. God is the creator of thousands of different varieties of wildflowers, insects, and galaxies. It appears that God, too, enjoys great variety. So, I think cultural and ethnic variety of people may remain, but language will be unified. The ability for all of the redeemed to pray together, rejoice together as a choir, and worship God together in harmony will greatly glorify his Holy Name throughout eternity.

NEW EARTH CONCLUSION

Deuteronomy 29:29 says that the secret things belong to the Lord our God. The exact details of what the new earth will be like, I do not claim to know. The last couple of chapters have been heavy with speculation. An excellent note at the end of the NIV Study Bible from which many of my Scripture quotes are taken says, "The Bible devotes much less space to describing eternity than it does to convincing people that eternal life is available as a free gift from God."[2] I must admit my own dubious hermeneutical endeavors, for we are engulfed within a sea of unanswerable questions. Instead of obtaining any dogmatic answers, I hope to provide only a hint of what the future may hold.

What I know for sure is that God has anointed us with the oil of joy (Heb 1:9) and that the splendor of this new world will be tremendous. I praise God that, just like the small church in ancient Colossae, we, too, have been qualified to share in the inheritance of the saints in the kingdom of light (Col 1:12).

ENDNOTES

1. Ashcraft, "Designed to Eat Plants Then Cursed to Be Unable."
2. *Life Application Study Bible*, "What We Know about Eternity," 2333.

14

Ezekiel's Temple

IN THE CLOSING PASSAGE of Ezekiel, chapters 40–48, the prophet describes the temple and the renewed priestly system of the restored Jerusalem. As the passage is nine chapters long, it is too lengthy to repeat here. I would suggest that you read it—in its entirety and in context—before continuing with this study. Until you have read that passage, do not read past the break below. That's right, put my book down and read your Bible. Use whichever translation of Scripture you prefer; the God of the universe is not bound or confined to a particular human language or dialect of any century.

Theologians have debated for decades whether this vision is literal or symbolic.[1] Premillennialists believe in an earthly kingdom—a Golden Age, as expected by the early Jews—to be ruled by the Messiah Jesus within our current cosmic system. This millennial age will occur before "the renewal of all things," as prophesied by Jesus in Matt 19:28 and before the "elements melt with fervent heat," as expected in 2 Pet 3:12. During this millennial time, sin, sickness and death will still exist; however, they will be in remission due to the righteous government and rule of the world. Humans will be born and will die. Lions will kill and eat antelopes. The sun will rise and fall. The moon will continue to shine over the night skies. The oceans will still encompass the separate continents, just as they do today. Some of this will (probably) ultimately change in the new earth. The millennium, however, will be the regular world as we know it, albeit greatly improved. The millennium, however, is *not* the topic of my study, but we must touch on it here to understand the differences between the millennial state and the eternal state. Additionally, this will set the stage for the next chapter on the new Jerusalem.

Ezekiel 40:2–4 states, "In visions of God he took me to the land of Israel and set me on a very high mountain, on whose south side were some buildings that looked like a city. He took me there, and I saw a man whose appearance was like bronze; he was standing in the gateway with a linen cord and a measuring rod in his hand. The man said to me, 'Son of man, look with your eyes and hear with your ears and pay attention to everything I am going to show you, for that is why you have been brought here. Tell the house of Israel everything you see.'"

As I have mentioned, my eschatology is of a historically premillennial and moderately dispensational persuasion. I also like to always read the Bible at face value and interpret words as normally as possible. In childlike faith we must simply take the word of God for what it says and rest upon the clear, normal, obvious meanings. This requires a literal interpretation, unless the context is impossibly hyperbolic. We must study all Scripture in context with itself. Picking out a verse and claiming that it must be literal, without reading dozens of others, is equally poor scholarship. We recognize that Bible writers frequently used figurative language, probably more frequently than we do today. This is a picturesque way of portraying the truth, and it is a problem for some literalists. They hate to give up ground on anything, and will occasionally stick to a literal interpretation even when the text clearly says, or common sense requires, a metaphorical meaning. As with most things in life, there is a middle ground between the extremes. This is where I stand.

There are at least six major interpretations for the temple passage found in Ezekiel's book. In order to review each possibility I have designed an identification key. In biology this would be called a dichotomous key, or sequential key, because each question point branches into two possibilities. Keys are common for bird, tree, and insect identification. This theological key also consists of couplets, or pairs of opposite descriptive statements. To use this key, start at the first lead and read the two statements. Decide which statement best describes your belief about the temple vision of Ezekiel. The note will direct you toward the next lead number to follow. Repeat the procedure until your doctrine is identified.

EZEKIEL'S TEMPLE: THEOLOGICAL DICHOTOMOUS KEY

1a The temple passage in Ezekiel is not inspired.

-ID=Secular. The most unbiblical doctrine would be that it is crazy nonsense that has no real meaning for us. It was written while the exiled prisoner was high on opium and heavily depressed about the recent destruction of his homeland. This is actually a common belief. However, since this present book is geared toward individuals of faith, I'm not even going to offer a reply to this objection. We pray that the Holy Spirit will tug at the heartstrings of people so impressed.

1b The temple passage in Ezekiel is God breathed. Continue to #2.

2a The passage is not literal and real, but is a parable or allegory.

-ID=Symbolic Vision. This is a legitimate theory. It is most commonly found among Reformed, Catholic, and most amillennialist theologians. They argue that the passage is a metaphoric figure of speech and never meant to be taken literally. The belief usually claims that the entire vision is symbolic of our Christian life and walk with Christ. The problem is that the passage is clearly addressed to Israel in 40:4 and again in 43:10. If it is meant to be symbolic, I have absolutely no idea what the details are supposed to mean.

2b The passage is literal and real. Continue to #3.

3a The temple is literal and real, but in a spiritual dimension, not on earth.

-ID=Spiritual Reality. This gnostic theory is that the temple's existence will be in heaven and our fellowship with Christ will be in some other dimension. We have previously discussed this and shown the non-scriptural basis. Our promise is on earth.

3b The temple is physically literal and real on earth. Continue to #4.

4a The text is a remembrance of the first temple that Solomon built.

-ID=Solomon's Memory. It was designed to preserve the Levitical heritage for a new generation of Israelites born in captivity. However, there are numerous contradictions between Ezekiel's temple and Solomon's temple as recorded in 1 Kgs 5—8 and 2 Chr 2—7.

4b In Ezekiel's day, the text was prophetic. Continue to #5.

5a The vision has now been fulfilled in the second temple.

-ID=Nehemiah's Charge. The passage provided a literal construction plan for the rebuilding of the temple by the returning exiles seventy years later. However, similar to above, there are significant differences in architectural dimensions, construction details, and priestly regulations with that of the second temple. Additionally, God says in 43:7 that his people will never again defile his name. That certainly did not happen.

5b The vision is still prophetic today. Continue to #6.

6a Ezekiel's temple will be fulfilled in the eternal state of the new earth.

-ID=New Earthly Vision. This theory is bolstered by the use of such terms as "forever," and "a lasting covenant." It is well noted that Christ's reign will not cease after the thousand years expire. A serious problem with this theory is the existence of death, sin, widows, disputes, and uncleanliness (chap. 44) within the eternal situation.

6b Ezekiel's temple will be fulfilled in the millennium.

-ID=Millennial Vision. My preferred view. It satisfies all of the conditions of the text.

The only theory above in opposition to the millennial theory that I can see as plausible is the argument for a symbolic vision. It is agreed that Ezekiel contains a number of parables, analogies, similes, and such (chaps. 15—17; 23—24; 34; 37). These passages are by intent meant to be understood figuratively. In 15:6, Jerusalem is as a worthless piece of wood to be burned in the fire. In chapter 16, she is an adulterous wife prostituting with strangers. In chapter 17, God says, "Set forth an allegory and tell the house of Israel a parable" about two eagles and a vine. Two adulterous sisters are described in chapter 23, then verse 4 identifies them as Samaria and Jerusalem. Chapter 24 compares the coming destruction of Jerusalem to a cooking pot charring on a raging fire. In chapter 34, there is a scathing judgment against shepherds and sheep, yet it is universally accepted as really being against the national leaders and the people. One last example clearly exists in the vision of dry bones in chapter 37. Fortunately, the text tells us in verse 11 that these bones are symbolically representing the house of Israel.

Randall Price, archaeologist and biblical historian, notes that the temple of Ezekiel's "text is crucial to futurism because if literal interpretation fails with respect to this prophecy, then there is no reason to insist on a literal interpretation of any Old Testament prophecy, including messianic prophecy, which is an inseparable part of the restoration prophecies."[2]

There are no literary clues that the temple vision is meant to be symbolic or parabolic. If it is, then it is anyone's guess as to what it is supposed to mean; it is never explained or clarified. The description of the temple toured by Ezekiel in chapters 40—48 is very detailed, and I believe it is a literal description of the restored temple to be built in Jerusalem during the millennium. Ezekiel is told to write down everything and to tell the house of Israel everything that he sees (40:4). He recounts measurements taken by the angel of bronze of the gates, alcoves, porches, courtyards, stairs, interior rooms, and every aspect of the physical building in chapters 40—42. Because Ezekiel is himself a Levitical priest, he is very familiar with and interested in the details of temple construction. These details are ignored as irrelevant or meaningless by the symbolic school. However, in chapter 43, we are given the reason that all of this detail is provided:

Ezekiel 43:10-11: "Son of man, describe the temple to the people of Israel, that they may be ashamed of their sins. Let them consider the plan, and if they are ashamed of all they have done, make known to them the design of the temple—its arrangement, its exits and entrances—its whole design and all its regulations and laws. Write these down before them so that they may be faithful to its design and follow all its regulations."

God wants the rebellious house of Israel to repent and to follow this design. Build it, do it, obey it. This is strong evidence for a literal construction of a temple complex. Such a temple was not built under the return with Nehemiah, nor did Herod's expansions fulfill this passage. If literal, it must still be future.

All of the measurements recorded by Ezekiel are normal dimensions, generous but reasonable. All of the construction materials are of wood and stone; these are normal components and even used today—again, further evidence for a literal building. When compared to the new Jerusalem in Rev 21, it should be noted that the new Jerusalem is of ridiculous dimensions and of unearthly materials. That should be the first clue that the eternal city is not literal.

Ezekiel 41:4: "And he measured the length of the inner sanctuary; it was twenty cubits, and its width was twenty cubits across the end of the outer sanctuary. He said to me, 'This is the Most Holy Place.'"

In this verse, the bronze angel and Ezekiel enter into the holy of holies. It is separated with a wall and doors (41:23) instead of a curtain. Again, this is evidence that if the temple is literal, it must be a future temple program because we know that in historic temples the holiest place was separated from the holy place with a curtain (Exod 26:33; 40:3; 2 Chr 3:14; Matt 27:51; Heb 9:3). Apparently, there is no problem with Ezekiel, who was not the high priest, entering the most holy place. I suppose this is because, during the millennium, Christ will reign as king and priest. There is no comment about seeing the ark. It will not be present during this period according to Jer 3:16. Maybe the holy of holies will serve as the throne room for His Majesty Jesus.

CUBITS OR REEDS?

Ezekiel 42:15-20: "When he had finished measuring what was inside the temple area, he led me out by the east gate and measured the area all around: He measured the east side with the measuring rod; it was five hundred cubits [KJV, reeds]. He measured the north side; it was five hundred cubits [KJV, reeds] by the measuring rod. He measured the south side; it was five hundred cubits [KJV, reeds] by the measuring rod. Then he turned to the west side and measured; it was five hundred cubits [KJV, reeds] by the measuring rod. So he measured the area on all four sides. It had a wall around it, five hundred cubits [KJV, reeds] long and five hundred cubits wide, to separate the holy from the common."

The measurements of the entire temple compound are given here. The Masoretic Hebrew text uses five hundred "reeds," as the KJV accurately translates. However, the Septuagint, translated in 250 B.C. and widely used during the time of Christ, uses five hundred "cubits." Which one is correct? If you are looking for a literal interpretation, we must agree with the Greek. The Septuagint is almost one thousand years older than the Masoretic text and makes common sense for a literal interpretation. A temple compound of five hundred cubits square would be about seventeen acres, a perfectly normal dimension. The current Temple Mount is about thirty-five acres.

If the KJV is correct in the reading of five hundred reeds, then we have a problem. The reed refers to the measuring rod stick held by the angel. Ezekiel 40:5 tells us that one reed equals six big cubits. The measuring rod that he was using was about ten feet long. This would yield a temple complex of about seven hundred acres—over one mile square.

Certainly this is larger then the entire ancient city of Jerusalem. A mile across the courtyard would be ridiculous. The Nazarites cutting their hair, the woodshed/oil storage, and the other corner kitchens would be impractically far away. When carried forward to the measure of the city walls (48:30–35 specifies forty-five hundred units) and the measure of the sacred territory surrounding the city, called the Oblation (45:1 specifies twenty-five thousand units), using the rod as the unit becomes silly. As a matter of fact, it is contradictory. Twenty-five thousand reeds multiplied by twenty thousand reeds would be a rectangle about fifty miles by forty miles for the sacred territory (not counting the tribes). This does not even fit within the boundaries of the promised land as specified by Ezekiel himself in 47:18, 20. "On the east side the boundary will run between Hauran and Damascus, along the Jordan between Gilead and the land of Israel, to the eastern sea and as far as Tamar. This will be the east boundary. . . . On the west side, the Great Sea will be the boundary to a point opposite Lebo Hamath. This will be the west boundary." The distance from the Jordan River to the Mediterranean Sea is only about forty miles. This is the entire land of Israel; there would be no room left for the "portion for the prince," or for tribal allotments, as directed in chapter 48. Modern translations have referenced the ancient Septuagint, which the apostles themselves used, and corrected this mistake. The proper, logical, and literal unit of measure is the big cubit, as defined in 40:5.

RETURNING GLORY TO DWELL AND ANIMAL SACRIFICES

Ezekiel 43:2, 4–5, 7a: "And I saw the glory of the God of Israel coming from the east. His voice was like the roar of rushing waters, and the land was radiant with his glory. . . . The glory of the LORD entered the temple through the gate facing east. Then the Spirit lifted me up and brought me into the inner court, and the glory of the LORD filled the temple. . . . He said: 'Son of man, this is the place of my throne and the place for the soles of my feet. This is where I will live among the Israelites forever. The house of Israel will never again defile my holy name.'"

The *shekinah* glory of God returns to this temple and will from now on dwell among the Israelites forever. *Shekinah* means dwelling. This dwelling of God also occurred in the tabernacle of the wilderness with Moses. Solomon's temple was overpowered by the dwelling presence of God, and the priests had to stop ministering due to the smoke and fire. This passage seems to remove any possibility that the prophecy has been literally and historically fulfilled in the second temple. Ezekiel was written about 570 B.C. during the Babylonian exile. The second temple was finished about 130 years later. Certainly Nehemiah and Zerubbabel would have been familiar with the prophet of Chebar. However, it is recognized that the *shekinah* glory never rested upon that structure. God did not personally reign from there as king, and obviously Israel continued to defile God's holy name after that second temple had been built. I safely assume that these prophecies were not fulfilled during the Second Temple period, and have not been fulfilled yet as of today.

Yet even while the millennial temple is the dwelling for the very presence of God, bloody animal sacrifices are said to continue. This is powerful evidence for a pre–eternal state earthly millennium, but the question needs to be addressed: why sacrifice animals when Christ was the ultimate sacrifice?

Ezekiel 43:18: "Then he said to me, 'Son of man, this is what the Sovereign LORD says: These will be the regulations for sacrificing burnt offerings and sprinkling blood upon the altar when it is built.'" He goes into quite a bit of detail with young bulls and male goats without defect as a sin offering, and exactly how to smear blood on the horns of the altar.

Ezekiel 46:13: "Every day you are to provide a year-old lamb without defect for a burnt offering to the LORD; morning by morning you shall provide it." It is undeniable that animal sacrifices will occur in this temple. This has been the most disconcerting reason, why some people feel that this is not a literal future temple. They correctly point to Heb 7:27: "Unlike the other high priests, he does not need to offer sacrifices day after day, first for his own sins, and then for the sins of the people. He sacrificed for their sins once for all when he offered himself." The same thought goes all the way through the book of Hebrews (see also Heb 9:12, 26–27). The old covenant is discarded. The new covenant is better. There are no more sacrifices for sin. Jesus was it once and for all. Because of this, many Christians believe that the Ezekiel passage must be non-literal and symbolic. They feel that actual sacrifices would be unnecessary bloodshed, possibly even blasphemous and sacrilegious. They believe that it would demean the work of God upon the cross of Calvary.

However, if you're reading the book of Hebrews, you also need to read 10:1–4: "The law is only a shadow of the good things that are coming—not the realities themselves. For this reason it can never, by the same sacrifices repeated endlessly year after year, make perfect those who draw near to worship. If it could, would they not have stopped being offered? For the worshipers would have been cleansed once for all, and would no longer have felt guilty for their sins. But those sacrifices are an annual reminder of sins, because it is impossible for the blood of bulls and goats to take away sins."

Even during the original temple and Aaronic days, animal sacrifices never provided for the forgiveness of sins. They never postponed any sins; the animal blood didn't really *do* anything. They were always, and will be in Ezekiel's future temple, symbolic of Christ's true redemption. Only faith in God brings salvation. Forgiveness is always a gracious gift, even during the Israelite dispensation of the Old Testament. Way back in Gen 15:6 it says that Abram believed God, and it was counted unto him for righteousness.

Dr. John Whitcomb, OT scholar and creationist author, points out, "It is a serious mistake, therefore, to insist that these sacrifices will be expiatory."[3] Expiatory means to extinguish. Animal sacrifices never extinguished sin. They never put an end to or atoned for sin. They were only a reminding ritual. They were performed out of obedience to God, who commanded them as a symbol pointing toward Jesus.

The only real difference in the historic sacrificial system and those of the millennium is the tense of the expectation for the Messiah. In Aaronic days, Israel waited for the sometimes not-so-well-understood promise of cleansing and atonement that the sacrifices so clearly embodied. During the millennium, righteous Israel will, with the benefit of 20/20 hindsight, remember Christ's death as the true reality of atonement.

The millennium has long been recognized as a dispensational period where God's physical, temporal promises to Israel are fulfilled. After the second coming (or rapture, depending on your preferred eschatology), the age of the Gentiles will be complete. The millennial age is a time of focus upon Israel; rightly it would include a context of distinctive Israelite worship. In Ezek 44:9, circumcision in both heart and flesh is referenced as a requirement. Festival of Tabernacles (45:25), Passover (45:21), and New Moons and Sabbaths (45:17) will be observed. These items are further evidence of a dispensational millennium wherein the Jewish protocol is the order of the day.

John Walvoord, the chancellor of Dallas Theological Seminary, has said, "Though it is objectionable to some to have animal sacrifices in the millennial scene, actually, they will be needed there because the very ideal circumstances in which millennial saints will live will tend to gloss over the awfulness of sin and the need for bloody sacrifice. The sacrifices offered will therefore be a reminder that only by the shedding of blood and, more specifically, the blood of Christ, can sin be taken away. Ezekiel was not alone in referring to a sacrificial system in the Millennium (cf. Isa. 56:7; 66:20–23; Jer. 33:18; Zech. 14:16–21; Mal. 3:3–4). The prophets therefore seem to be united in referring to literal sacrifices in connection with a literal temple in the Millennium."[4]

In conclusion, I believe that bloody animal sacrifices will occur in the millennial temple. That's okay, because they are a memorial, a remembrance of Christ. In our own day we take the cup of communion. The wine is said to be the blood of Jesus. We do not think of ourselves as vampires drinking human blood, because we understand the symbolism behind the ritual. The wine of the Eucharist is a memorial to the blood of Christ under a Christian framework. Animal sacrifices will be a very similar idea under a millennial Jewish framework.

WHO IS THE "PRINCE"?

There is a man who rules Israel called the prince. He is mentioned in chapters 44—46 and 48. There has been a lot of speculation as to his identity. One possible candidate is that the prince is King David himself resurrected in a glorified body.

Several scriptural verses appear to say this.

Ezekiel 34:23–24 (KJV): "And I will set up one shepherd over them, and he shall feed them, even my servant David; he shall feed them, and he shall be their shepherd. And I the LORD will be their God, and my servant David a prince among them; I the LORD have spoken it."

Ezekiel 37:24–25 (KJV): "And David my servant shall be king over them; and they all shall have one shepherd: they shall also walk in my judgments, and observe my statutes, and do them. And they shall dwell in the land that I have given unto Jacob my servant, wherein your fathers have dwelt; and they shall dwell therein, even they, and their children, and their children's children for ever: and my servant David shall be their prince for ever."

Hosea 3:5: "Afterward the Israelites will return and seek the LORD their God and David their king. They will come trembling to the LORD and to his blessings in the last days."

Jeremiah 30:9: "Instead, they will serve the LORD their God and David their king, whom I will raise up for them."

Ezekiel 44:3 tells us that the prince will eat meals in the gatehouse of the temple. No other people are allowed to be there; this is quite an exclusive privilege just for the prince. He is not eating inside the temple, and certainly not in the throne room of the holiest place. The prince is only in the gatehouse. So it is not referring to the Messiah, who would be eating in a much higher-status location than a gatehouse at the periphery of the temple compound. The prince of the millennium is definitely a man and not the Messiah. Further evidence that this cannot be Jesus is found in 45:22: "The prince is to provide a bull as a sin offering for himself and for all the people of the land." Jesus would not be making a sin offering for himself. But then again, neither would the resurrected David, for Paul says in 1 Cor 15 that our bodies will be incorruptible and without sin.

For this reason, I tend to think that the prince is a regular human mortal son (not resurrected and glorified). He is a descendant of David who will be born during this period. On this point, I remain uncertain.

PRIESTS IN THE TEMPLE

Ezekiel 44:10–16: "The Levites who went far from me when Israel went astray and who wandered from me after their idols must bear the consequences of their sin. They may serve in my sanctuary, having charge of the gates of the temple and serving in it; they may slaughter the burnt offerings and sacrifices for the people and stand before the people and serve them. But because they served them in the presence of their idols and made the house of Israel fall into sin, therefore I have sworn with uplifted hand that they must bear the consequences of their sin, declares the Sovereign LORD. They are not to come near to serve me as priests or come near any of my holy things or my most holy offerings; they must bear the shame of their detestable practices. Yet I will put them in charge of the duties of the temple and all the work that is to be done in it. But the priests, who are Levites and descendants of Zadok and who faithfully carried out the duties of my sanctuary when the Israelites went astray from me, are to come near to minister before me; they are to stand before me to offer sacrifices of fat and blood, declares the Sovereign LORD. They alone are to enter my sanctuary; they alone are to come near my table to minister before me and perform my service."

Ezekiel 44:10–16 speaks of the resurrection. These priests will live again. Some of the sinful, idolatrous Levites who had lived during Israel's monarchy and temple period will apparently be saved. I'm sure that there will also be some wicked Levites who do not receive part in this resurrection, but some at least are resurrected to life in the first resurrection, to live and work in the kingdom of the Messiah. Those who had defiled themselves with idolatry will serve in menial capacities, but I'm sure that with resurrected, glorified bodies (as we have already seen) they will be perfectly happy, immortal, sinless, and incorruptible. Also raised from the dust are those descendants of Zadok who remained pure during the time when Israel went astray. Zadok was made high priest in the days of Solomon. He had always remained loyal to David, Solomon's father. Hundreds of years later, some of Zadok's descendants remained holy to Yahweh, even while the rest of the nation was mired in idolatry. Even during the most apostate periods, God always retains a remnant for himself. They will receive a higher calling in their glorified bodies.

All of these priests mentioned are actual, literal, historic men, or possibly contemporaries of Ezekiel. By the time of the millennial temple, they will have been long dead, about twenty-five hundred years and counting. But in this temple, they live. This is confirming evidence that Ezekiel's temple is yet future. It must be after the resurrection, which occurs at Christ's appearance (1 John 3:2).

Alongside these resurrected and glorified ancient priests and Levites will also be regular mortal humans, who continue to live and breed during the millennium. Toward the end of Ezek 44 are several commands given to the priests that mark this period as millennial. It cannot be the eternal state.

Ezekiel 44:22: "They must not marry widows or divorced women; they may marry only virgins of Israelite descent or widows of priests." In Matt 22:30, Jesus says that in the resurrection, glorified people will not marry at all, but be nonsexual, as the angels. So at least some of these priests in Ezekiel must still be unglorified humans who are marrying. This is not the eternal state.

Ezekiel 44:24a: "In any dispute, the priests are to serve as judges and decide it according to my ordinances." As we will be like Christ, there will be no disputes in the new earth of eternity. All will have the mind of God. These disputes are clearly happening after the resurrection but before the eternal state. This fits with the dispensational doctrine of the millennium.

Ezekiel 44:25: "A priest must not defile himself by going near a dead person; however, if the dead person was his father or mother, son or daughter, brother or unmarried sister, then he may defile himself." There will be no such thing as death in the eternal state, according to Rev 21:4. So this must be millennial.

Ezekiel 44:29a: "They will eat the grain offerings, the sin offerings and the guilt offerings." Since there will be no sin in the eternal state of the new world order, there will be no need for sin offerings. After the millennium is complete in the new world of eternity, the temple will continue, but the animal sacrifices will cease. We will more fully explain this shortly.

Ezekiel 44:30 (KJV): "And the first of all the firstfruits of all things . . . shall be the priest's: ye shall also give unto the priest the first of your dough, that he may cause the blessing to rest in thine house." Tithing will be reinstituted to support the Levitical priesthood, as it had been in antiquity. This is very much an Israelite custom, with which we are not involved during our current age of the Gentiles. Unfortunately, some Christian preachers like to make you think that you are still obliged to tithe.

Ezekiel 44:31 (KJV): "The priests shall not eat of any thing that is dead of itself, or torn, whether it be fowl or beast." Again, this is further evidence for an occurrence on the regular earth of today during the millennium. This is referring to a time period before the cessation of death, and before the herbivorization of all animals.

Many Christians today deny the literal nature of Ezekiel's temple passage. They claim it is allegorically speaking of our Christian walk. These verses make absolutely no sense when one attempts to interpret them as a symbolic, nonliteral parable.

RIVER FROM THE TEMPLE

Ezekiel 47:1–2, 8–10: "The man brought me back to the entrance of the temple, and I saw water coming out from under the threshold of the temple toward the east (for the temple faced east). The water was coming down from under the south side of the temple, south of the altar. He then brought me out through the north gate and led me around the outside to the outer gate facing east, and the water was flowing from the south side. . . . He said to me, 'This water flows toward the eastern region and goes down into the Arabah, where it enters the [Dead] Sea. When it empties into the [Dead] Sea, the water there becomes fresh. Swarms of living creatures will live wherever the river flows. There will be large numbers of fish, because this water flows there and makes the salt water fresh; so where the river flows everything will live. Fishermen will stand along the shore; from En Gedi to En Eglaim there will be places for spreading nets. The fish will be of many kinds—like the fish of the Great Sea.'"

The description of the temple river seems hard to believe. It starts off as a minor trickle offset toward the south side of the temple. Within a mile and a quarter it becomes a raging torrent that cannot be crossed on foot. It descends to the Dead Sea, which will no longer be dead of life, but now contains many fish. There are clear geographical references made in connection with this river (i.e., south of the altar, Arabah, En Gedi, En Eglaim), which definitely give credibility to a literal interpretation. A few other references to a temple river also appear in the Bible.

> Joel 3:18: "In that day . . . all the ravines of Judah will run with water. A fountain will flow out of the LORD's house and will water the valley of acacias."
>
> Zechariah 14:8 (KJV): "And it shall be in that day, that living waters shall go out from Jerusalem; half of them toward the former sea, and half of them toward the hinder sea: in summer and in winter shall it be."
>
> Psalm 46:4 (KJV): "There is a river, the streams whereof shall make glad the city of God, the holy place of the tabernacles of the most High."

Joel lived 250 years before Ezekiel. Zechariah wrote about 90 years after Ezekiel. They both use language wherein both context and vocabulary demand a literal interpretation. "In that day," this and that will happen. I understand this river to actually be a literal river gushing from the temple during the millennium, and probably into eternity upon the new earth.

Its perennial flow in summer and in winter will bring lush vegetation to the Judean wilderness and also toward Ashdod/Ashkelon on the coast. A lot more could be said about this river and the changes in topography and geography of Israel at the second coming. I'll leave this fertile field for commentators discussing the millennium. My main reason for bringing up the river is to observe its similarity to the river of life in Rev 22. We should not equate this temple river with the river flowing from the new Jerusalem. We look at that river in the next chapter.

EZEKIEL'S TEMPLE INTO THE NEW WORLD

The temple built by the Messiah is promised to last forever. Mount Moriah will always for eternity be the throne of the mighty king. However, some big changes, mostly in ritual worship, will occur at the close of the thousand years. After the millennium is over, there is a massive cosmic change to the universe. The melting of elements with fervent heat may or may not be partly metaphorical, but out of it, the new earth is created from this old earth. The world merges with the fourth dimension. This is the birth of the promised new world. Ezekiel's temple will, like all other holy things, remain, yet be totally changed. It is a resurrection from carnal to sublime. It will, however, remain recognizable as the millennial temple, just as Jesus remained recognizable to those to whom he revealed himself. If you are a Christian today, you will certainly visit the temple during the millennium on a regular basis. When heaven and earth merge at the start of eternity, I think that you will still remember details of the beautiful millennial temple that are now perceivable in the new eternal temple.

Remember, we will throughout eternity live on earth. We don't go to heaven forever. You have probably figured out by now that the thought of "we are going to live in heaven forever" is one of my pet peeves. Instead heaven comes to us. This world is re-created heavenly. In the eternal world, there will be no sin, no death. The new world order will be perfect. At that point, some ritual modifications will be necessary in the Jerusalem temple.

Admittedly, I have no Bible verses backing this up, so it is speculative opinion. I think that there will be no need for sin or guilt offerings. Sin will have been exterminated, along with those who practiced it. Sin and guilt offerings are of meat. They sacrifice a lamb or kid goat. The priest eats a portion of it as part of the ritual. In the new world of eternity, as we have already learned, carnivorous predation shall cease. People will no longer eat flesh during eternity future. As a matter of fact, I think animal sacrifices will cease entirely, because death will not exist (at least for higher animals, lambs included). So the shedding of blood as part of the temple rite will be discontinued. I'm sure King Jesus will come up with some other clever activity to keep the priests and Levites busy.

EZEKIEL'S TEMPLE SUMMARY

The Bible contains numerous prophecies that expect the renewal of Jerusalem and the temple to take place someday. I do not discount them. I fully anticipate a renewed city of Jerusalem here on earth. This temple passage in Ezekiel is, in my opinion, one of the most compelling and powerful in favor of a premillennial chronology because it is so lengthy and detailed. I owe many insights to John Schmitt, who has been studying Ezekiel's temple vision for many years. He has written an excellent book, *Messiah's Coming Temple, Ezekiel's Prophetic Vision of the Future Temple*. He has also built a very detailed model, which has been on display at the Temple Institute in Jerusalem.

However, dispensational millennialism, also known as chiliasm, is not the point of my study. To verify the prophetic expectation of a nationalistic golden age for Israel, I'd also recommend another good book, *The Millennial Kingdom* by John Walvoord. Our study is to review the eternal abode of those with Christ, the terminal state of the saved. Let us now reason together and study the final and glorious new Jerusalem.

ENDNOTES

1. For a helpful study of Ezekiel's millennial temple, see Feinberg, *Prophecy of Ezekiel*, 233–79. See also Couch, *Introduction to Classical Evangelical Hermeneutics*, 300–317.
2. Price, "Ezekiel's Prophecy of the Temple."
3. Whitcomb, "Christ's Atonement and Animal Sacrifices in Israel," 210.
4. Walvoord, *Every Prophecy of the Bible*, 202.

15

New Jerusalem

Figure 3
Guernica, Pablo Picasso, 1937

PABLO PICASSO, THE GREAT Cubist artist of the twentieth century, painted a monumental work in 1937 called *Guernica*. The painting is a protest against the bombing of a small village called Guernica in northern Spain by the fascist, pro-Nazi Francisco Franco during the Spanish Civil War. *Guernica* powerfully displays the tragedies of war and the human suffering that war inflicts upon people. However, it makes its statement in a very abstract way. This style of art is called Cubism. It was a popular mode of expression in the 1930s world of avant-garde art.

This painting is huge, like a wall mural. It is eleven feet by twenty-five feet, painted on canvas. It is all black and white. Picasso's choice to paint in only black and white conveys a very somber mood. The painting is located at the Reina Sofía Museum in Madrid. I've been to Madrid twice, and I've made the effort to see it both times. I love this painting.

Allow me to give you a quick tour of this masterpiece. At the left, a woman cries over a dead baby in her arms. This is one of the most poignant figures. There are tiny daggers coming out of her mouth, which suggest screaming. Beside her is a bull running wild through the streets. During the chaos of the bombing, the animal has escaped his pasture, suggesting anarchy. The center is occupied by a large and prominent horse falling in agony as it has just been pierced by a spear or javelin. The shape of a human skull forms the horse's nose and upper teeth. Even the horse has an expression of pain.

A dead body appears in the street below the horse, another very emotional image. The mouth of the corpse is agape in a frozen scream. Apparently, he is a fallen soldier. His open hand is still clutching at air as he tries to grasp for the freedom that he had wanted for his village, before he was mercilessly cut down by the Fascists. The other hand still grasps in death on a broken sword. They didn't really use swords in the 1930s. The battle was fought with machine guns, bazookas, and high-powered rifles. The shattered sword is horrifically graphic and symbolic of utter defeat.

To the right is a building going down in flames. A man leaps in suicide from its heights. All is lost. He is falling to dead people covering the streets below. Beneath him and entering the scene from the right is a panicking woman. She staggers toward the center below a strange ghostlike head, which is trapped in the burning building.

Guernica presents a horrific scene of death, violence, brutality, suffering, and helplessness. These atrocities are carried out against innocent civilians and children. *Guernica* clearly depicts suffering people, animals, and even buildings wrenched by violence and the chaos of war, yet the painting is not clear at all literally. It is all black and white. It has strange deformed shapes. For example, the bull has both eyes on the same side of its head. The heads of most human figures shown are entirely too large to be proportionally accurate.

If I only understand photography, and if I expect literal realism in painting, then this scene isn't going to make much sense. If I were to stand on the streets of Guernica and snap a photograph during this battle, then I might capture the building burning down or the dead soldier, or maybe the stray bull. I'm not going to catch all of this action in the same frame. This painting is powerful in that it captures so much chaos on one canvas. If I had a photo of a woman with a dead baby, certainly that would be disturbing. However, outdoor photographs almost always have a background that includes green trees and blue sky. This would be reassuringly consistent. But in *Guernica*, because of the Cubist approach, everything is reduced to geometric and abnormal shapes. Triangles, oblong figures, and amoebic shapes dominate the canvas. The very background, the palette, of this painting is disturbing and alarming.

Even if you knew nothing of the Spanish Civil War, after viewing this great painting you are going to be disturbed. It is emotional, strong, and very evocative. Seeing it in person is much better because it is so huge, towering over your head. *Guernica* is overpowering.

This book is about heaven and hell. This chapter is about the new Jerusalem. You may ask, "Why is the author describing a Cubist painting to me?" I believe that we can learn something about biblical literature by studying modern art. Literature is art. The Apocalypse of Jesus Christ given to John of Patmos is one of the finest pieces of literature ever written in the Greek language. If you can understand and appreciate the use of figurative and symbolic representations in Picasso's *Guernica*, then you will be better suited to properly interpret the new Jerusalem, as well as many other symbolic passages of Scripture.

In Rev 21, John records a fantastic vision of the new Jerusalem. The traditional conservative, dispensational interpretation is that of a literal new city, but before we consider my thoughts, let's read the passage:

Revelation 21:2, 9–27: "I saw the Holy City, the new Jerusalem, coming down out of heaven from God, prepared as a bride beautifully dressed for her husband. . . . One of the seven angels who had the seven bowls full of the seven last plagues came and said to me, 'Come, I will show you the bride, the wife of the Lamb.' And he carried me away in the Spirit to a mountain great and high, and showed me the Holy City, Jerusalem, coming down out of heaven from God. It shone with the glory of God, and its brilliance was like that of a very precious jewel, like a jasper, clear as crystal. It had a great, high wall with twelve gates and with twelve angels at the gates. On the gates were written the names of the twelve tribes of Israel. There were three gates on the east, three on the north, three on the south and three on the west. The wall of the city had twelve foundations, and on them were the names of the twelve apostles of the Lamb. The angel who talked with me had a measuring rod of gold to measure the city, its gates and its walls. The city was laid out like a square, as long as it was wide. He measured the city with the rod and found it to be 12,000 stadia in length, and as wide and high as it is long. He measured its wall and it was 144 cubits by man's measurement, which the angel was using. The wall was made of jasper, and the city of pure gold, as pure as glass. The foundations of the city walls were decorated with every kind of precious stone. The first foundation was jasper, the second sapphire, the third chalcedony, the fourth emerald, the fifth sardonyx, the sixth carnelian, the seventh chrysolite, the eighth beryl, the ninth topaz, the tenth chrysoprase, the eleventh jacinth, and the twelfth amethyst. The twelve gates were twelve pearls, each gate made of a single pearl. The great street of the city was of pure gold, like transparent glass. I did not see a temple in the city, because the Lord God Almighty and the Lamb are its temple. The city does not need the sun or the moon to shine on it, for the glory of God gives it light, and the Lamb is its lamp. The nations will walk by its light, and the kings of the earth will bring their splendor into it. On no day will its gates ever be shut, for there will be no night there. The glory and honor of the nations will be brought into it. Nothing impure will ever enter it, nor will anyone who does what is shameful or deceitful, but only those whose names are written in the Lamb's book of life."

The beauty of the new Jerusalem is legendary, supremely expressed as best as human language is capable. The vision has a breathtaking, arresting allure. The standard dispensational understanding of this passage is that this is a literal city, created by God, to be the new home of the saints throughout eternity. However, I think that explanation falls short of the correct intended meaning. I'm inclined to see this new Jerusalem passage as figurative for the bride of Christ, the redeemed of all ages. The twelve tribes represent the OT saints, the apostles represent the church-era Christians, and let's not forget the tribulation saints, who more than anybody will suffer for the name of Jesus. We are the new Jerusalem. The literal city of Jerusalem that we inhabit upon the earth is described at the end of Ezekiel and other places.

The preeminent reason for an allegorical understanding of this passage is simply because the text says so. The escort angel announces to John, "Come, I will show you the bride, the wife of the Lamb." Everything that John describes after that is in reference to the vision of the bride.

Notice that the dimensions are all expressed as divisors of 12. There are 12 foundation stones, 12 gates, 12,000 stadia for length/width/height, and 144 cubits (12 x 12). There are 12 tribes of Israel and 12 apostles of Christ. Twelve appears to be the number of God's people, so this numerology most likely represents all the redeemed of God in both the OT and NT periods.

The city comes down out of heaven, presumably toward the earth. It is 12,000 stadia. A stadion was a Greek measurement of about 600 feet. An arena containing the track for footraces in ancient Greece was originally one stadion in length. (The English word "stadium" comes directly from the Greek.) Twelve thousand stadia yields an object roughly 1,450 miles in a cube shape.

Verses 15 and 16 say the angel "had a measuring rod of gold" and "he measured the city with the rod." Measuring rods were typically a 10-foot-long, very straight stick of wood. In Ezek 40:5, the rod is 6 cubits. This is where the literal interpretation starts to have logical problems. Gold is a very soft, malleable metal. For a 10-foot-long rod to hold its shape and not deform every time it gets bumped, it would need to be about a minimum 2 inches in diameter. A rod of gold 10 feet long by 2 inches thick would weigh 263 pounds—rather awkward to wield as a measuring stick, but since he is an angel, I guess he is really strong. Measuring a city of 1,450 miles with a 10-foot surveying stick, a rod at a time, would be very time consuming—but since he is an angel, I guess he is really fast. Good thing it is an eternal city, because measuring it with a 10-foot stick would just about take an eternity.

Verse 16 says that the city is as high as it is long. It probably means cubic. It may possibly be a square-based pyramid shape, but the text does not specify. However, a pyramid harkens back to slavery in Egypt. I do not favor that imagery and geometry. A cube, on the other hand, is the perfect geometry for the inner sanctuary, also known as the holy of holies, in Solomon's temple of Jerusalem. See 1 Kgs 6:20: "The inner sanctuary was twenty cubits long, twenty wide and twenty high."

Twelve thousand stadia cubed is about half the size of the moon. It would be similar in size to the recently downgraded dwarf planet Pluto. The city has a wall around it, so it looks sort of like a disembodied piece of real estate floating in the sky. Possibly the city lands on the earth and is melded into and merged with the existing planet Earth. I suppose, if literal, it must be the newly redeemed new earth with which the new Jerusalem merges, because the old earth gets destroyed and reborn with fervent heat in 2 Pet 3:10. Assumedly the new Jerusalem would not be destroyed by fire in judgment of sin by God's wrath, so that any potential merger must be after the purging of sin.

The current Jerusalem is upgraded, so to speak, with the new Jerusalem. However, this seems unlikely. A literal view continues to have more problems in this verse. If we want to be literal, we need to be scientific. A planetelle of this size has a footprint of over 2.1 million square miles (1450 miles x 1450 miles). Texas, my huge home state, is a paltry 269,000 square miles. This planetelle is twice the size of the entire Mediterranean Sea, and roughly the same size as greater Europe or the eastern half of the United States. This is about the footprint of the entire known world in the first century A.D. Not only would it replace

Jerusalem and Ezekiel's temple; it would usurp all of Israel and the entire Mediterranean world.

That cannot happen, according to Scripture. The land of Israel according to the Bible will be inhabited perpetually (a previous chapter in this book addresses that issue). I think "perpetually" means eternally—that the earth will be forever. Remember, I believe in a literal bodily resurrection and a literal new earthly/heavenly inheritance. I do not think a literal new Jerusalem planet will descend from heaven to obliterate and replace the land of Israel.

A literalist's next possible idea is for the glorious new city, which he interprets as literal, to become a satellite of the new earth. Maybe it will orbit our planet. Maybe it will defy gravity and centrifugal force and park stationary and permanently above the Temple Mount. If it is really made of solid gold, I think the gravitational balance could shift, and the Earth might revolve around it. If you believe in a physical, bodily resurrection and actual, real redemption of earth, then this theory is so far out there in fanciful imagination that I can offer no logical recourse. Such ideas are fueled by the SciFi Channel.

It is hard to fathom, but the size of this city is absolutely huge. It is 1,450 miles high. That is far outside of Earth's atmosphere. The troposphere, where the vast majority of gases and all of earth's life reside, is only about 12 miles deep. The far outer reaches of ionosphere, the recognized limit to outer space, is about 70 miles high. If we take the description literally, and assume that the city is tridimensional and that the full cubic volume will all be inhabited and that each story of the city is, let us assume, 1 mile high, then the total cubic volume is over 3 billion square miles of habitable land. The earth is slightly over 500 million square miles of surface area. So in this literal scenario the new Jerusalem is about 15 times larger than the current earth.

A more likely interpretation: I think the vast size of the city in the vision represents that the grace of God extends to a huge host of believers. Certainly, not all humans will be saved, but the scope of God's mercy may very well surprise many Christians.

A third possible option for a literal-city viewpoint is the spiritual-city home. This theory says that the envisioned new Jerusalem will be the future eternal home for our spirit/soul. It is a real place, and we will literally live there, but it is in another dimension, a spiritual world. This appears to explain the otherworldly attributes such as transparent gold and huge pearls. This view is blatantly nonbiblical. As we have already investigated, we are promised to have a bodily, physical life, as Jesus has a tangible glorified body. We shall rule with him upon a real, terrestrial new earth.

STREET OF GOLD

In verse 18 and again in verse 21, John tells us that he sees that the city and the street were of pure gold, clear and transparent as glass. First of all, this may sound silly, but in Greek it says "street"—singular. A city this huge only has one street? This appears to be another deliberate attempt to be illogical, because the passage is meant to be taken symbolically. Second, gold is not a chemically translucent element. Natural gold has an atomic number of 79, which means that a single gold atom has a total of 79 protons and neutrons at its nucleus. This is far too dense and heavy to allow photons of light to refract and pass through. Simply put, gold is not transparent. Obviously, John is not talking about a literal vision.

Third and most important, God does not honor the same things that people honor. An oft-repeated message in Psalms and Proverbs is that wisdom, godly knowledge, and obedience to the law are better than gold, silver, and gems. An omnipotent God could create a million metric tons of gold with a single word. God does not value riches the way that humans do.

Job 28:15–17: "[Wisdom] cannot be bought with the finest gold, nor can its price be weighed in silver. It cannot be bought with the gold of Ophir, with precious onyx or sapphires. Neither gold nor crystal can compare with it, nor can it be had for jewels of gold."

Psalm 19:9–10: "The fear of the LORD is pure, enduring forever. The ordinances of the LORD are sure and altogether righteous. They are more precious than gold, than much pure gold."

Proverbs 8:10–11 (KJV): "Receive my instruction, and not silver; and knowledge rather than choice gold. For wisdom is better than rubies; and all the things that may be desired are not to be compared to it."

Isaiah 55:9 (KJV): "For as the heavens are higher than the earth, so are my ways higher than your ways, and my thoughts than your thoughts."

Ezekiel 7:19: "They will throw their silver into the streets, and their gold will be an unclean thing. Their silver and gold will not be able to save them in the day of the LORD's wrath. They will not satisfy their hunger or fill their stomachs with it, for it has made them stumble into sin."

First Corinthians 1:27-29: "But God chose the foolish things of the world to shame the wise; God chose the weak things of the world to shame the strong. He chose the lowly things of this world and the despised things—and the things that are not—to nullify the things that are, so that no one may boast before him."

First Peter 1:18-19 (KJV): "Forasmuch as ye know that ye were not redeemed with corruptible things, as silver and gold, from your vain conversation received by tradition from your fathers; But with the precious blood of Christ, as of a lamb without blemish and without spot."

Why then would God build his city out of earthly treasure? He wouldn't. Gold is really quite meaningless to God. It is not the stuff that he desires, values, or treasures. The city of gold and jasper undoubtedly represents something incredibly precious, something of super, inestimable value—something so dear to the mind of God that he is willing to die for it. The golden city that shines with the glory of God (Rev 21:11) represents the redeemed human believers of earth. A city has never been built at such a high price, being the price of the Mediator's blood.

WALLS OF THE NEW JERUSALEM

The wall is made of solid jasper (Rev 21:18). John writes that the wall is 144 cubits, but is unclear if he means tall or thick. One hundred forty-four cubits are about equal to 216 feet. Jasper is a gemstone mineral in the silica family. It is usually red, yellow, brown, or green, depending on its mineral content. Revelation 21:11 mentions that this jasper is clear as crystal. However, earthly jasper is opaque, setting forth yet another literal contradiction. If this is to be interpreted as a literal city, why does it have walls? Who will attack or lay siege during eternity?

A better understanding of this city wall might be achieved if we study another famous walled city: The great city of Babylon on the plain of Shinar had immense walls of astounding height. The city was surrounded by two walls: an outer wall and an inner wall. Between them lay an open area thought by some to be filled with lions, which would be an adversary to any invading army. It is thought that this boundary between the walls may be the lion's den into which the prophet Daniel had been cast. We know that the walls were crenellated and had bas-relief animals sculpted into the clay brick. Gates and high-profile areas were painted blue. Many U.S. soldiers stationed in Iraq have in recent years toured the archaeological ruins of Babylon, which include sections of original wall.

The Greek historian Herodotus (about 450 B.C.) claimed the outer walls alone were 80 feet thick and 320 feet high. The walls were solid and had a flat surface on top that could be used as a road. According to Herodotus, the walls were wide enough to allow a four-horse chariot to make a complete U-turn. Herodotus records in his *History* that the inner walls were "not so thick as the first, but hardly less strong." Inside the walls were fortresses and temples containing immense statues of solid gold. Towering above the city were the great ziggurat and numerous temples to the god Marduk and others of the Babylonian pantheon. While archaeological examination has disputed some of Herodotus's claims (the outer walls seem to be not nearly that high), his narrative does give us a sense of how awesome the features of Babylon appeared to those who visited.

More realistically, the Greek historian Strabo (64 B.C.–A.D. 24), a contemporary of Jesus, says that the walls were 50 cubits high (75 feet).[1] Another Greek historian, Diodorus, about 50 B.C., agrees with the 75-foot height when describing the famed hanging gardens of the city.[2]

Accounts indicate that the walls were built to these heights by King Nebuchadnezzar, who ruled the city for forty-three years at its peak of power and fame. The walls of the Golden City (Isa 14:4) were credited as being impenetrable. In fact, they were never breeched. The Persians entered through the Euphrates River, under the floodgates, but the walls have been since destroyed. Babylon was continuously occupied thru the Persian, Hellenistic, Roman, Parthian, and Sassanid periods. In approximately A.D. 650 at the Arab expansion, the city was abandoned and the walls destroyed. It has not been occupied for the last thirteen hundred years.

As prophesied in Jer 51:58a (KJV), "Thus says the LORD of hosts; The broad walls of Babylon shall be utterly broken, and her high gates shall be burned with fire." Verse 62 (KJV) of the same passage continues, "Then shalt thou say, O LORD, thou hast spoken against this place, to cut it off, that none shall remain in it, neither man nor beast, but that it shall be desolate for ever."

The mighty city of Babylon had very impressive defensive walls, although it eventually came to an end with the ravages of time. The walls of the new Jerusalem will be even bigger and better. We are promised that they will never fail. Instead of 75 feet high, they are seemingly 216 feet high. Instead of being made with clay brick, they are made of jasper stone. Instead of painted blue gates, the new Jerusalem has pearly gates. The vision of the wall is symbolic. It clearly says that the inhabitants of the new Jerusalem are secure, safely protected by the Holy One of Israel.

GATES OF THE NEW JERUSALEM

Only twelve gates for a massive city of this size would be an eternal traffic jam, if this city is literally to be our heavenly abode. The minuscule island of Manhattan has seventeen traffic bridges accessing it to the rest of New York and New Jersey. However, traffic engineering is not the point in John's vision. There are twelve portals in the wall oriented to the compass, with three in each cardinal direction. There is an angel stationed at each gate, or gatehouse (Rev 21:12). These gates are each made of a single pearl. Maybe this is where pop Christianity derived the name of the "pearly gates." If these are intended to be literal natural pearls, then it would take a whopper of an oyster to produce them.

These pearls remind us of the parable in Matt13:45 where a merchant sells everything that he owns in order to buy the pearl of great price. The parable represents Christ giving up his life to redeem the precious church. The pearl of great price in the parable is the church, as the pearly gates of the vision are the bride of Christ.

The orientation of gates facing in every direction suggests pilgrims from every corner of the globe. All nations, all tongues, and all races are within. Revelation 21:25 tells us that the gates of the city will never be shut. Allegorically, then, salvation is open to all who wish to receive part of this position of splendor. Notice that every sentence has meaning. It is symbolic and nonliteral, but full of glorious truth.

Revelation 21:12 states, "On the gates were written the names of the twelve tribes of Israel." And then verse 14 says, "The city had twelve foundations, and on them were the names of the twelve apostles." The passage does not describe which name is inscribed on which gate and foundation stone, or if all of the names of the tribes and apostles are inscribed on all of the gates and foundation stones, respectively. That aspect of the arrangement is open to speculation. I tend to think that it will be one name per gate or stone. Although we must remember that this vision is not literal but symbolic of the redeemed church, it is fun to enhance the details of the picture, as a fine artist puts shoelaces and cufflinks on his imaginary characters in a painting. In this vein, I propose that Levi will receive a gate and Joseph will have only one gate. Furthermore, I feel that Judas Iscariot's name will be absent from the foundations, replaced by that of Matthias (Acts 1:26).

The names of the twelve tribes of Israel are written on these gates. Although it does not specifically mention, the layout of the gates is possibly parallel to that of the tribes as described in Num 2 while they were encamped around the ark during the forty years of wandering. Another possibility (my allegorical preference) is that the gates remain similar to the layout of gates in Ezek 48 in the literally restored Jerusalem of the millennial future.

Arrangement of Tribes from Numbers 2

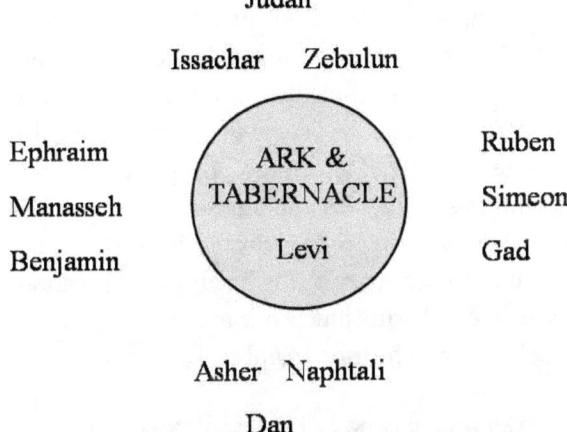

Arrangement of Gates from Ezekiel 48

Judah

Ruben   Levi

Joseph	RESTORED CITY	Gad
Benjamin	4500 cubits sq (1.25mile x 1.25mile)	Asher
Dan		Naphtali

Simeon

Issachar   Zebulun

Figure 4

ISRAEL AND APOSTLES UNITED

The columns and beams of the magnificent metroplex have engraved upon them the names of the tribes of Israel and the disciples of Christ. This is clear evidence that OT believers and NT saints are both members of the bride of Christ. Israel and church are finally united in the eternal state of the new earth. Dispensational theology has long observed a dichotomy between Old Testament Israel and the New Testament church. The splitting asunder of God's people was caused by Dead Soul Syndrome. The fall of Adam also caused the death of all human souls, the separation of God and people by the sea, and the invisibility of the fourth dimension. All righteous people of the kingdom will be restored to unity at the restoration of all things, at the merging of heaven and earth, at the synthesis of the seen and unseen. This is the time when the entire curse, including Dead Soul Syndrome, is overturned.

I hope that a deeper study of the healing of this catastrophic split within God's people will bring much-needed reconciliation between dispensational believers and historic mainline Evangelical Christians.

FOUNDATION STONES OF THE NEW JERUSALEM

Ephesians 2:19–22: "Consequently, you are no longer foreigners and aliens, but fellow citizens with God's people and members of God's household, *built on the foundation of the apostles* and prophets, with Christ Jesus himself as the chief cornerstone. In him the whole building is joined together and rises to become a holy temple in the Lord. And in him you too are being built together to become a dwelling in which God lives by his Spirit" (emphasis added).

This passage is another municipal metaphor likening the apostles to monolithic structural components of a building. In Rev 21:14, the names of the apostles are carved into the foundation stones of the walls. The stones are decorated with gems (vv. 19–20). The Greek word used for "decorate" is *cosmeo*, from which we derive our English word "cosmetics." The rich adornments garnishing the foundations cause them to sparkle. The imagery of the vision conveys that the way into Christ was forged by the apostles, and their faith shines as gems.

Matthew 16:18a (KJV): "And I say also unto thee, That thou art Peter, and upon this rock I will build my church." Here, Jesus uses another foundation-stone analogy. Whether Peter or Jesus himself was intended as the antecedent is not my current interest; my point is that the setting of foundation stones is the first work on the new construction site and will create an enduring monument. The apostles were the foundation of the new Jerusalem, of which all Christians take part. The variety of color on these multi-hewed foundations represents the broad diversity of redeemed saints who are components of the holy bride, the new Jerusalem.

The list of gems given alludes to the list of gems given twice in Exodus, at chapters 28 and 39. The breastplate of the high priest had twelve gems mounted in it on gold filigree settings. The breastplate was approximately nine inches square. The gems were mounted in four rows of three. The names of the twelve tribes were engraved onto the stones, like a seal for making a wax impress. John's list includes eight of the stones from Exodus and four different gems not mentioned in the breastplate. The two arrangements are in different order.

Note: The New International Version and the King James Version agree fully on the translation of the Greek gemological words found in Revelation; however, the Hebrew gem names vary. I have used the NIV. The precise identification of some of these precious stones is uncertain.

	Revelation 21:19–20	Color	Exodus 28:17–20; 39:10–13 (NIV)	Color
1	Jasper	Varies	Ruby	Red
2	Sapphire	Blue	Topaz	Opaque yellow
3	Chalcedony	Varies	Beryl	Blue green
4	Emerald	Green	Turquoise	Aquamarine
5	Sardonyx	Red banding	Sapphire	Blue
6	Sardius	Translucent red	Emerald	Green
7	Chrysolite	Olive	Jacinth	Dark blue/black
8	Beryl	Blue Green	Agate	Varies
9	Topaz	Opaque yellow	Amethyst	Purple quartz
10	Chrysoprasus	Apple green	Chrysolite	Olive
11	Jacinth	dark blue/black	Onyx	Banded multi
12	Amethyst	Purple quartz	Jasper	Varies

Five of the Greek words used in John's catalog are used only here, nowhere elsewhere in the NT. The only other enumeration in Scripture that gives so many gemstones is found in Ezek 28, with a description of the king of Tyre. We looked at that passage in chapter 6. It is really speaking of Satan. He is adorned with nine gemstones. Again the Ezekiel passage is symbolic. Satan doesn't really wear a rhinestone suit glittering with precious gems. The meaning is that he had been of very high rank. He had previously been one of the anointed cherubs that covered the throne of God with his wings.

NO TEMPLE

In Rev 21:22, John notes that he sees no temple in the new Jerusalem descending from heaven. If literal and if earthly, this is in direct contradiction to Ezek 40—48, as studied in the last chapter. The newly remodeled Jerusalem is said by Ezekiel to have a glorious temple in which the *shekinah* presence of God will dwell with his people forever, and they will never again defile his holy name.

In light of this passage, a literal city interpretation for the new Jerusalem erases the biblical doctrine of the perpetuity of Jerusalem and the temple, as the capital of Israel and God's kingdom. A spiritual city interpretation is infected with gnosticism, denying the physical reality of our inheritance. Those hyperliteralists who attempt to show a nonfigurative nature for the new Jerusalem passage hold the gold medal for exegetical gymnastics. Attempting to make logical, literal sense out of the extreme hyperbole only weakens the dispensationalist case for a simple reading when it should be rightfully applied elsewhere, like Ezekiel's temple. The only interpretation that I am aware of that satisfies all criteria is the municipal metaphor for the bride of Christ. We, the redeemed, are the glorious citadel.

The verse goes on to say that the Lord God almighty and the Lamb are its temple. This is the place where God lives. Where does God live? He lives in us, the bride of Christ, the new Jerusalem. Paul clearly says in 1 Cor 3:16 that our bodies are the temple of God.

WATER OF LIFE AND TREE OF LIFE

Revelation 22:1–2: "Then the angel showed me the river of the water of life, as clear as crystal, flowing from the throne of God and of the Lamb down the middle of the great street of the city. On each side of the river stood the tree of life, bearing twelve crops of fruit, yielding its fruit every month. And the leaves of the tree are for the healing of the nations."

Revelation 22:14: "Blessed are those who wash their robes, that they may have the right to the tree of life and may go through the gates into the city."

Revelation 22:17, 19: "The Spirit and the bride say, 'Come!' And let him who hears say, 'Come!' Whoever is thirsty, let him come; and whoever wishes, let him take the free gift of the water of life. . . . And if anyone takes words away from this book of prophecy, God will take away from him his share in the tree of life and in the holy city, which are described in this book."

In the book of the prophet Ezekiel, we read verses about a river of water full of fish issuing forth from south of the altar out of the literal millennial temple of the future that the Messiah himself shall build. Those verses started off with exclamatory prophetic declarations, such as "In that day . . ." I believe that river should be understood as factual and real. Now, in the closing verses of Revelation, Jesus makes a clear allusion to that famous prophetic passage, with which everyone should be familiar. This passage however is different.

Christ himself is the water of life. Jesus is bubbling through the middle of the city. He is the refreshing fountain that sustains the city. He also claims to be the living water in John 4 when speaking with the Samaritan woman by the well. The water gives eternal life. Again in John 7, Jesus talks about living water, but this time the reference is to the Holy Spirit. There is no contradiction; this is a complementary supplementation. The Holy Spirit and eternal life go together. Whenever the first is received, the second is granted.

Today, we turn a faucet, and water squirts out into the sink. I have personally never drawn water from a hand-dug well. Have you? But Israel is a dry country. Ancient Israelites had to work hard to supply their daily water needs. The winter rains recharge the aquifers, but during the long, hot, dry summers, a water source is critical for human existence. It is easy to understand how in such a country a well, a spring, or a river could be used as a symbol for life.

Other verses that speak of God as free, clear, life-giving water are as follows:

Isaiah 55:1: "Come, all you who are thirsty, come to the waters; and you who have no money, come, buy and eat! Come, buy wine and milk without money and without cost."

Jeremiah 2:13: "My people have committed two sins: They have forsaken me, the spring of living water, and have dug their own cisterns, broken cisterns that cannot hold water." See also Jer 17:13.

Simultaneously with the water of life, another allusion to the tree of life is presented here. The tree of life in the garden of Eden from Gen 2 provided the unrealized potential for Adam to live forever. Solomon uses multiple references to wisdom and righteousness as the tree of life in Proverbs (3:18; 11:30; 13:12; 15:4). Jesus is the tree of life. It is by symbolically eating of the tree that we are granted entrance into the eternal city of the new Jerusalem. The hyperbole is knee-deep. To claim that to be granted passage through the "gates into the city" (Rev 22:14), immigration control will literally require an individual to consume some certain special magical fruit would be amounting to salvation by dietary works. Hallelujah for the tree of life, for by his leaves we are healed! I think all can agree that the washing of robes is also obviously metaphorical. Admittance to the city is also not gained by doing laundry. (This is a very good thing for me. My wife has stories about my attempt at laundry.)

OUTSIDE ARE THE DOGS

Revelation 22:15: "Outside are the dogs, those who practice magic arts, the sexually immoral, the murderers, the idolaters and everyone who loves and practices falsehood." These words are spoken by Jesus, the captain of our salvation (Heb 2:10), almost immediately after the new Jerusalem vision. They are commonly used to argue that the sinners are still in existence somewhere outside the walls, even after the literal new Jerusalem has set into its planetary orbit for its eternal duration. However, when the new Jerusalem is correctly understood not to be a place, but a people, then it makes perfect allegorical sense that the wicked are not within the city. In other words, the wicked are not part of the redeemed bride of Christ.

These are not really canine animals, of course. This is a derogatory remark; they are unredeemed evil people, as in Phil 3:2: "Watch out for those dogs, those men who do evil, those mutilators of the flesh." Possibly it is an allusion to Deut 23:18 (KJV), wherein male prostitutes are referred to as "dogs." "Thou shalt not bring the hire of a whore, or the price of a dog, into the house of the LORD thy God for any vow: for even both these are abomination unto the LORD thy God." For these doglike people, only oblivion follows death. Death will be followed by a temporary resurrection to the throne of the Holy One and ultimate termination in the lake of fire on earth.

On a lighter note, this verse is not a prohibition against having a pet Fido on the new earth, which brings up a question my dog-loving mother used to ask me. She had five or six dogs at the same time at one point. Will there be animals in heaven? People have actually written books on this subject. Since animals are physical bodily creatures without a spiritual essence, and since we have learned in our studies that the current heaven is a spiritual place indwelt by God and his angels, technically the answer is no. However, we will not be in heaven either. We will be on earth, which will have merged with heaven to become a heavenly new earth. There will definitely be animals on earth. There will be a multitude of species and variety, for the whole earth will be a vibrantly life-filled place. So the practical answer to Mother's question is "yes." There will be friendly, loving animals in your eternal home.

COMING DOWN OUT OF HEAVEN

If we are willing to accept that this entire passage is metaphorical for the bride of Christ, then it is interesting to note (and it corroborates my theories) that John observes the city "coming down out of heaven from God." Where are the redeemed stationed during this intercalary period between bodies? My hypothesis has been that the souls of the righteous abide in heaven until the resurrection.

CONCLUSION

I am personally fascinated with the vision in Rev 21 and 22 of the new Jerusalem. In summation, either the passage is referring to a literal city built with unearthly components or it is allegorical. If I am mistaken, and it is intended to convey an actual, nonfigurative description using nonexistent and indescribable building components (e.g., transparent gold, giant pearls, clear jasper), then the passage is somewhat uninterpretable. It doesn't make sense; it can't make sense. It would be as inexplicable as a Zen koan. You must just believe that God can do it. If, on the other hand, the passage is intended to be allegorical, then it is rich in meaning and intended for people of all ages to ponder and consider what their savior has done for them. God's grace will be extended to a huge number of people; saints come from every direction on the compass;

sainthood is free and open to everyone; God's protection is better than the mightiest fortified walls. The bride of Christ gleams brighter than any imaginable gem and is more radiant than the purest gold. It shines with the very glory of God. We are that which God loves. We are the gleaming city "whose builder and maker is God" (Heb 11:10). But the best reason to understand the new Jerusalem passage as an allegory of the bride of Christ is simply because the word of God says that it is such. Please reread that critical verse from where we started, Rev 21:9: "Come, I will show you the bride, the wife of the Lamb."

ENDNOTES

1. Strabo, *Geographies*, book 16, chap. 1.
2. Wellard, *Babylon*, 156.

16

Epilogue

ORTHODOX JEWS HAVE FOR two millennia defended the oral law as being the word of God on par and equal with Torah. They claim that at Mount Sinai, Moses received two laws: one written, the Torah, and one oral. The oral law was passed down verbally for over a millennium to the rabbis. From about 200 B.C. to about A.D. 500, the rabbis gathered and wrote down this longstanding oral law in a great corpus of writings known as the Mishnah and Talmud. Thus, today, Orthodox Judaism has essentially two canons: the biblical one and the traditional one. It is believed that the oral law interprets and defines the Bible. The oral law is thought to be divinely inspired. Many Jewish laws and doctrines are derived from the oral law.

Among both Jews and Christians, possibly the most violated commandment of the entire Bible is found in Deut 4:2: "Do not add to what I command you and do not subtract from it, but keep the commands of the LORD your God that I give you."

It is easy for us humans to see the fault in our neighbors' lives. Evangelical Christians would unanimously agree that the rabbinic Jewish devotion to oral law is nothing more than a devotion to tradition. When speaking to the Pharisees about ritual hand washing, our savior Jesus said in Mark 7:7b–8, "'Their teachings are but rules taught by men.' You have let go of the commands of God and are holding on to the traditions of men." See also Matt 15:9.

It is a simple step for a conservative Christian to view an Orthodox Jew as intellectually indefensible in the treatment of tradition. However, it is so much harder to recognize the very same traits in our own life. We humans are creatures of our personal biases. The traditions with which we grew up are nearly branded into our psyche. May the Holy Spirit soften our hearts and minds so that we may be molded in all biblical truth!

It has been noted that "apart from [the authority of the Bible] evangelical faith does not exist. Yet the irony is that many conservative evangelicals act as if they do not really believe it. When a new idea pops up, they react immediately to counter it solely because it is new and not what has always been believed. No matter how much it is based on biblical scholarship and interpretation, if it is not traditional most conservatives oppose it . . . [snip]. . . . Surely all truth has not been captured already!"[1] I respectfully request that as this book is read, we will not be as the Pharisees and cling to the traditions of our childhood just because they were ours.

Each and every doctrinal teaching that we hold must be integrated and harmonious with all of our other teachings. They must help to explain each other. Doctrines are like a spider's web, with all strands interweaving with each other. Every strand of doctrine leads into another doctrine. That is why it is important to ensure doctrinal integrity. The reason we study doctrine is applicational. It should never be an academic pursuit for which there is zero application in life. That was the mistake of the Pharisees. They were so wrapped up in their studies of Torah that they forgot to love their brethren. Practice flows from theory. Our lives are based on the attitudes of our teachings. That was another mistake of the Pharisees. They believed that observant Jews were favored by God, and they became proud of their position. However, we know that God is no respecter of persons (Acts 10:34; Col 3:25), so there is no place for our arrogance. Incorrect doctrines usher in wrong attitudes, and ultimately a diseased and warped Christian life.

Ephesians 4:1 contains an interesting principle hidden within the Greek word *axios*, translated as "worthy" in the KJV: "I therefore, the prisoner of the Lord, beseech you that ye walk worthy of the vocation wherewith ye are called." It has been noted that the word includes a dimension that relates to doctrinal integrity and is something we should strive for in our relationship with God. Dr. Martyn Lloyd-Jones, a famous British evangelist of the twentieth century, in his commentary on Ephesians, tells us the word has the meaning of "equal weight." Imagine a scale with objects of equal weight on opposite sides, so that it does not tilt. If the scale balances perfectly, it is "worthy." If it tilts, it is "not worthy." In context and in practical application in life, Paul is saying that doctrine must perfectly balance with practice for us truly to walk worthily of our calling. However packed one's head may be with truth, if it is not being used, that person is unbalanced—not walking worthily. It is equally true that, if one says that Christianity is no more than living a good life and that learning doctrinal truths is not important, and thus that person fails to search and expand the understanding of truth through the Scriptures, that person is also not walking worthily.[2]

This book has addressed an intellectual and somewhat heavy theology. It is not exactly parlor reading. After reviewing the manuscript, a friend asked me, "What is the point?"

How does this technical, intellectual knowledge make us better Christians? How can it be applied to my daily life? In 1 Cor 13:2, the rightly celebrated "love" chapter, the Apostle Paul declares that if we understand every deep mystery of the cosmos but do not love our neighbor, then our life has been wasted.

The doctrines that this book addresses—lack of human immortality, soul sleep, spiritual quickening, life in Christ, eternal torment, glorious beauty of the Bride, reigning forever on earth, and others—when understood through my lens, hopefully will result in the behavior of humility due to the frailty of our human soul, a joyous expectation of resurrection and communion with God, and a somber yet judicial retribution for wickedness. In short, I hope we build up love, humility, and an expectant hope.

The doctrines that I argue against will, I believe, ultimately work an arrogance of human invincibility in their perceived immortality, callousness toward those suffering an unfairly punitive vengeance, and a forgetfulness of the resurrection of our Lord Jesus.

An important lesson that I have learned from the study and preparation of this book, and I hope it does not go unnoticed by each of you, is that no single group or denomination of believers has all the right answers. In these pages, I have quoted and gleaned from the doctrines and writings of the Church of Christ, Baptists, Seventh-day Adventists, Armstrong's Church of God, Anglicans, and many others. I wonder if God has deliberately given each denominational clique a small piece of truth that he gave only exclusively to that one group. If Christians never read or listen outside of their own personal comfort zone, then they will never be exposed to that morsel of knowledge. Baptists can learn from Anglicans. Anglicans can learn from Seventh-day Adventists. Seventh-day Adventists can learn from the Church of Christ. I can learn from all of them.

A major goal of this book is to be a bridge between these denominational hinterlands. Adventists and Baptists alike will traditionally agree with parts of my theories and disagree with other sections. But a bridge connects opposite sides of a chasm. I pray that this study will assist in bringing together brother and sister Christians of variant traditions. A hope for unity among Christians and an open-mindedness that all denominations can contribute valuable insight for accurate doctrine is my motivation in teaching.

I believe the majority of born-again Evangelical Christians have never thought the doctrine of the afterlife through to its conclusion. They arrived at their beliefs by tradition and culture. It is what they were told. It is the tradition of men. Those doctrines were not forged by reading the Bible. When people do turn to the Bible, to justify what they already know, I'm afraid many Christians just quote two or three texts (e.g., "undying worm" and "forever and ever"—case closed) without ever making the slightest effort to view them in the light of other passages. In other words, people often lack a systematic insight.

Throughout history, there have always been Christians who have held the positions that I advocate today. What I am teaching is nothing new. Most of these doctrines were declared heresy by the Roman Church around A.D. 550. At this time the Roman Church aggressively destroyed competing teachings and so-called heresies within the church. Along with the destruction of unorthodox teachings came the destruction of Jews, and ultimately anyone who stood in the way of the Inquisition and the Crusades.

Today there is an attitude among Evangelical Christians that is frighteningly similar to the Inquisition. The immediate thought and conclusion are that if a person admits to not believing in hell for the wicked and heaven for the saved, then they must be an atheist or a modernist. Granted, modernism is a serious problem in our society. Elements of it can water down even born-again Christians. However, from the many pages of Bible study shown here, I hope that everyone will realize that I am no atheist or modernist. My intent is to discover the true meaning of infallible Scripture that was inspired by the Almighty God of Israel. I hope traditional immortal-soul thinkers as well as fellow Christians of a soul-sleep persuasion will put aside all biases and preconceived notions. Instead, let us pray to the Eternal God for understanding. Let his Spirit fill our regenerated souls with love, peace, and joy.

This concludes my study on the nature of the human soul and afterlife. Since I have never been there myself, I cannot be too dogmatic about this topic. However, I prayerfully believe that this compendium of hypotheses fits neatly with the character of God and revelation of Scripture.

Here is my challenge that I promised in the opening pages of this book to anyone who may disagree with my hypothesis of the afterlife: If you have questions that I did not satisfactorily answer, or if you have comments, rebuttals, or additions of any type, please contact me at the email address below. I promise, Lord willing, to answer or at least to reply to every inquiry. If your question is exceptionally difficult, I retain the right to plead ignorance and claim Ps 35:11 as my own: "They question me on things I know nothing about."

If you disagree with any part of this book, hopefully you will be able to offer fresh verses that I have overlooked. I do require biblical citations, please. We can all learn from each other. The compendium of all human knowledge has been gained one person at a time.

I hope you have gleaned a few bits of fresh knowledge and wisdom from this book. I, too, can learn from you. By no means do I have a monopoly on doctrine. Whether you are a theology professor or a manual laborer; whether you are an amillennialist or a dispensationalist; whether you are a soul immortalist or a soul sleeper; no matter your doctrine or profession—God can use you as a vessel to reveal a little bit more truth to the world. So, please reply . . . and together we can forge a holistic and correct view of the afterlife as revealed by Scripture.

I eagerly await your opinion. Thank you very much for any assistance, guidance, and commentary that you may offer.

In Christ Jesus, my Savior,
Jay Altieri
jay@deadsoulsyndrome.com
March 2010

ENDNOTES

1. Olson, *How to Be Evangelical without Being Conservative*, 40.
2. Ritenbaugh, "Eating."

Selected Bibliography

Many of these books overlap between topics. I categorize them based on the topic that I found most helpful. Most of these books and sources were extremely helpful in my study; some others that I read or reviewed were totally worthless.

THE SOUL

Bacchiocchi, Samuele. *Immortality or Resurrection? A Biblical Study on Human Nature and Destiny*. Berrien Springs, MI: Biblical Perspectives, 1997.
Ball, Berry. "What Happens to My Soul When I Die?" http://www.detailshere.com/soul.htm (accessed June 2, 2007).
Ball, Bryan W. *The Soul Sleepers: Christian Mortalism from Wycliffe to Priestly*. Cambridge, UK: James Clarke, 2008.
Barth, Karl. *Resurrection of the Dead*. Eugene, OR: Wipf & Stock, 2003.
Bible Truth Keys: Where Are the Dead? Hartford, CT: Hartford Bible Students, 1909.
Bloch-Smith, Elizabeth. *Judahite Burial Practices and Beliefs about the Dead*. Sheffield, UK: JSOT, 1992.
Boettner, Loraine. *Immortality*. Phillipsburg, NJ: P & R Publishing, 2000.
Canright, Dudley Marvin. *A History of the Doctrine of the Soul*. Battle Creek, MI: Seventh-day Adventist Pub. Association, 1882.
Chapman, John. "Tertullian, A Treatise on the Soul, Chapter 55." *The Catholic Encyclopedia*. Vol. 14. New York: Robert Appleton Company, 1912. Online edition edited by K. Knight, http://www.newadvent.org/fathers/0310.htm (accessed September 15, 2008).
Coombs, Peter B. *Life after Death*. London: Falcon, 1962.
Cullmann, Oscar. *Immortality of the Soul or Resurrection of the Dead? The Witness of the New Testament*. London: Epworth, 1960.
Finley, Mark. "The Real Truth about Near-Death Experiences," http://www.maran-ata.it/english_studies/discoveries_profhecy/htm/the_real_truth_about.htm (accessed January 18, 2008).
Habermas, Gary R., and J. P. Moreland. *Immortality: The Other Side of Death*. Nashville: Thomas Nelson, 1992.
Hough, R. E. *The Christian after Death*. Chicago: Moody, 1947.
Hughes, Philip Edgcumbe. *The True Image: The Origin and Destiny of Man in Christ*. Grand Rapids: William B. Eerdmans, 1989.
Jackson, Wayne. "Do Human Beings Have an Immortal Soul?" http://www.christiancourier.com/articles/1446-do-human-beings-have-an-immortal-soul (accessed November 18, 2008).

Johnston, Philip. *Shades of Sheol: Death and Afterlife in the Old Testament*. Downers Grove, IL: InterVarsity, 2002.

Larkin, Clarence. *Dispensational Truth or God's Plan and Purpose in the Ages*. Philadelphia: Clarence Larkin Estate, 1920.

Nee, Watchman. *The Spiritual Man*. Anaheim, CA: Living Stream Ministries, 1998.

Sale-Harrison, L. *Judgment Seat of Christ*. London: Pickering & Inglis, 1938.

Smith, F. LaGard. *Afterlife: A Glimpse of Eternity beyond Death's Door*. Nashville: Cotswold, 2003.

Strauss, Lehman. *We Live Forever: A Study of Life after Death*. Neptune, NJ: Loizeaux Brothers, 1947.

White, Ellen. *The Great Controversy*. Mountain View, CA: Pacific, 1950.

HELL

Blanchard, John. *Whatever Happened to Hell?* Darlington, UK: Evangelical Press, 1992.

Buis, Harry. *The Doctrine of Eternal Punishment*. Nutley, NJ: P & R Publishing, 1957.

Crockett, William, ed. *Four Views on Hell*. Grand Rapids: Zondervan, 1992.

Dixon, Larry. *The Other Side of the Good News: Confronting the Contemporary Challenges to Jesus' Teaching on Hell*. Tain, UK: Christian Focus, 2003.

Fernando, Ajith. *Crucial Questions about Hell*. Wheaton, IL: Crossway, 1994.

Froom, L. *The Conditionalist Faith of Our Fathers*. Washington, DC: Review & Herald, 1966.

Fudge, Edward William. *The Fire That Consumes: A Biblical and Historical Study of Final Punishment*. Houston: Providential Press, 1982.

———. "Putting Hell in Its Place." *Christianity Today* 6 (August 1976): 14–17.

———, and Robert Peterson. *Two Views of Hell: A Biblical and Theological Dialogue*. Downers Grove, IL: InterVarsity, 2000.

Gerstner, John H. *Jonathan Edwards on Heaven and Hell*. Grand Rapids: Baker House, 1980.

———. *Repent or Perish*. Morgan, PA: Soli Deo Gloria Ministries, 1997.

Kenyon, E. W. *Identification: A Romance in Redemption*. Seattle: Kenyon's Gospel Publishing Society, 1968.

Leckie, J. H. *The World to Come and Final Destiny*. Edinburgh: T & T Clark, 1936.

Moore, David George. *The Battle for Hell: A Survey and Evaluation of Evangelicals' Growing Attraction to the Doctrine of Annihilationism*. Lanham, MD: University Press of America, 1995.

Morey, Robert. *Death and the Afterlife*. Minneapolis: Bethany House, 1984.

Morgan, Christopher W., ed. *Hell under Fire*. Grand Rapids: Zondervan, 2004.

Moriarty, Michael G. *The New Charismatics*. Grand Rapids: Zondervan, 1992.

Neil, William. *More Difficult Sayings of Jesus*. Grand Rapids: Eerdmans, 1981.

Peterson, Robert A. *Hell on Trial: The Case for Eternal Punishment*. Phillipsburg, NJ: P & R Publishing, 1995.

Pink, Arthur W. *Eternal Punishment*. Swengel, PA: Reiner Publications, ca. 1970s.

Pinnock, Clark H. "The Destruction of the Finally Impenitent." *Criswell Theological Review* 4 (Spring 1990): 243–59.

———. "Fire, Then Nothing." *Christianity Today* 31 (March 20, 1987): 40–41.

———, ed. *The Openness of God*. Downers Grove, IL: InterVarsity, 1994.

Shedd, William. *The Doctrine of Endless Punishment*. New York: Scribner's Sons, 1886.

Stott, John. *Basic Christianity*. Grand Rapids: Eerdmans, 1958.
———. *Our Guilty Silence*. Downers Grove, IL: InterVarsity, 1970.
Walls, Jerry L. *Hell: The Logic of Damnation*. Notre Dame, IN: U of Notre Dame P, 1992.
Wiese, Bill. *23 Minutes in Hell*. Lake Mary, FL: Charisma House, 2006.

HEAVEN

Alcorn, Randy. *Heaven*. Wheaton, IL: Tyndale House, 2004.
Ambassador College Correspondence Course. Lesson 7, "Will You Go to Heaven When You Die?" Charlotte: Worldwide Church of God, 1977.
Baker, Don. *Heaven: A Glimpse of Your Future Home*. Portland, OR: Multnomah, 1983.
Beam, Joe. *The Real Heaven: It's Not What You Think*. Webb City, MO: Covenant, 2006.
Connelly, Douglas. *After Life: What the Bible Really Says*. Downers Grove, IL: InterVarsity, 1995.
Criswell, W. A. *Heaven*. Wheaton, IL: Tyndale House, 1991.
Dixon, Larry. *Heaven: Thinking Now about Forever*. Camp Hill, PA: Christian Publications, 2002.
Ice, Thomas. *What the Bible Says about Heaven and Eternity*. Grand Rapids: Kregel, 2000.
MacArthur, John. *The Glory of Heaven*. Wheaton, IL: Crossway, 1996.
Piper, Don. *90 Minutes in Heaven: A True Story of Death and Life*. Grand Rapids: Revell, 2004.
Schmitt, John. *Messiah's Coming Temple: Ezekiel's Prophetic Vision of the Future Temple*. Grand Rapids: Kregel, 1997.
Smith, W. M. *The Biblical Doctrine of Heaven*. Chicago: Moody, 1968.
Tada, Joni E. *Heaven: Your Real Home*. Grand Rapids: Zondervan, 1995.
Walls, Jerry L. *Heaven: The Logic of Eternal Joy*. New York: Oxford Press USA, 2007.
Wright, N. T. *Surprised by Hope*. New York: Harper One, 2008.

REFERENCE MATERIALS

Aquinas, Thomas. *Summa Theologica of St. Thomas Aquinas*. 5 vols. Notre Dame, IN: Christian Classics, 1981.
———. *The Summa Theologica of St. Thomas Aquinas*. Supplement 69:2, online edition edited by K. Knight, http://www.newadvent.org/summa/5069.htm (accessed April 15, 2007).
Brodeur, Arthur Gilchrist, trans. *Prose Edda of Snorri Sturlson*. Mineola, NY: Dover, 2006.
Brown-Driver-Briggs Hebrew and English Lexicon to Old Testament. Peabody, MA: Hendrickson, 1996.
Buttrick, George A., ed. *The Interpreter's Bible*. Nashville: Abingdon, 1957.
Cohen, Abraham. *Everyman's Talmud*. New York: E. P. Dutton, 1949.
Couch, Mal, ed. *An Introduction to Classical Evangelical Hermeneutics*. Grand Rapids: Kregel, 2002.
Davis, John. *A Dictionary of the Bible*. Philadelphia: Westminster, 1907.
Gaebelein, Frank, ed. *The Expositor's Bible Commentary*. 12 vols. Grand Rapids: Zondervan, 1992.

Gill, John. *Exposition of the Entire Bible.* Online Edition BibleClassics.com, http://www.ewordtoday.com/comments/isaiah/gill/isaiah60.htm (accessed December 12, 2008).
———. *Exposition of the Old and New Testaments: Complete and Unabridged.* 9 vols. Paris, AR: Baptist Standard Bearer, 2006.
Hamilton, Edith. *The Greek Way.* New York: W. W. Norton, 1942.
Hoekema, Anthony A. *The Bible and the Future.* Grand Rapids: Eerdmans, 1979.
Holy Bible. King James Version and New International Version.
Horn, Siegfried. *Seventh-day Adventist Bible Dictionary.* Washington, DC: Review & Herald, 1979.
Jewish Study Bible: Complete TANAKH. Jewish Publication Society Translation. New York: Oxford Press USA, 2004.
Jurgens, William. *The Faith of the Early Fathers.* Collegeville, MN: Liturgical Press, 1979.
Kittel, G., ed. *Theological Dictionary of the New Testament.* Grand Rapids: Eerdmans, 1964.
Lawler, T. C., ed. *Ancient Christian Writers Series: The Case against the Pagans.* Mahwah, NJ: Paulist, 1949.
Life Application Study Bible. New International Version. Grand Rapids: Zondervan, 1991.
Lipman, Eugene, ed. *The Mishnah: Oral Teachings of Judaism.* New York: Viking, 1970.
McHugh, John. "Particular Judgment." In *The Catholic Encyclopedia.* Vol. 8. New York: Robert Appleton Company, 1910. Online edition edited by K. Knight, http://www.newadvent.org/cathen/08550a.htm (accessed April 15, 2007).
Neusner, Jacob. *The Mishnah: A New Translation.* New Haven, CT: Yale UP, 1991.
Nichol, Francis. *Seventh-day Adventist Bible Commentary.* Washington, DC: Review and Herald Publishing Association, 1978.
Parry, Aaron. *Complete Idiot's Guide to the Talmud.* Indianapolis, IN: Alpha Books, 2004.
Singer, I., ed. *The Jewish Encyclopedia.* New York: Funk & Wagnalls, 1925.
Smith, William. *Dictionary of the Bible.* Boston: Houghton, Mifflin, 1869.
Talmud—Schottenstein English Complete Full-Size Edition. 72 vols. New York: Mesorah Publications, 2005.
Thayer's Greek-English Lexicon of the New Testament. Peabody, MA: Hendrickson, 2007.
Wesley, John. *Explanatory Notes upon the New Testament.* Westville, FL: Alec R. Allenson, 1958.

OTHER READINGS

Abbott, Edwin Abbott. *Flatland: A Romance of Many Dimensions.* Mineola, NY: Dover, 1992.
Ashcraft, Chris. "Designed to Eat Plants Then Cursed to Be Unable," http://www.nwcreation.net/plantcellulose.html (accessed December 1, 2008).
Biederwolf, William. *Seventh-day Adventism.* Knoxville, TN: Evangelist of Truth Publishers, c. 1920.
Caram, Paul. "The Double Portion of the Firstborn," http://zion.ph/articles/dportion.pdf (accessed March 9, 2010).
Feinberg, C. L. *The Prophecy of Ezekiel: The Glory of the Lord.* Chicago: Moody Press, 1969.

Gill, Dan. "How They Met: Geology Solves Long-Standing Mystery of Hezekiah's Tunneler." *Biblical Archaeology Review* 20, no. 4 (July/August 1994): 20.
Jackson, Wayne. "Are Some Sins 'Greater' Than Others?" http://www.christiancourier.com/articles/966-are-some-sins-greater-than-others (accessed March 9, 2010).
Kioulachoglou, Tassos. "Lazarus and Rich Man," http://www.jba.gr/Articles/jbajan07a.htm (accessed February 9, 2008).
Kleiman, Mark A. R. "Remembering Amalek," http://www.spa.ucla.edu/faculty/kleiman/REMEMBERING%20AMALEK.doc (accessed March 9, 2010).
Meyers, Eric. "The Jesus Tomb Controversy: An Overview." *Near Eastern Archaeology* 69, nos. 3/4 (September–December 2006): 116.
North, Gary. *75 Bible Questions Your Instructors Pray You Won't Ask*. Tyler, TX: Spurgeon, 1984.
Olson, Roger. *How to Be Evangelical without Being Conservative*. Grand Rapids: Zondervan, 2008.
Patching, J. "Rich Man and Lazarus," http://www.tentmaker.org/books/RichManandLazarus-Patching.html (accessed February 9, 2008).
Price, Randall. "Ezekiel's Prophecy of the Temple," http://www.worldofthebible.com/Bible%20Studies/Ezekiel's%20Prophecy%20of%20the%20Temple.pdf (accessed October 10, 2008).
Ritenbaugh, John. "Eating: How Good It Is! (Part Six)." Forerunner Commentary, http://bibletools.org/index.cfm/fuseaction/Library.sr/CT/PERSONAL/k/2/Eating-How-Good-Is-Part-Six.htm (accessed August 9, 2007).
Russell, Bertrand. *Why I Am Not a Christian*. New York: Touchstone, 1957.
Shakespeare, John. "What N. T. Wright Really Said." In *Question from Surprised by Hope*, http://groups.yahoo.com/group/Wrightsaid/message/21808 (accessed July 14, 2008).
Strabo. *Geographies*. Cambridge, MA: Harvard UP, 1978.
Walvoord, John. *Every Prophecy of the Bible*. Colorado Springs: Chariot Victor Publishing, 1999.
———. *The Millennial Kingdom*. Grand Rapids: Zondervan, 1959.
Wellard, James. *Babylon*. New York: Saturday Review Press, 1972.
Whitcomb, John C. "Christ's Atonement and Animal Sacrifices in Israel." *Grace Theological Journal* 6, no. 2 (Fall 1985): 201–17.
Wolters, Albert. *Creation Regained: Biblical Basics for a Reformational Worldview*. Grand Rapids: Eerdmans, 1985.

www.ingramcontent.com/pod-product-compliance
Lightning Source LLC
Chambersburg PA
CBHW062015220426
43662CB00010B/1341